P9-CCP-339

MAKING SIMPLE MUSICAL INSTRUMENTS

Editor: Deborah Morgenthal
Art Director: Dana Irwin
Production: Elaine Thompson, Dana Irwin
Illustrations: Charlie Covington
Photography: Richard Babb

Published in 1995 by Lark Books
Altamont Press
50 College Street
Asheville, NC 28801

Hopkin, Bart, 1952–
Making simple musical instruments / Bart Hopkin.
p. cm.
Includes bibliographical references (p. 144) and index.
ISBN 0-937274-80-1
1. Musical instruments--Construction. I. Title.
ML460.H77 1994
784.192'3--dc20 94-3543
CIP
MN

10 9 8 7 6 5 4 3 2 1

Forward
by Robert Moog

Many people of my generation learned to play a musical instrument in their younger years. We dutifully practiced scales and chords on the piano (while our luckier friends got to play baseball!). Or we wailed away on trumpets and clarinets so we could march around the football field at half time in those funny uniforms. And when we became adults, we usually forgot all of it, preferring instead to get our musical enjoyment passively—through records, CD's, or by attending an occasional concert.

Still, most of us, young and old alike, wish we could find a musical activity that we could actively participate in. We're not interested in becoming virtuoso performers or major stars. Rather, we just want to do something that's fun, something that feels good, and puts us in touch with our musical culture. And we want to do this without having to invest in expensive, delicate instruments, or in hours upon hours of practice.

Well, we need look no further than this book. Bart Hopkin is a talented musician who has a powerful interest in musical instrument design and building, and in the tremendous diversity of musical forms and sounds enjoyed by cultures around the world. Through his own research, as well as in his role as editor of the quarterly journal *Experimental Musical Instruments*, Bart has come up with an amazing array of simple and highly playable instruments that you can make. In clear and easy-to-understand language, Bart tells you the basics of musical sound, then explains how to build his designs using ordinary shop tools and basic building skills. Although you will need to special order the ostrich egg to make the ocarina, most of the materials are readily available from your local building supply store.

So what does building a musical instrument have to do with making music? Simple: Once you've built an instrument, you will want to play it. Many of the instruments, such as the xylophone and hand drum, require no previous musical study. Others, like the saxophone and the bowed psaltery will take some practice, and Bart explains the playing technique of each instrument. Thus, the book is rewarding in three ways: you'll learn how simple structures and materials can be put together to make musical sounds; you'll learn how to produce sounds out of your finished instrument; and you'll discover the personal satisfaction of playing music for yourself or with friends.

As a professional musical instrument designer who really enjoys playing Bart's instruments, I invite you now to partake of the musical resources that he has prepared for you. Have fun!

Musician and musical instrument maker, Robert Moog (left), talks with author, Bart Hopkin.

Table of Contents

Preliminary Thoughts and Ideas

THE AUTHOR, BART HOPKIN, PLAYING HIS SEAWEED HORN MADE FROM BULL KELP, DRIED AND FINISHED

Throughout the world and over the centuries, musical instruments have flourished in an endless diversity of forms. Leaf through a book on historical instruments, or stroll through a really good collection of instruments from many lands, and you will begin to sense the breadth of the possibilities. And although most musical instruments represent recognizable and familiar types, it is also true that instruments need not be fashioned in imitation of preexisting models. An instrument can be as unique as a piece of sculpture. The photographs appearing on these opening pages show where this kind of thinking has taken a few particularly creative, contemporary instrument makers.

This is the spirit in which I have made this book. Yet the instrument plans included here are not as idiosyncratic as all this might suggest. Most of them, by design, relate closely to familiar instrument types and are fully playable as such. Plans for about 30 musical instruments are given, including representatives of most of the widely played basic types in the world's music. You can use them to make familiar sorts of music if that is what you want or let them serve as a starting place for more exotic musical travels.

An Invitation to Explore

You will find that the materials and dimensions for each instrument in this book appear with some specificity, as if the reader were expected to do things in just such a manner. I have presented them in this way because it is easier and clearer to describe something as taking a certain form than it is to suggest that it could take this form or that form, or could be varied in a million other ways. But the last of these is closer to the truth: there is nothing unchangeable about these plans, and there are countless ways you can alter them to make them your own. Follow them in detail and you will be sure to end up with a playable instrument. Rethink them according to your own ideas and purposes, and you will arrive at something different and perhaps superior.

On a more prosaic level, you will often be able to substitute lumber of slightly different dimensions, reflecting the sizes available at your local lumberyard, rather than cutting and planing many pieces to precisely match the dimensions recommended in the plans. Let common sense be your guide in these matters. I have tried to present enough underlying principle (stopping short, I hope, of being burdensome) that you will be able to think intelligently about design options as you go.

An Emphasis on Sound, Not Woodworking

This is not a woodworking book, and it doesn't provide a background in shop technique. The emphasis is not on fine craft, but on the making of things that have value in the sounds they make and the feel of the playing—things that work musically and have distinctive musical personalities of their own. If you have the skill to make each instrument a work of high craft as well, so much the better.

You will find some of the instruments given here are easy to make, while others are more demanding. Each project is identified at the start as easy, moderate, or difficult. In addition, some of the finished instruments will be easier to play than others. A few require special skill in playing, and this information is given in the introductory notes. With the others, most people will be able to produce a musical sound without too much difficulty and develop their playing facility from there.

Access to a good work space and a range of power tools will make the construction work quite a bit faster and easier, but they are not essential for most of the plans. For more on this, see Appendix 1, Tools and Materials, on page 139.

Sound Basics

Before getting down to the business of building, we need to establish common ground in a couple of areas, particularly regarding tunings and note-naming conventions.

Sound is the brain's interpretation of vibration in the atmosphere impinging on the eardrums. The stronger the vibration (the greater its amplitude), the louder the perceived sound. Pitch, which is the sense of how high or low a sound is, is a function of vibrational frequency: the higher the frequency (the more oscillations per second), the higher the perceived pitch. As an example, a steady vibration at 440 cycles per second yields the pitch western musicians identify as A above middle C.

Most sounds, however, do not take the form of a smooth oscillation at a single frequency. Rather,

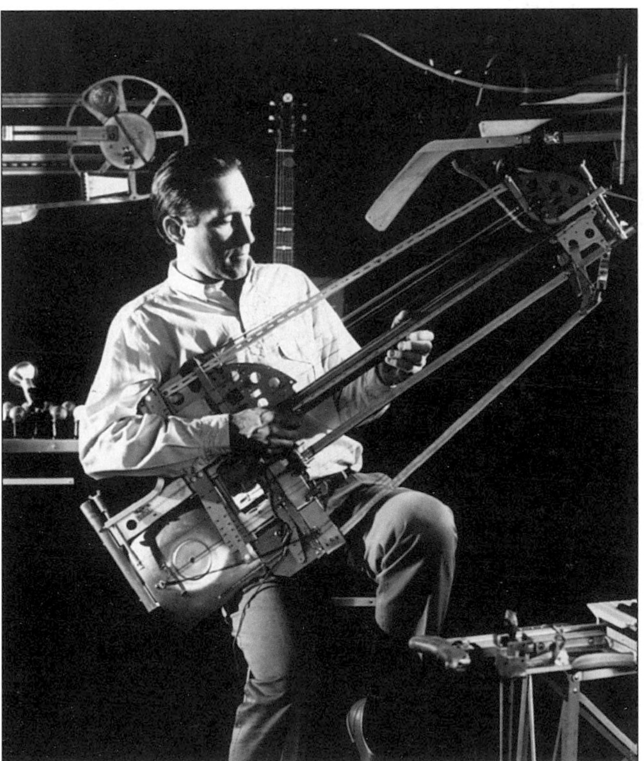

KEN BUTLER PLAYING HIS UNIQUE DESIGN, THE SHIP, ASSEMBLED FROM METAL MATERIALS AND OBJECTS

they take the form of a complex pattern of vibratory movement that can be interpreted as being the sum of many frequencies happening simultaneously. With experience you can learn to hear the pitches of component frequencies within a complex sound, but more typically your brain will hear the complex pattern as a single sound with a single pitch. The perceived pitch is usually that of the lowest of the frequencies present, often called the *fundamental*. The other frequencies, called *partials* or *overtones*, blend in and help lend the sound its characteristic tone quality. Noiselike sounds, not seeming to have any clear pitch, are generally those in which the vibration pattern is too erratic or complex for the ear to focus on any single frequency as the fundamental. Sounds that strike people as having the most musical quality are usually, though certainly not always, those in which the vibration patterns are relatively simple. They typically have an easily recognized fundamental frequency, plus a nice blend of overtone frequencies to lend a bit of color.

Musical instruments are the devices that people have come up with for generating such sounds. They take many forms, because the physical world has provided us with many ways to make these mechanisms. Each produces its own characteristic patterns of vibration, overtone mixes, and resulting sound qualities. Their diversity enriches the world with a happy abundance of musical flavors. Learning about musical sound mechanisms as we try our hand at making a few of them is the business of this book. A sense of how to listen—an awareness of the sonic components as described above—will be valuable in the process and is rewarding in itself as well.

The exquisitely carved O'Ele'n Strings made by William Eaton

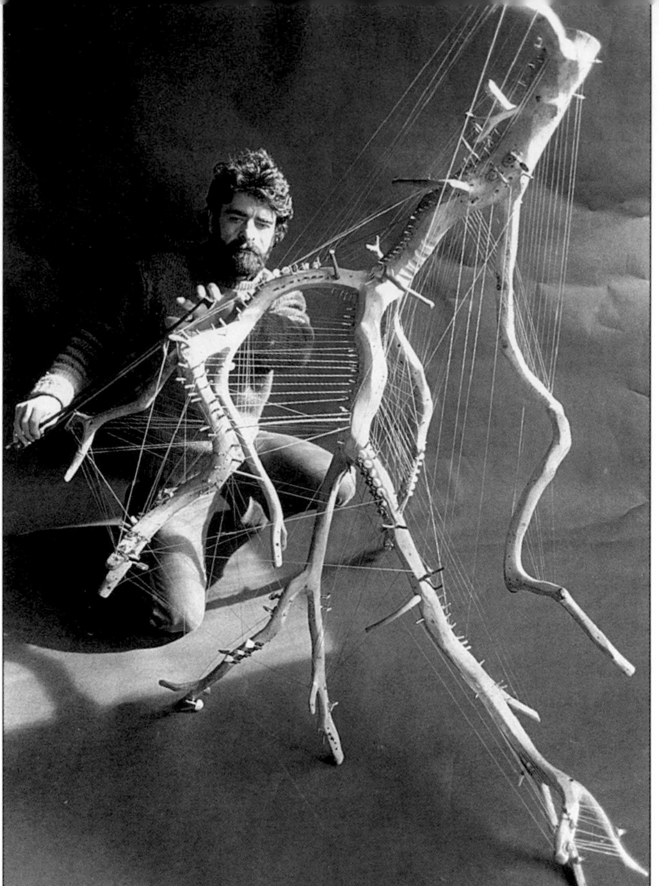

The Semi-Civilized Tree, made by Nazim Ozel, using hundreds of strings and a large oak branch

Tuning Theory

The subject of scales and tuning can become fantastically involved and convoluted. For the current purposes, we will do with the most general and practical sort of overview.

Most of the instruments in this book are designed to produce particular pitches and scales, so that people will be able to play recognizable melodies with them. One of your jobs as instrument maker will be to decide what pitches you want a given instrument to produce, and to tune the sounding elements to those pitches. Tuning procedures are different for different instruments, but there are some common principles. In the following paragraphs I will talk briefly about different sorts of scales. Then I will describe some basic applicable tuning procedures. You will be able to refer to these ideas when the time comes for tuning the instruments in this book.

A musical scale is a set of pitches available, by convention, for use in a particular piece or style of music. You can think of a scale as a set of pitch relationships: each successive note of the scale is higher than the one before by some amount, and specifying those intervals defines the scale. Those relationships give the scale its particular sound and mood, but you can further pin things down by specifying a certain frequency for one of the steps of the scale. Then you have defined not only a set of relationships, but a set of absolute pitches.

The vast majority of western musical instruments are made to produce the pitches of a particular scale known as *12-tone equal temperament*, at a standard pitch of A-440. The scale is made up of 12 equally spaced pitches in each octave, corresponding to the seven white keys and five black keys in an octave's worth of piano keyboard. (The familiar major and minor scales are subsets, each using seven pitches from the 12-tone scale.) It would be easy to assume that these 12 pitches per octave are the only pitches available for making music, but this is an artificially restricted way of looking at things. The range of possible pitches is a continuum, and between any two frequencies—between the tones of any two keys on the piano—there are other frequencies to be heard. You can devise a musical scale using whatever points along the continuum you wish, with as many tones per octave as you wish, and using it make all the music you wish. Throughout history and around the world people have created music in a great variety of scales.

The musical instrument plans I devised for this book are based on the assumption that most people will be inclined, initially at least, to stick with the standard 12-equal or its seven-tone subsets, if only to provide common ground for playing in tune with other instruments. But there is a great deal of leeway here. With little or no modification to the plans, you can alter the tunings of any of the instruments as you see fit. You can, if you wish, create alternative scales simply by freely following the inclinations of your ear. Or you can replicate other nonstandard scales with which you may be familiar. Or you can tune an instrument to realize some theoretical scale that you or someone else may have devised. There is a world of possibilities. See the Bibliography on page 140 for sources of further information on tuning theory.

Tuning Procedures

And now, some notes on the tuning process. Imagine that you have an instrument before you, and you are at the stage where you are ready to adjust the sounding elements to produce the pitches that you want, be they the pitches of 12-equal or some other scale. This pitch-adjusting process may be a matter of using a tuning peg to adjust string tensions, determining fret locations on a string instrument's neck, adjusting the lengths of xylophone bars, or adjusting the size or placement of a wind instrument's tone holes. You will find those specifics discussed in each of the instrument plans.

THE ECCENTRIC PIKASSO GUITAR WITH 42 STRINGS, MADE ON COMMISSION FROM PAT METHENY BY LINDA MANZER

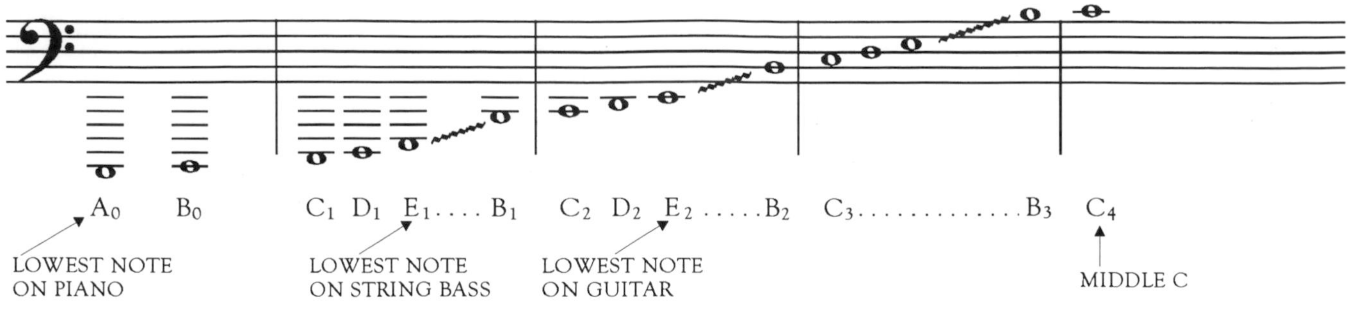

FIGURE 1

STANDARD NOTE-NAMING SYSTEM. THE PITCH CLASS NAMES USE THE FAMILIAR LETTER NAMES (A–G) AND ACCIDENTALS (#, ♭) OF STANDARD MUSIC NOTATION. THE OCTAVE IS DESIGNATED BY A SUBSCRIPTED NUMERAL.

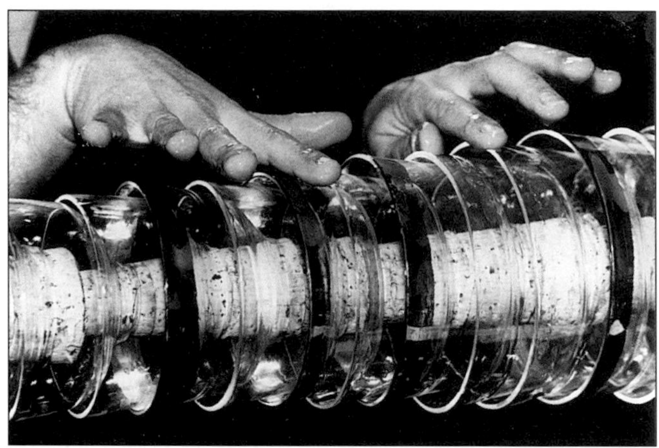

GERHARD FINKENBEINER'S RECREATION OF THE GLASS HARMONICA INVENTED BY BEN FRANKLIN

Whatever the tuning mechanism, unless you have great ears, you will benefit by having some sort of tuning guide to help you in the process—something to help you recognize when the sounding element you are tuning is at the desired pitch. There are several approaches to this.

One is to buy special tuning equipment. In recent years electronic tuners have come on the market that are accurate, easy to use, and moderately priced, at least compared to what such things cost not too long ago. They have meters to visually indicate the pitch of a particular sounding tone, and many also have a small built-in speaker to produce a range of pitches for reference or comparison purposes. These instruments are available through large music stores or through the piano tuner supply or school music supply outlets listed in Appendix 1.

Another approach—a reasonable one for anyone new to the game and lacking special equipment—is to tune by comparing pitches from the new instrument to those of an existing instrument whose tuning you have decided to duplicate. If you have decided to stay with 12-equal, you can use a portable electronic keyboard, well-tuned piano, guitar, or whatever else you can get your hands on. I suggest starting with the lowest pitch to be tuned. Play the intended pitch on the reference instrument, then compare it to the pitch of the thing-to-be-tuned. Adjust the thing-to-be-tuned (turn the tuning peg, shorten the xylophone bar, or whatever) to try to bring its pitch into agreement with the reference tone. Keep at it until you are satisfied that the two match in pitch; then go on to the next pitch. Some people have an inborn knack for hearing whether the note-to-be-tuned is above, below, or right on the reference pitch. Others find it difficult, especially with odd or noisy tone qualities. Everyone improves with practice.

Finally, let us suppose that you have chosen not to replicate a prescribed scale but to come up with a tuning of your own by instinct. In that case, the tuning process is primarily an intuitive one. Excite the sound, listen to the pitch, and adjust it according to the preferences of your ear. Intermittently during the process, refer for comparison and context to other pitches already tuned on the instrument. Continue this adjustment operation until the instrument produces a set of pitch relationships that strike you as right.

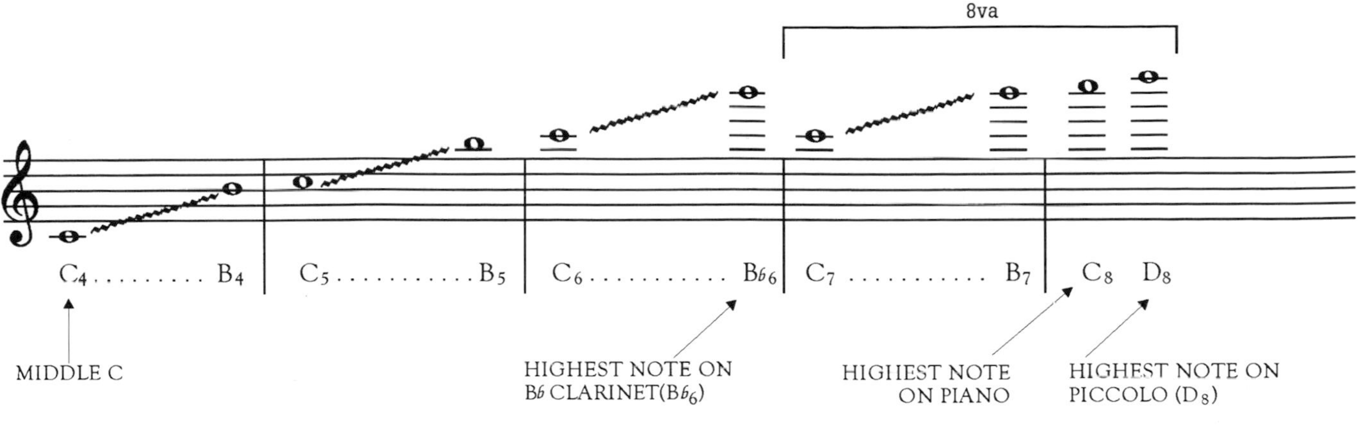

Pitch Names

There is broad agreement in western musical practice as to how to name the pitches within the octave, using the familiar note names C, C#, or D*b*, D, D#, or E*b*, and so forth. But distinguishing between like-named pitches in different octaves remains confusing. For the purposes of this book, it will be important to get this business straight, so we can describe the musical ranges of the instruments to be built. We will use the note-naming system that is generally accepted among people who study musical acoustics, and that has been sanctioned by the American Standards Association. Figure 1 provides the details.

Classification of Musical Instruments

The most widely used system for classifying musical instruments has four primary categories: *aerophones* (wind instruments), *chordophones* (string instruments), *membranophones* (drums), and *idiophones* (defined in the following pages). The plans in this book are grouped according to these categories, and I have placed a few comments at the start of each grouping. Those comments will be helpful as you move on to the individual instruments.

Acknowledgments

It has been my special privilege to meet, correspond with, and study the work of a great many skilled, innovative, and knowledgeable instrument makers, as well as scientists, theoreticians, and scholars. This book is full of things that I have learned from them. In fact, there is scarcely an idea here that I can claim as uniquely my own. I won't try to list all of these people here. Perchance if they see this book they will recognize their contributions. My sincere thanks to all.

Richard Waters playing his elegant Waterphone by bowing its vertical bronze rods

Idiophones

Idiophones are musical instruments in which the vibration originates in some solid, inherently rigid material. This differentiates idiophones from wind instruments, in which the original vibrating material is air (not solid), and from string instruments and drums, in which the original vibrating material is stretched (not inherently rigid). Xylophones are idiophones; so are gongs, bells, tuning forks, and mbiras. So is the floor when you stomp on it and the desk when you pound it.

Idiophones—admittedly a rather motley group—can be divided into subcategories based on the characteristic pattern of vibration in the sounding elements. For instance, marimba bars, tubular chimes, and other similarly long and narrow sounding bodies all show similar motions when they vibrate. Based on this they can be grouped together under the name *free-bar instruments*. Instruments having vibrating tongues, such as music boxes, mbiras, and tongue drums, can similarly be grouped together under the formal name *lamellophones*; and the list could go on through several more subgroups. At the end of the list would be a large catchall grouping containing irregularly shaped oddities with idiosyncratic patterns of vibration not so easily categorized.

Among the instrument plans in the following pages are representatives of most of the major groups, and we will learn more about each of them as we get into the plans. But before getting into specifics, here are two general observations that will help you think more clearly about the forces at play in idiophones.

General observation number one: A moment ago I mentioned characteristic patterns of vibration. In any idiophonic vibrating body, there are regions of maximum vibratory movement and regions where there is almost no movement at all. If anything touches the vibrating body in a way that inhibits the movement of a region that needs to vibrate, then the sound will be damped, and the instrument will sound poorly. Instrument makers must take this into account when they devise the mountings for their sounding elements. To allow it to vibrate with the least possible inhibition, the sounding body should be held at one of its points of minimum vibration. Bells, gongs, and free-bar instruments all benefit greatly from proper mounting in this way. The key is knowing how to find those points and designing a mounting that takes advantage of them. Conversely, when you excite the vibration—by striking or other means—it helps greatly to inject the energy in a region that will show strong vibration, and not at one of those no-vibration points.

Yet the situation is a bit more complex than I have

implied, for virtually all idiophonic vibrating bodies are capable of several different modes or patterns of vibration, each having different points of maximum and minimum movement. Different mounting arrangements and ways of exciting the vibration will bring out different modes, altering the tone color and sometimes the perceived pitch. Usually, though not always, the goal will be to bring out the fundamental mode most strongly. The trick, then, is to set the mountings and inject the energy at the right points to give that mode free reign.

General observation number two: Two factors are most important in determining the vibrating frequency of any idiophonic vibrating element and thus its pitch. They are the mass of the portions of the body, and the rigidity of the portions that must flex to allow vibration. By reducing the mass of the active parts, you can raise the instrument's pitch. This is what happens when you shorten a xylophone bar or an mbira prong (effectively removing mass from the ends of the bar or prong). Conversely, by making the flexing parts less rigid, you can lower the pitch. This is what happens when you thin a xylophone bar at its center or an mbira prong near its base (effectively making the flexing portions more flexible). When the two considerations seem to conflict—when removing mass also reduces rigidity—thc rigidity factor usually dominates, and pitch is lowered. Most idiophonic instruments can be tuned following these rules.

We will see these principles at work in several of the plans that follow.

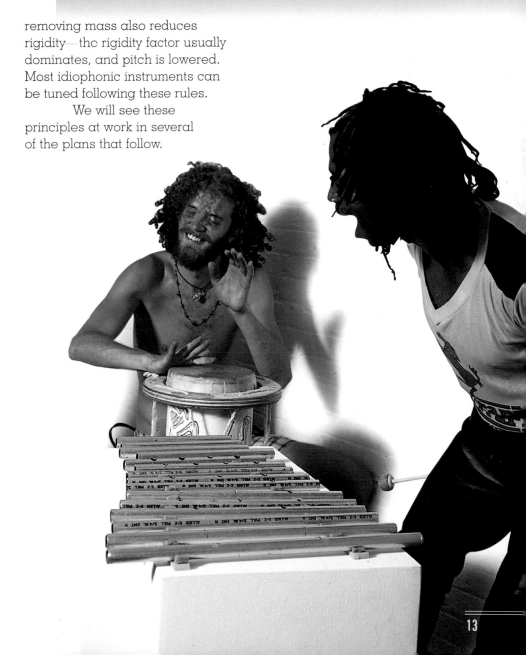

The Simplest Possible Xylophone

EASY

This simplest possible xylophone consists of 15 wooden bars of different lengths with support pads glued to their undersides, so that they can be laid out on a floor or table and struck with mallets. You may be surprised at the volume and clarity of tone this unassuming arrangement yields. The instrument's range as given here is *diatonic* (comprising a seven-note major or minor scale), covering two octaves. This is in keeping with the phrase "simplest possible," but you easily could add more bars at either end to extend the range, or fill in the missing bars for a complete *chromatic* scale of 12 tones per octave. Or, if you wish, you can tune the bars to some entirely different scale.

Free-bar instruments manifest certain characteristic modes of vibration. In the fundamental mode (which is the one we want to bring out in this xylophone), the pattern involves flexing at the center. When you strike the bar, the middle goes down when the ends go up and vice versa, as shown in Figure 1. The bar pivots at two points of minimal movement somewhere between the middle and each end. For a bar of uniform rectangular or cylindrical shape, these points are typically about 22% of the bar length in from each end. In this xylophone, the support pads under each bar will be attached at these points, so as to minimize damping on the remainder of the bar.

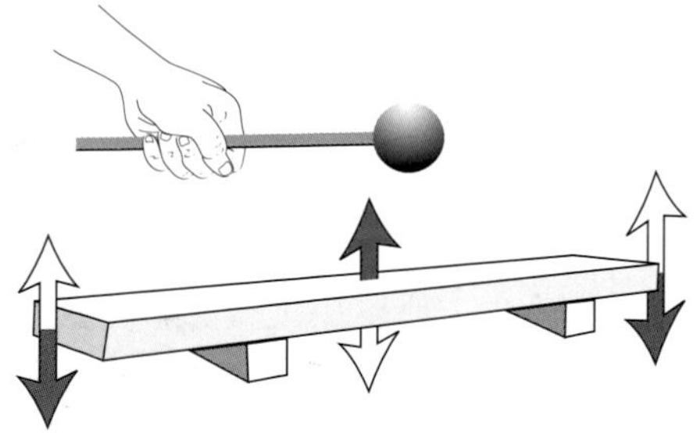

FIGURE 1

VIBRATIONAL MOVEMENT FOR A FREE BAR IN ITS FUNDAMENTAL MODE OF VIBRATION. THE CENTER MOVES UP WHILE THE ENDS MOVE DOWN, AND VICE VERSA. PORTIONS OF THE BAR DIRECTLY OVER THE SUPPORT PADS DO NOT MOVE EXCEPT TO PIVOT.

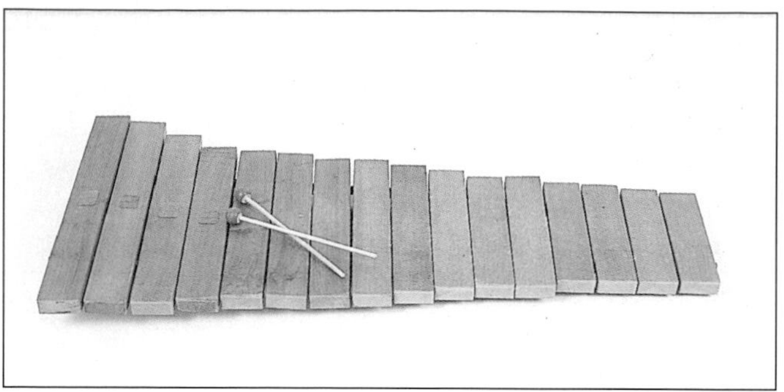

The one slightly fancy thing about this xylophone is that the support pads are different heights for different bars. With rectangular bars resting close to a floor or table top, reflected sound waves can affect the bar's vibration. At certain heights the reflected waves counteract the vibration and deaden the sound. At other heights they can reinforce the vibration to strengthen and enrich the sound. The ideal height varies depending on the pitch of the bar. Our xylophone has each of its bars set at a height that works to its advantage.

The most highly prized xylophones are made with dense tropical hardwoods. For this plan I have suggested making the bars of redwood, simply because it is one of the better-sounding among widely available and affordable temperate woods. It also is easy to work and not prone to splitting; it looks nice and ages well. You may choose to use some other wood, and perhaps you will come across one with a truly superior tone. If you do use another wood, your bar lengths for given pitches may be well out of agreement with the approximate lengths given in Figure 2. Whatever you use, be sure that your wood is kiln-dried or otherwise well-seasoned. Look for straight, close grain, particularly on the broad face of the bar, and avoid knotty wood, or discard knotty sections when making the bars.

Instructions

1. If you intend to put any sort of finish on the wood, do this as a first step. (Adding wood finish after cutting the bars would add weight which might affect their tuning.)

2. When the finish is dry, you are ready to tune the bars. Tuning is simply a matter of cutting the bars to the right lengths to produce the desired pitches. The chart in Figure 2 gives a very approximate idea of what lengths to expect if you are working with the suggested kiln-dried redwood. As you proceed through the tuning process, don't be concerned if your tuned bar lengths don't match the chart closely: each piece of wood is different. Review "Tuning Procedures" on page 9 for important background information on the following procedure, and review "Pitch Names" on page 11 for the meanings of the subscripted pitch designations below and in Figure 2. Now we'll start to cut and tune:

Begin with the longest and lowest bar, which is to produce the pitch G_4. Cut this first bar about 2" longer than the length given in Figure 2. Cut two scrap pieces of foam rubber, and lay the bar across them as shown in Figure 3. Tap the bar sharply at the center with the tips of your fingers, and listen for the pitch. Be sure to focus your ear on the fundamental—the lowest sounding pitch—

FIGURE 2

VERY APPROXIMATE BAR LENGTHS AND PITCHES FOR KILN-DRIED REDWOOD 2 X 4. ACTUAL LENGTHS WILL VARY DEPENDING ON THE CHARACTER OF THE WOOD. SIZES FOR THE FOAM SUPPORT PADS FOR EACH BAR ARE GIVEN AS WELL, IN THE FORM *HEIGHT* X *THICKNESS* X *WIDTH*.

Bar #	Pitch	Approx. Length	Foam Pad Size
1	G_4	26-1/4"	2-7/8" x 2" x 3-1/2"
2	A_4	24-3/4"	2-1/2" x 2" x 3-1/2"
3	B_4	23-3/8"	2-1/4" x 2" x 3-1/2"
4	C_5	22-3/4"	2-1/8" x 1-1/2" x 3-1/2"
5	D_5	21-3/8"	1-7/8" x 1-1/2" x 3-1/2"
6	E_5	20-1/4"	1-5/8" x 1-1/2" x 3-1/2"
7	F_5	19-5/8"	1-1/2" x 1-1/2" x 3-1/2"
8	G_5	18-1/2"	1-3/8" x 1" x 3-1/2"
9	A_5	17-1/2"	1-1/4" x 1" x 3-1/2"
10	B_5	16-1/2"	1-1/8" x 1" x 3-1/2"
11	C_6	16"	1-1/8" x 1" x 3-1/2"
12	D_6	15-1/8"	1" x 1" x 3-1/2"
13	E_6	14-1/4"	7/8" x 1" x 3-1/2"
14	F_6	13-7/8"	7/8" x 1" x 3-1/2"
15	G_6	13-1/8"	3/4" x 1" x 3-1/2"

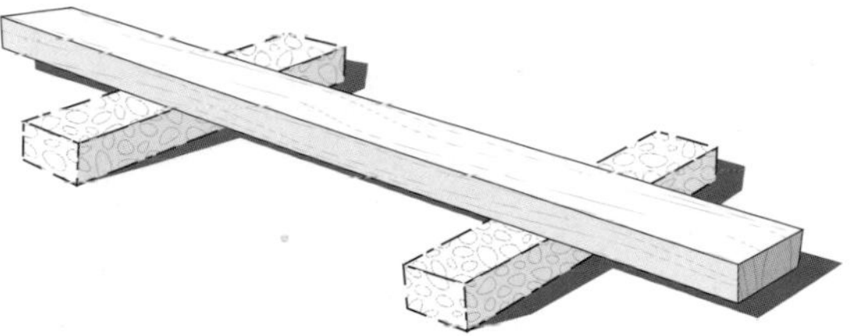

FIGURE 3

FOR PITCH TESTING, LAY THE BAR ACROSS TWO SCRAP PIECES OF FOAM RUBBER WITH ABOUT A FOURTH OR FIFTH OF THE BAR'S LENGTH OVERHANGING AT EACH END, AND STRIKE AT THE CENTER WITH A MALLET.

Materials List

Lumber

30' of 2"x 4" kiln-dried redwood *Bars*

Hardware & Supplies

3-1/2" x 2' x 3' foam rubber (Notes-1) *Pads*

3/8" x 1/8" x 2' lightweight foam weather strip *Side pads*

Glue gun with hot melt glue, or white craft glue

Wood finish (optional) (Notes-2)

Moleskin, one package (optional) (Notes-3)

Suggested Tools

Carpenter's handsaw or circular saw

Utility knife, hacksaw, or band saw (See comments in step 4)

Sharp scissors

Paintbrush or rag

Sandpaper

Notes

1. This is approximately the total amount of foam rubber you will use, but you don't need that precise shape because you will be cutting it into small pieces. There are various types and densities of foam; any medium-dense foam will do. Available at foam shops and other outlets.
2. Your choice. An oil finish that sinks into the wood is preferable to one that coats the surface.
3. Moleskin is a foot care product sold at pharmacies.

and not on the higher tone of the first partial, which is likely to be fairly prominent in this longest bar. Because you cut the bar long, the pitch should be below the intended G_4. Carefully shorten it bit by bit, testing the pitch again after each shortening, until you bring it up to the desired pitch.

If you shorten it too much and find yourself sharp of the intended pitch, put that bar aside to use for the next higher pitch, and try again with a new bar. Alternatively, you can bring the pitch of a too-short bar back down by cutting a shallow kerf across the center of the bar on the underside. Occasionally you may get a funky bar that, due to structural flaws that may or may not be visible on the outside, simply doesn't produce a good tone. Put it aside and try another piece.

Cut and tune all 15 bars in this manner.

PLACING THE XYLOPHONE BARS CLOSE ALONGSIDE ONE ANOTHER IMPROVES THE TONE OF THE LOWER BARS, AS IT CREATES IN EFFECT A RESONATING AIR CHAMBER BENEATH. NOTICE THE MOLESKIN PADS (DYED BROWN, FOR HARMONIOUS APPEARANCE) ON THE LOWER-PITCHED BARS.

3. To improve the appearance and reduce splintering, use sandpaper to ease the edges of the bars where you have made the cuts. Then, if you applied wood finish to the bars earlier, retouch the newly cut ends. These two steps may have minor effects on pitch, but they should cancel out one another, leaving the pitch not appreciably altered.
4. The chart in Figure 2 also gives dimensions for the two foam pieces that support each bar. To cut the foam to these sizes, you can use any of several tools. A band saw makes an easy and very neat cut, but be careful: the foam offers almost no resistance going through, making a slip of the hands a dangerous possibility. Not as neat, but still functional, are very sharp scissors (for pieces 1" thick or less), a very sharp utility knife, or a hacksaw. If the foam cuts are not neat, the instrument will play just as well.

   For each bar, follow these steps: Measure the length of the bar, and multiply that length by .22 (22%). Mark that distance in from each end of the bar with a perpendicular line across on the underside. (Either side can be the underside; choose the nicer looking side to be the top.) Cut two foam pieces to the dimensions given in Figure 2 for the bar in question. Using white craft glue or hot glue from a glue gun, glue the foam pieces on, centered over the line (Figure 4). Put the bar aside to dry, resting on its foam pieces to assure gluing surface contact.
5. When the bars are set out on the floor and played, they will dance around a bit. To prevent their rattling against one another, place two pads of the

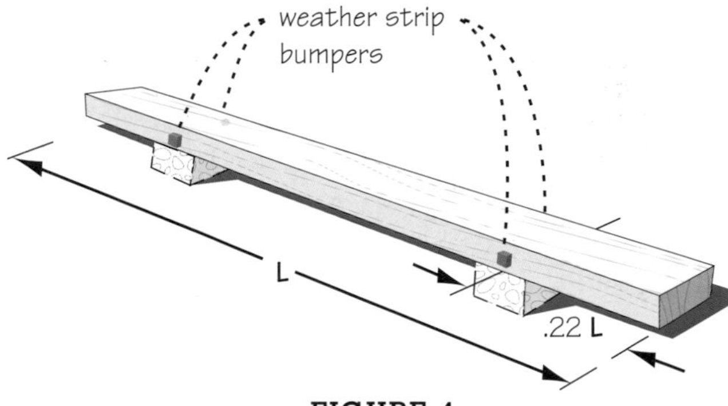

FIGURE 4

BARS WITH FOAM PIECES GLUED TO THE BOTTOM, AND THE LOCATIONS FOR THE FOUR BUMPER PADS ON THE SIDES OF EACH BAR

adhesive-backed, lightweight weather strip on each side of the bars, to serve as bumpers (Figure 4). Use scissors to cut the weather strip, making each pad about 3/8" x 3/8" square.

6. The instrument is now complete. Arrange the bars beside one another on a floor or table. You can lay them out in any sequence you wish, and there is a lot to be said for random or irregular sequences that tend to bring out fresh and unexpected melodic patterns. However, if you arrange them in ascending order with the bars pushed close together so that the side pads touch, an air chamber is formed underneath that greatly improves the tone of the lower bars.
7. Over a period time the moisture content of the bars may change, causing them to go out of tune. The most radical change, if there is to be such, is likely to occur in the days or weeks immediately after the bars are cut. As described in step 2 above, you can retune them at any time by shortening the bars to raise the pitch, or making a small saw kerf across the midpoint of the underside to lower it.
8. Optional improvement: place a bit of thin padding, in the form of a 2" square of moleskin, at the center of the lowest three or four bars. Striking on this padding will be similar in effect to striking with a slightly softer beater, helping to bring out the fundamental in these lowest bars.

Playing Technique

Strike the bars at their centers with mallets. Different mallets will bring out different sound qualities. Medium hard, moderately heavy percussion mallets probably will be best all around. Slightly softer mallets bring out the best in the longer bars; slightly harder mallets work well in the higher bars. Plans for several types of mallets appear on pages 50–53. From among those plans, try the wooden-headed mallet of 1-1/2" diameter or larger, with an over-wrap of moleskin.

Variations

Marimba- and xylophone-making are fine arts, and good makers have developed a great many methods for bringing the best out of a bar of wood. I will just mention two of the most important here.

1. Removing wood from the underside of the bar to make it thinner at the center lowers the pitch. Especially with heavier, harder woods, it also allows the bar to ring longer after being struck, and makes the fundamental more prominent for clearer pitch and a deeper tone quality. By thinning not just at the center, but at several particular locations, experienced marimba bar tuners also can alter the pitches of the overtones relative to the fundamental, for a more musical tone quality and clearer pitch sense.
2. Lower bars in particular benefit from added air resonance. This can be done by placing tuned resonators below the bars. The resonators usually take one of two forms: a) they may be tubes closed at the lower end, with their lengths adjusted so that the air within naturally resonates at the fundamental frequency of the bar above; b) they may be globular shapes—usually gourds or calabashes—with openings at the top. Their air resonances can be tuned by selecting the right size gourd and adjusting the opening size.

Metallophone

MODERATELY EASY

The metal tubular chimes described here, are very similar, in principle, to the xylophone of the last plan, but their tone quality and musical effect are entirely different. The plan calls for two octaves' worth of tubular steel chimes tuned diatonically. You easily can add more tubes to extend the range or complete the chromatic scale, or alter the tunings to realize other scales. As we did with the xylophone plan, we will save ourselves the trouble of constructing a frame; instead, we'll mount each of the 15 tubes on its own pair of foam pads and arrange them on a floor or table for playing. Reflection from the surface below, which was an important consideration for the broad, rectangular xylophone bars, is not a concern with the narrow cylindrical chimes, so we can make all the mountings the same height.

For a more adventurous version of this instrument—harder to make, more interesting in concept, and fuller and richer in tone—see the suggestion under "Variations" at the end of this plan. (The materials list appears on page 20.)

Instructions

1. We will start by cutting and tuning the chimes. As with the xylophone bars, the initial tuning of the chime pitch will be simply a matter of cutting and possibly grinding to the right length to produce the desired pitch. Review "Tuning Procedures" on page 9, if need be, for important background information on the following procedure. Review "Pitch Names" on page 10 for the meanings of the subscripted pitch designations below and in Figure 1.

   Start with the longest chime, to be tuned to C_4. Cut the metal tubing a little longer than the length suggested in Figure 1. Test its pitch as follows:

   Lay the chime across two scrap pieces of foam, and strike it near the center with any moderately hard beater (the handle of a screwdriver will do). Be sure to focus your ear on the fundamental—the lowest sounding pitch—and not on the higher tone of the first partial, which is likely to be fairly prominent in this longest chime. The pitch will probably be below the intended pitch, because the chime was cut long. Shorten the tube bit by bit, checking its pitch after each shortening, until you've got it up to pitch. Referring to Figure 1, repeat the above procedure for the remaining 14 chimes.

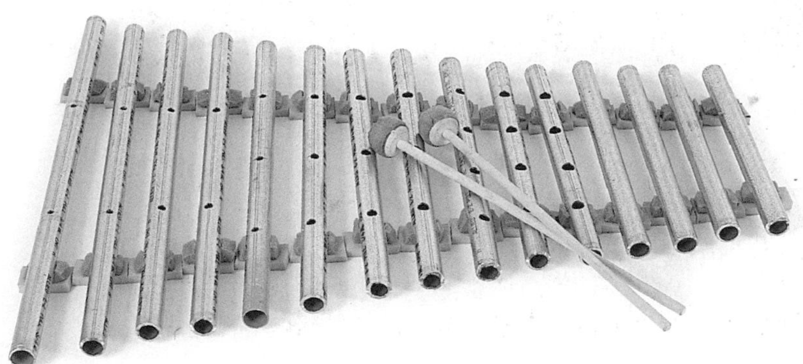

THE LOWER BARS IN THIS METALLOPHONE SET HAVE THE AIR RESONANCE TUNING HOLES DESCRIBED UNDER "VARIATIONS." IF YOU MAKE A SET WITHOUT THE AIR RESONANCE HOLES, THEN ALL YOUR BARS WILL RESEMBLE THE HOLE-LESS UPPER BARS.

CHM #	FINAL PITCH LENGTH	APPROX.
1	C_4	20-5/8"
2	D_4	19-7/16"
3	E_4	18-5/16"
4A_4		15-3/4"
7	B_4	14-13/16"
8	C_5	14-7/16"
9	D_5	13-9/16"
10	E_5	12-3/4"
11	F_5	12-3/8"
12	G_5	11-5/8"
13	A_5	11"
14	B_5	10-7/16"
15	C_6	10-1/4"

FIGURE 1

CHIME PITCHES AND THEIR APPROXIMATE EXPECTED LENGTHS. THIS IS TO SERVE AS A GUIDE; YOUR ACTUAL LENGTHS MAY VARY.

2. When all 15 chimes are tuned, you can mount them. Follow this process for each chime:
   A. Measure the chime length, multiply by .22, and mark that distance in from each end.

B. Cut two 2" segments of the lightweight foam rubber weather strip. Stick one segment at each of the marks, wrapping part way around the chime, as shown in the top drawing in Figure 2A. Do not stretch it on tight, but let the sticky-tape side of the weather strip pucker, allowing the outer surface to spread without stress.

C. This next step is easy if your scissors are good and sharp. If they're not, it's not. Snip off the convex tops of the weather strip bands (Figure 2B). The cuts need not be perfectly neat and square, but try to make them reasonably flat.

D. Cut two strips of the 3/8" foam rubber, 1" wide and 2" long. Use the rubber glue to attach them to the flat surface of the two weather strip bands (Figure 2C). Put the chime aside for the adhesive to dry, resting in playing position on its dual foam pads to assure gluing surface contact.

3. This completes the instrument. For playing, lay the chimes out in whatever sequence you wish on a floor or table.

Materials List

Hardware & Supplies

1 3/4" internal diameter x 20' electrical metal tubing, commonly called EMT (Notes-1) ***Chimes***

1 3/4" x 1/2" x 10' roll of lightweight foam rubber weather strip ***Support pads***

1 3/8" x 12" x 12" moderately dense foam rubber pad (Notes-2)

Adhesive for rubber or flexible plastics

Suggested Tools

Hacksaw (optional: tubing cutter)

Files and/or grinder (Notes-3)

Sharp scissors

Notes

1. This is a galvanized steel tubing, named for its primary intended use as a protective conduit for electrical wiring. It is inexpensive and widely available at hardware stores. There are slight differences between tubing from different manufacturers. If you have a choice, avoid tubing having a prominent seam along the side, and look for the sort with a shiny alligator skin surface rather than the dull, smooth surface.
2. The exact shape of this 3/8" thick pad isn't important, as long as you have enough to cut into 1" wide strips totaling 8' in length.
3. A bench grinder is recommended. A less effective but more affordable option is a grinder bit for an electric hand drill. Hand files (a flat file and a narrow half-round file or rat-tail file) will suffice but will be slow.

Playing Technique

Strike the chimes at their centers with mallets. Different mallets will bring out different sound qualities, with slightly softer mallets bringing out the best in the longer tubes and slightly harder mallets working well for the higher ones. Among the mallets described on pages 50–53, the best all-around for these chimes will probably be the wooden-headed mallet of 1-1/4" diameter, with one or two overwraps of moleskin.

Variations

You can easily augment this chime set with additional chimes for greater range and different tunings. If you wish to extend the range downward, use larger diameter tubing.

Use tubing of metals other than steel for different tone qualities. Brasses and bronzes will produce a slightly more round tone and aluminum a tone that is gentler still.

The chimes, as described in the above plan, are a bit thin-sounding in the lower part of their range. For a chime set that will be richer and louder in the lower octave, consider adding the special feature described in the following paragraphs.

A tubular chime encloses a column of air, much like the air column in a wind instrument. That air column has its natural resonant frequencies, which depend primarily on the length of the tube. For chimes of typical dimensions, the fundamental air column resonance is far below the ringing pitch of the metal, and so it doesn't come into play when the chime sounds. But if the air resonance pitch can somehow be raised to where it matches the fundamental chime pitch—ah, yes! Then the air resonance will reinforce the chime tone, making it both fuller and louder.

One way to do this is to tune the air resonance in the same manner that air resonances are controlled in many wind instruments: by drilling tone holes in the side of the tube. Here is an approach to air resonance tuning that will work for the chimes just described. Each of the four longest chimes (C_4–F_4) will have two evenly spaced holes drilled along the top, as shown in Figure 3. The next four chimes (G_4–C_5) have three. The remaining chimes (the upper octave) will have no holes; they will not be air-tuned, as the additional resonance is not as effective or as necessary in the upper register.

Fine-tuning of the air column is done by adjusting the hole size: the larger the holes, the higher the air resonance pitch. Start by drilling relatively small holes, then gradually enlarge them, repeatedly comparing the air resonance pitch to the chime pitch. To hear the air resonance pitch, hold the chime crossways in front of your mouth, an inch or two away, and blow a narrow airstream across one of the holes. You will hear a tone that is breathy, yet recognizable in pitch. When the air pitch is just barely below the chime pitch, try striking the chime. The added resonance will make its tone fuller and louder. You can test the effect by covering one of the holes (which defeats the coupling by throwing off the air resonance pitch). If the coupling was good, covering a hole will cause a marked loss in tone and

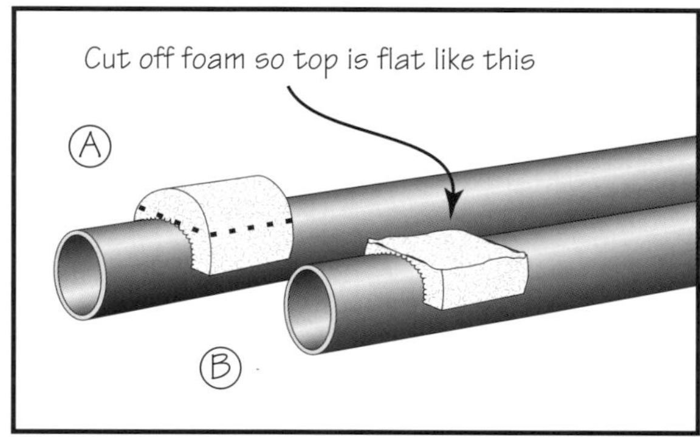

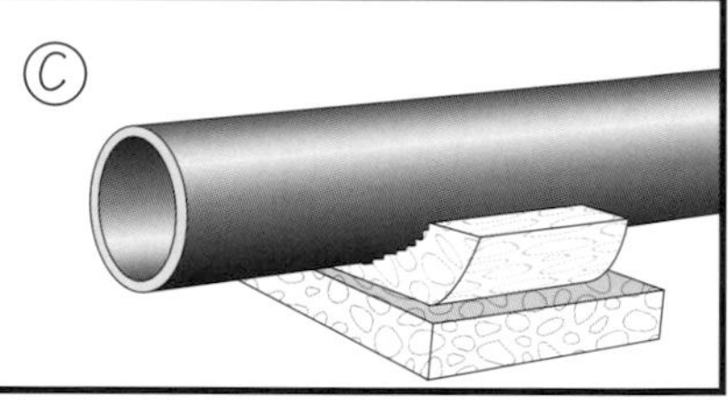

FIGURE 2

THE ADHESIVE-BACKED WEATHER STRIP. A, POSITIONING THE STRIP ON THE CHIME; B, CUTTING A FLAT SURFACE ON THE STRIP (IT IS O.K. IF YOUR CUT DOES NOT COME OUT PERFECTLY FLAT); C, THE STRIP GLUED TO THE FOAM RUBBER PAD THAT PROVIDES A FOOT FOR THE CHIME.

FIGURE 3

TYPICAL CHIMES WITH AIR RESONANCE TUNING HOLES. WHETHER THERE ARE TWO OR THREE HOLES, THE HOLES ARE TO BE EQUALLY SPACED ALONG THE CHIME.

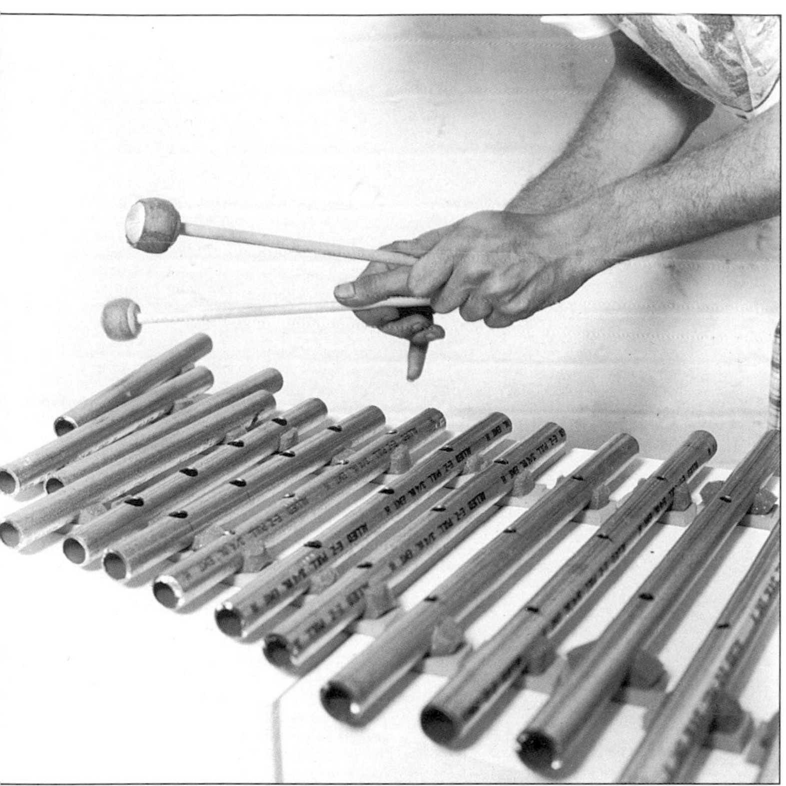

volume. Repeatedly tapping over the hole very lightly with your finger will yield a vibrato similar in both effect and principle to that of a vibraphone. The approximate expected size for the air resonance tuning holes on the longest tube (C_4) will be about 7/32" diameter. Progressively higher pitches will require progressively larger holes, up to about 7/16" at C_5.

Two caveats: 1) Adding the air-tuning holes will weaken the tube, causing the chime pitch to drop. The effect is small on the longer tubes with smaller holes, and greater for the shorter, larger-holed tubes. As a result, you probably will have to retune the chime after drilling by shortening it, and then fine-tune the air resonance pitch again. 2) The drilling process heats the tube and the enclosed air, which temporarily alters their tunings. After doing the initial air resonance tuning, you may find that the acoustic coupling is lost when things have cooled down. In that case go back and refine the tuning by enlarging the holes a bit more.

Acknowledgments: Several builders in recent years have worked with instruments using the same sort of metal conduit used here, finding it especially useful in alternative tuning explorations. Prominent among those explorers: Ivor Darreg, Erv Wilson, Stephen Smith, Bill Colvig, and Buzz Kimball.

Free-Bar Length Calculations

In place of trial-and-error tuning of free-bar instruments, it would be useful to be able to calculate in advance the bar length required to produce a particular pitch. In some cases this turns out to be impractical: the math is too complex or the physical situation is too variable or ambiguous. In other cases it is a fairly simple matter.

The manageable cases are those in which all the bars of a given instrument are to be of the same material and of the same thickness. In that case, most of the factors determining pitch are constant from one bar to the next, leaving bar length as the only variable. Knowing that, you can cut a sample bar and test its pitch empirically. Then use a little math, outlined below, to calculate required lengths to achieve the desired pitches in the other bars relative to the sample bar's pitch. The calculations yield accurate results for highly uniform materials, such as manufactured metal tubing, and considerably less accurate results for natural materials that vary in mass and rigidity, such as wood. They don't work at all for bars of irregular shape (e.g., wooden bars which are hollowed out underneath).

The physical principle at work is an inverse square rule. Bar frequency is inversely proportional to the square of the length. In practical terms, that leads to these rules:

TO PRODUCE A NEW BAR OF THIS PITCH	MAKE IT THIS LONG RELATIVE TO THE SAMPLE BAR
1 octave higher	0.7071 x as long
1octave lower	1.4144 x as long
1 semitone higher	0.9715 x as long
1 semitone lower	1.0293 x as long

The semitone values assume you are working in the standard 12-tone equal temperament scale. You can determine lengths for other steps within an octave in 12-equal by applying the semitone-up or the semitone-down factor repeatedly. Ambitious people with a mathematical background and some knowledge of tuning theory will be able to apply the inverse square rule in a more general way to calculate bar lengths for intervals outside of 12-equal.

Tuned Gong Set

MODERATELY EASY

A gong, according to the standard definition, is an idiophone with a plate-like shape, having its point of maximum vibration at the center. Accordingly, gongs are struck near the center and supported from points of minimal vibration a little distance in from the edges. You can distinguish gongs in this way from cymbals and bells, which are supported at the center and have their strongest vibration near the edge.

The beautiful gongs of Asia and the adjacent Pacific islands are usually made of bronze, by casting or cold-hammering or both. They may have *bosses*, raised bumps in the center, and rims folded back, or they may be slightly convex in shape. These characteristics contribute to a satisfyingly rich gong sound. Yet even the simplest unadorned metal disk, struck at the center with the right sort of beater, will produce a pleasing tone.

The description that follows is for gongs just a little more elaborate than the unadorned disk. I have suggested using aluminum disks because they produce an attractive sound and are easy to work.

For these gongs, a small boss will be hammered in the center of the disk. The boss has two effects: it controls the disk's vibration in a manner that makes the fundamental fuller and the nonharmonic overtones less prominent, and it raises the pitch of the gong. The pitch-raising effect means that you can tune the gong to a desired pitch by making a larger or smaller boss.

Instructions

1. Begin with a trip to a scrap metals yard. You will want to pick up several gongs-to-be, with the idea of creating a tuned set. Disks of aluminum hide in odd corners of most large scrap yards. Bring two or three moderately soft beaters of different weights (see the mallet plans on pages 50–53). In a pinch you can use your knuckle or fingertips. Take up each prospective gong and drop it, tapping it at the center in free fall, to get some sense of its sound. Look for disks in a range of sizes, thicknesses, and pitches.

If aluminum proves unavailable, you can try steel disks. They produce good sound but are harder to work. Whatever the metal, if you do not find any disks, you may end up cutting disks from rectangular sheets. Cutting moderately thick sheet metal to a disk shape with tin snips may prove arduous or, for thick metal, impossible. Cutting aluminum with a jigsaw or band saw and the proper blade is easier. On the other

Materials List

Lumber

Wood or other materials for a support frame of your own design

1 piece of scrap wood (Notes-1)

Hardware & Supplies

5-10 6" to 14" diameter x 1/16" to 1/8" thick aluminum disks (See step 1) ***Gongs***

1/16" diameter strong cord ***Support cords***

Suggested Tools

2 hammers, one of which is a ball peen hammer

Drill with 1/8" bit and countersink bit

Optional: hole cutter or circle saw drill attachment for 2" circles

Tools to make the support frame

Optional: jigsaw or band saw with aluminum cutting blade (Notes-2)

Eye protection (goggles)

Notes

1. Any piece of board at least 4" wide and 1' long will do.
2. For cutting disks in the event that ready-cut disk shapes are not available.

Aluminum disks as they come from the scrap yard are usually weathered and dull in color, often with unattractive marks or scratches. The gongs shown here have been given a more attractive "brushed" surface by sanding lightly with an orbital disk sander using coarse sandpaper. This was followed by a clear acrylic spray finish, to enhance and preserve the sheen.

hand, you can also try making gongs in a square shape, or hexagonal shape, or any other shape you may come across, as long as the form is not so long and narrow as to behave acoustically like a bar rather than a gong. The rules of the gong game for squares are not very different from disks nor, surprisingly, are the sounding results.

2. The simplest mounting for gongs is to suspend them vertically from some sort of framework, with two cords passing through 1/8" holes drilled in the gong (Figure 1). Back in the workshop, the first step for each gong will be to drill those holes. They should be at points of minimum vibration for the gong's fundamental vibrational mode. This mode has a region of minimum vibration in the form of a ring somewhere around 30% of the gong's radius in from the edge. (Its precise location depends upon the size of the boss and other factors, but this 30% figure will yield good-enough results.) Locate and mark the center of the gong, then mark the two hole locations, located 30% of the radius from the edge, at about 10 o'clock and two o'clock (imagining the disk as a clock face). Drill, then slightly ease the edges of the holes on both sides with the countersink bit. This will reduce wear on the support cord.
3. For each gong, tie a loop of cord through each hole. Start with cords of equal length to make loops of equal size. Suggested cord length: one and a half times disk diameter.
4. Raise a boss at the center of the gong (Figure 2) by hammering over a concave mold. Many things can serve as the mold. My suggestion is to use a hole cutter or a circle saw (available as an inexpensive drill accessory) to cut a 2" hole in a piece of scrap board. Place the center of the gong over the hole. Use a heavy ball peen hammer directly on the gong, or, for more control, hold the ball end of the hammer against the gong and strike it with another hammer. Before doing this, cover the head of one hammer with electrician's tape to reduce the chance of metal-against-metal chipping. Wear gloves and safety goggles. Watch your fingers.

   Hammering a small boss in a previously unbossed gong brings the pitch up considerably. Progressively enlarging the boss continues to raise the pitch but more and more slowly, until at some point the results become inconsistent. The breadth of the boss is more important than the depth for pitch purposes, and easier to control. The simplest approach to gong tuning, then, is to start with a flat gong that produces a tone somewhat below the desired tone (a musical fourth, perhaps?) and hammer a small boss at the center, gradually enlarging the boss to bring the gong up to pitch. To check the pitch intermittently as you hammer, hold it by the support cords and tap it at the center. If you overshoot and tune too high, you can lower the pitch by hammering around the periphery of the boss to reflatten it.

   What pitches to tune to? It's up to you, except that you will find that the disks you are working with will have a lot of say-so in the matter. A given disk will sound good only over a certain tuning range. For that reason, it is likely that you will develop your tuning as you proceed, arriving at something well-suited to your particular collection of disks.
5. I leave to you the design of a support framework from which to hang the disks, but here are a few considerations:

   —The cords should angle out and away from the gong so they won't damp or rattle against the gong when it vibrates.

   —It would be easy to hang the gongs by simply looping the support cords over a 2 x 4 set horizontally, but with such a system the gongs are hard to remove without untying or disassembling things. Consider an alternative like that in Figure 2, which allows for easy removal and replacement.

   —Gongs take up space. To keep things from getting out of hand, you can make many gongs tuned to many different pitches, but use a frame that holds only a few at a time. Hang those gongs that you want to use at a particular time, and replace them with others as the need or the urge strikes.

   —Consider setting your gongs up outdoors. They look nice in the yard; the sound carries well; the aluminum will not suffer too much in the rain. If you take this approach, choose an especially durable weatherproof cord, as constant motion from wind tends to rapidly fray the support cords.

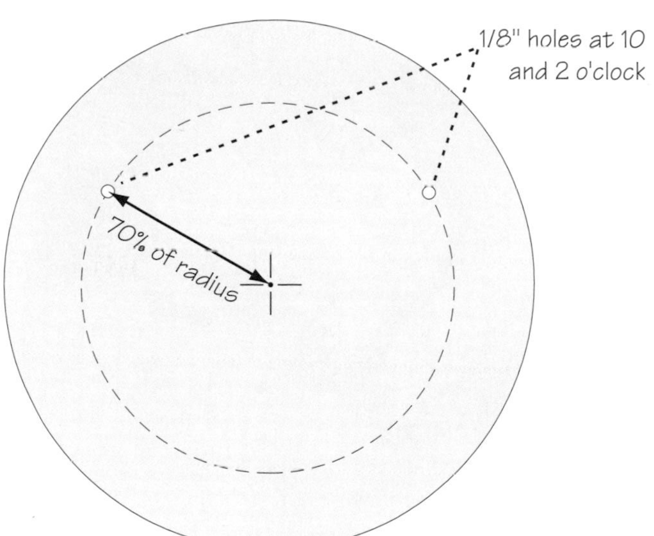

FIGURE 1
SUPPORT-HOLE LOCATIONS

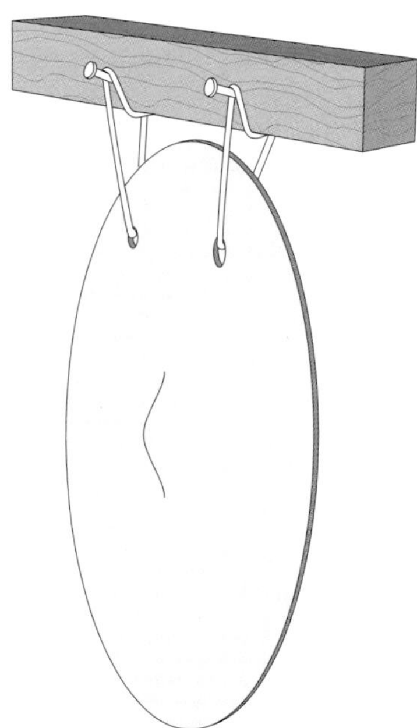

FIGURE 2
GONG HANGING FROM MOUNTING SYSTEM. NOTE THE SMALL BOSS RAISED AT THE CENTER OF THE GONG. NOTICE THAT THE CORDS ANGLE OUT AND AWAY FROM THE GONG, AND THAT THE CORDS ARE LOOPED OVER NAILS IN THE SUPPORT BEAM IN A WAY THAT ALLOWS THE GONG TO BE EASILY HUNG OR REMOVED.

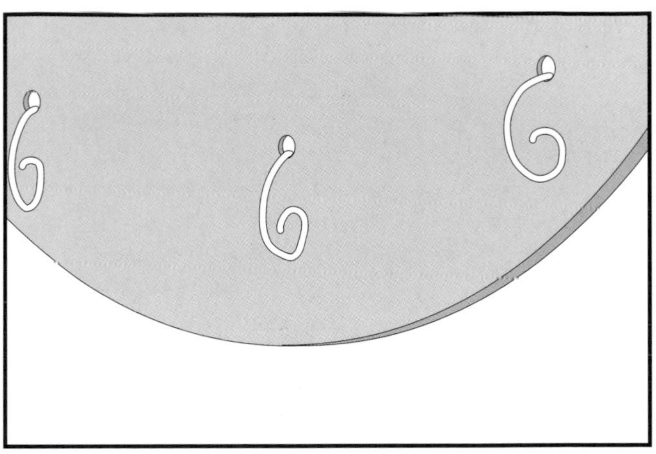

FIGURE 3
SHORT SEGMENTS OF FINE WIRE PASSING THROUGH SMALL HOLES ADD SIZZLE TO THE GONG TONE, ESPECIALLY WITH CYMBALLIKE STAINLESS STEEL GONGS. THE LOOPED ENDS OF THE WIRE SEGMENTS PREVENT THEM FROM SLIPPING OUT OF THE HOLES.

PLAYING TECHNIQUE

Strike the gongs at the boss using moderately soft beaters such as the high-bounce rubber ball beaters described on page 51. If possible, use a larger and/or slightly softer mallet for large gongs, and a smaller, slightly harder mallet for small gongs.

VARIATIONS

Because they are so easy to make and play, these simple gongs offer a lot of opportunities for exploration. For example, large steel disks (not hard to find at scrap yards) will yield a bigger, longer-sustaining sound. If you keep the steel disks outdoors they will rust dramatically, without noticeable effect on the sound. At the opposite extreme, thin sheets of stainless steel (which is much harder than common steel) will produce a splashy sound without clear pitch, similar to a cymbal sound—a nice complement to the pitched gong sounds. You probably won't find stainless disks, but rectangles are just as good. You can make a sizzle gong by adding a rattle, in the form of a loop of fine wire as shown in Figure 3. For more sizzle, add several of them. This is especially effective with a stainless steel splash gong.

Acknowledgment: Reinhold Banek and Jon Scoville describe this sort of gong in their book *Sound Designs*, and this plan owes a great deal to them.

Bell Tree

MODERATELY EASY

We will not be making any bells in this book. Instead, we will find them. Among the secondhand goods to be found at thrift stores everywhere, and among the oddities lurking in industrial scrap yards, are many cup-shaped things of metal. These include various sorts of bowls and cups, metal lamp shades, steel fence post caps, and lots of miscellaneous components from defunct industrial or household items. Whatever their original purposes, many of these objects will produce an excellent bell tone if held properly and struck with a lightweight metal rod. For the bell tree described here, you will gather a collection of scrap and secondhand bell-like objects and array them before the player on a special bell holder in the form of the most twisted, knotted tree branch you can find.

On page 24 I contrasted gongs with bells, saying that bells vibrate most strongly near the rim and minimally at the center. Accordingly, bells sound best supported at the center and struck near the rim. This will be your guiding principle both in searching for potential bells and in affixing them to the branch.

The bells, as they come to you, will ring at whatever pitches they happen to ring at. You may enjoy the random tonality that results. On the other hand, if you wish, you can retune them, either to create a prescribed scale or just to find a more pleasing variety of pitches.

Here are rudimentary principles of bell tuning. (These rules are for tuning the fundamental pitch in small bells. The centuries-old art of overtone tuning in large bells is fascinating but not a topic for the current book.) To raise the pitch of a bell, reduce the mass in the regions of large vibrational movement—that is, at the rim. The easiest way to do that is to grind the rim uniformly all around, in effect shortening the bell. Lowering the pitch is more difficult: you need either to add weight near the rim somehow or reduce the rigidity in the areas that must flex when the bell vibrates. These areas include most of the bell, but you can have the most effect by thinning the walls nearer the base, being sure once again to remove material uniformly all around.

Instructions

1. Cut two 10" lengths of 1/8" or 3/16" metal rod to serve as beaters. Remove any burrs and round the ends by filing, grinding, or sanding.
2. Make a trip to a metals scrap yard and/or a big, well-stocked secondhand store. Take the metal beaters. Look for anything roughly bell-shaped or cup shaped. One item that works well: steel fence post caps (made in a range of sizes to cap the steel poles on cyclone fences; often found in scrap yards or new, for not too much money, at fencing supply outlets).

   Whenever you come across a likely candidate, hold it or let it rest at the center or base, strike the side near the rim with the beater, and listen to the tone quality. Keep those whose sound you like. Anything larger than about 5" in diameter or depth is probably too large for the current project, unless you intend to use a particularly large branch. Nothing is too small if it sounds good. Look for bells of diverse pitches. Try to get at least 10 bells. If possible, purchase more than you think you will need; you will be glad to have plenty to choose from.
3. Do you like the pitch relationships between the bells you have found? If not, consider altering the pitch for some or all of them once you've brought them home or to the shop. Bell tuning procedures are described in the introduction to this plan on page 28.
4. Find a suitable tree branch. A single branch, if it has some bends, can be attractive. A branch that divides into a number of smaller branches might be nicer still. For my bell tree, shown in the photograph, I used the wood of a local shrub called manzanita, whose God-given nature it is to be as convoluted and ornate in form as possible. Oak branches often have an attractively twisted form, and other local species may serve the purpose in your area. Driftwood, too, can be lovely.

   And how big should it be? You can decide based upon your aesthetic inclinations and the space available in your living room. The one shown in the photos is about 20" high and 26" wide. You will need to trim the ends of the branches because the natural tips would be too thin to support the bells. Choose your piece so that at the point where the branches are to be cut off, they are no less than 5/16" thick.

Materials List

Lumber

1 10" x 14" board or plywood (approximate size) *Base*

Hardware & Supplies

10 to 20 salvaged bell forms (See step 2) ***Bells***

An attractively twisted branch, with several sub-branches (See step 4) ***Bell holder***

1/8" or 3/16" dia. x 20" metal rod ***Beater***

#6 machine screws (Notes-1)

#6 cap nuts, one for each bell

Flat rubber washers, such as faucet washers, one or two per bell

2 #10 wood screws, 2-1/2" long (Notes-2)

4 furniture glides

Sandpaper

Epoxy glue

Wood finish of your choice

Alcohol for cleanup

Paintbrush or rag

Suggested Tools

Bow saw or pruning saw

Hacksaw

Carpenter's saw or power saw

Drill with 5/32", 1/8", and 3/16" bits

Center punch and hammer

Screwdriver and adjustable wrench

Optional: Bench grinder for tuning the bells

Notes

1. The machine screw lengths you use will be determined by the thickness of your branch and its sub-branches, which will vary from place to place along the branch. With this in mind, get several each of several lengths: 3/4", 7/8", 1", 1-1/4", 1-1/2", etc.
2. Depending on the form and mounting arrangement of your branch, shorter wood screws may be called for. See Figure 2.

5. After you've chosen a branch and got it back home, look at it critically. Consider how it should ultimately look, how it should be oriented, and where along its limbs the bells can best be located. Then trim accordingly. At the point where the base should be, make a cut such that the cut surface will rest flat on the base when the branch is in the desired orientation. Double-check this after cutting by holding the branch on a flat surface. If the bottom is not cut level or won't sit flush, then file, trim or recut as necessary.
6. Typical bell mounting is shown in Figure 1. For each bell, follow these steps:
   A. Drill the 5/32" mounting hole through the center of the bell.
   B. At the point along the branch where the bell is to be mounted, make an indentation with a center punch, then drill through the branch with the 5/32" bit.
   C. Affix the bell to the branch using a #6 machine screw and cap nut, with a rubber washer serving as a spacer (Figure 1). The length of the machine screw will depend on the thickness of the bell and the branch at the point in question.
7. Cut the wood for the base. Its size will depend on the size of your branch. For the bell tree in the photo, with its 26" spread, I found a 9" x 14" board to be adequate. Sand the wood and round the edges as needed. Place the four furniture glides at the corners of what is to be the underside.
8. Hold the branch on the base in its intended position, and trace around the bottom of the branch to mark its location on the base. Remove it, and drill two 3/16" screw holes within the marked periphery. The exact location of these holes will depend on the way the branch sits on the base (Figure 2).
9. Hold the branch in place again, insert two #10 wood screws through the holes in the underside of the base, and tap them with a hammer to mark the screw locations on the cut surface at the bottom of the branch. Predrill the screw holes at those locations with a 1/8" bit.
10. Mix some epoxy glue and spread it on the cut surface. Use two #10 screws to assemble the branch to the base, with the glue to reinforce it. The length of the screws you use will depend on the shape and angle of the bottom of the branch, as shown in Figures 2A and 2B. After tightly screwing the branch to the base, use alcohol and a rag to remove excess glue that squeezes out of the joint. When the glue has dried, the bell tree is finished.

Playing Technique

Strike the bells near the rims with the metal beaters.

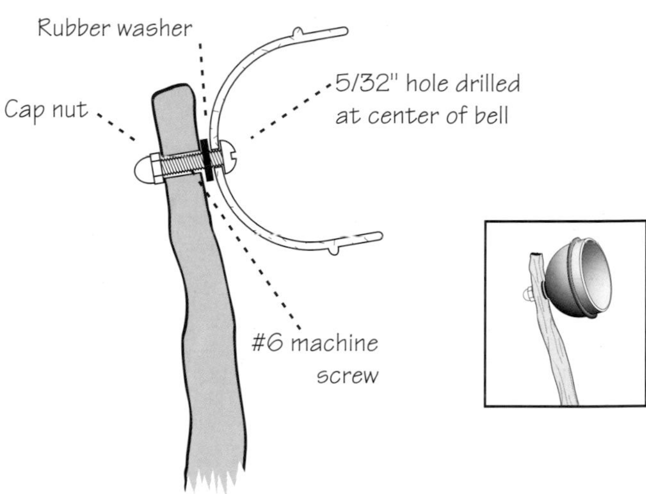

FIGURE 1

Attaching the bells to the tree. The length of the machine screw depends on the thickness of the branch and the bell. A machine screw that is a bit too long can be made to fit by adding another rubber washer as a spacer.

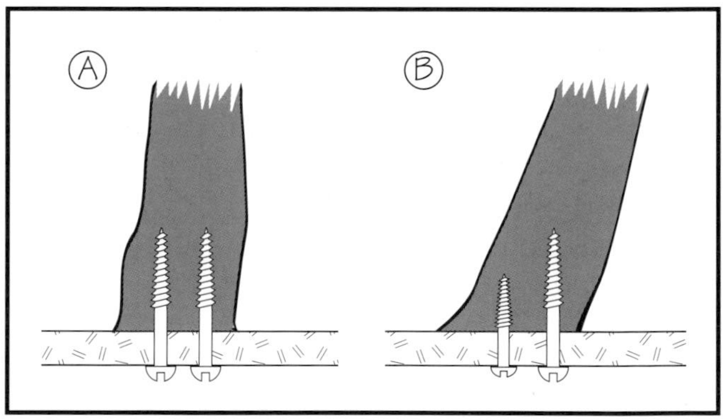

FIGURE 2

Attaching the branch to the base. A, if the branch rises roughly at a right angle to the base, use two fairly long wood screws to secure it; B, if it rises from the base at an angle, use one long screw for maximum strength and one shorter one.

Rumba Box

DIFFICULT

THIS RUMBA BOX HAS A CARRYING HANDLE ADDED ON THE SIDE (OFF-CENTER FOR BETTER BALANCE), AND DECORATIONS IN OPAQUE BLACK AND WHITE ACRYLIC.

You may be familiar with the plucked prong instruments sometimes called (inaccurately) thumb pianos. They exist in diverse forms throughout most of Africa south of the Sahara, known by various local names including *sansa, kalimba, mbira,* and others. They have become increasingly popular in the West as well, but only in recent years, as relatively few of the instruments seem to have come to the New World with the slave trade. Yet a few do appear in parts of South America and the Caribbean. Interestingly, these New World versions usually appear as large bass instruments—something only rarely seen in Africa. The Jamaican name for the big bass kalimba is *rumba box.* Elsewhere, other names are used, most common being the Cuban *marimbula.* Rumba boxes in Jamaica are used primarily for ensemble playing in Calypso and Mento bands, much like a string bass. They work wonderfully in that role, having a satisfyingly rhythmic quality—lots of oomph, even if the volume is fairly modest.

The instrument presented here is even bigger than the Jamaican rumba box (it has a lot more prongs too). The idea is to create an instrument that will project strongly well down into the bass clef. Having the big soundboard and air chamber does make a difference in delivering those low frequencies.

The design has room for 25 prongs, enough for two chromatic octaves. The suggested range is A_1 to A_3, putting the lowest note a fourth higher than the lowest on a string bass. The bridge on which the prongs are mounted has a two-tier configuration, which allows (at your option) a piano-keyboard-type layout for the pitches. As a simpler alternative, you can make your instrument with a single-tier prong mounting, allowing for two octaves of a diatonic scale (seven tones per octave). See notes for this option under "Variations" on page 38.

The rumba box player here is using wooden picks as described under "Playing Technique" and shown in Figure 8.

Materials List

Lumber

1 3/4" x 4' x 8' plywood (Notes-1) ***Sound box***
1 1/8" x 26" x 26" plywood (Notes-2) ***Soundboard***
1 1/2" x 1" x 6' any wood ***Struts***
1 1/2" x 4" x 18" ***Bottom of bridge base***
1 1" x 1" x 18" ***Top of bridge base***

Hardware & Supplies

1 1/8" x 3/4" x 36" steel bar ***Top of bridge***
3 1/8" x 3' spring-tempered steel rod (Notes-3) ***Prongs***
1 3/32" x 3' spring-tempered steel rod ***Prongs***
25 1/4" x 20 hex head machine screws with washers
2 #10 x 2-1/2" machine screws with nuts and washers
2 #10 x 1-1/2" machine screws with nuts and washers
2" finishing nails
Epoxy glue
Wood glue
Wood finish of your choice

Suggested Tools

Carpenter's saw or circular saw
Jigsaw or coping saw
Hacksaw
7/16" wrench (box wrench, ratchet, or adjustable crescent wrench)
Hammer
Sander or sandpaper
Drill and 7/32" bit
1/4" x 20 tap and tap wrench (Notes-4)
Bench grinder (Notes-5)
Vise
4 C-clamps
Paintbrush or rag

Notes

1. Low-grade plywood will do. For better appearance use a higher grade, or substitute 1" x 12" board for the top, bottom, and sides.
2. Most of the available 1/8" plywoods, with their veneers of various attractive hardwoods, will be of adequate quality.
3. This rod is sold under the name "music wire" in 3' lengths and a range of diameters in model shops and hobby stores.
4. Taps are special bits for cutting threads in a predrilled hole. They're widely available and not too expensive.
5. Cutting the tempered steel rods with a saw is almost impossible, but you can grind through them without difficulty. Alternatively, if you don't have access to a grinding wheel, consider purchasing a grinding bit for an electric drill. Hand files will do the job, but laboriously.

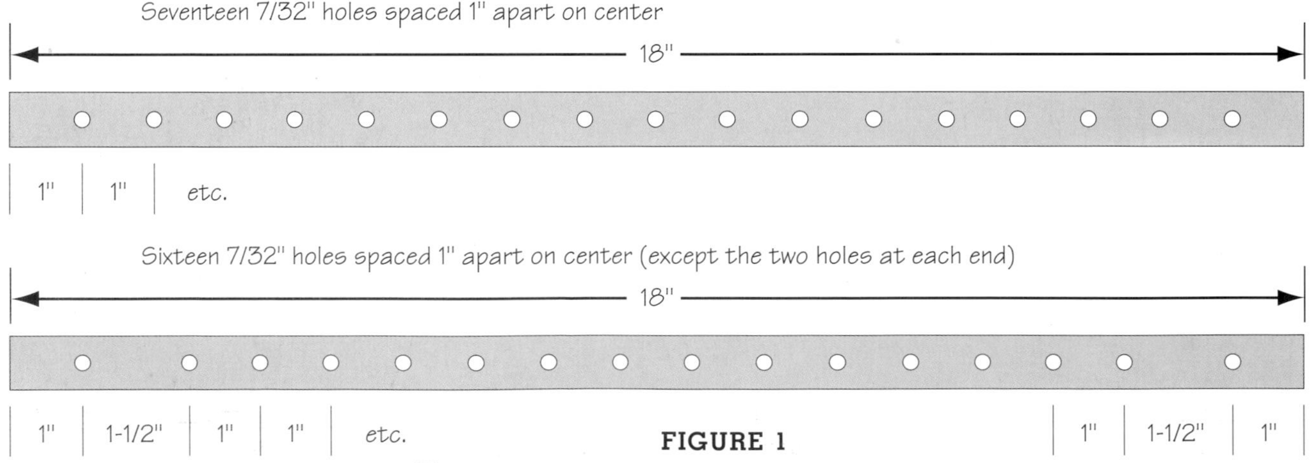

FIGURE 1
Hole spacings in the two metal bridge-top pieces

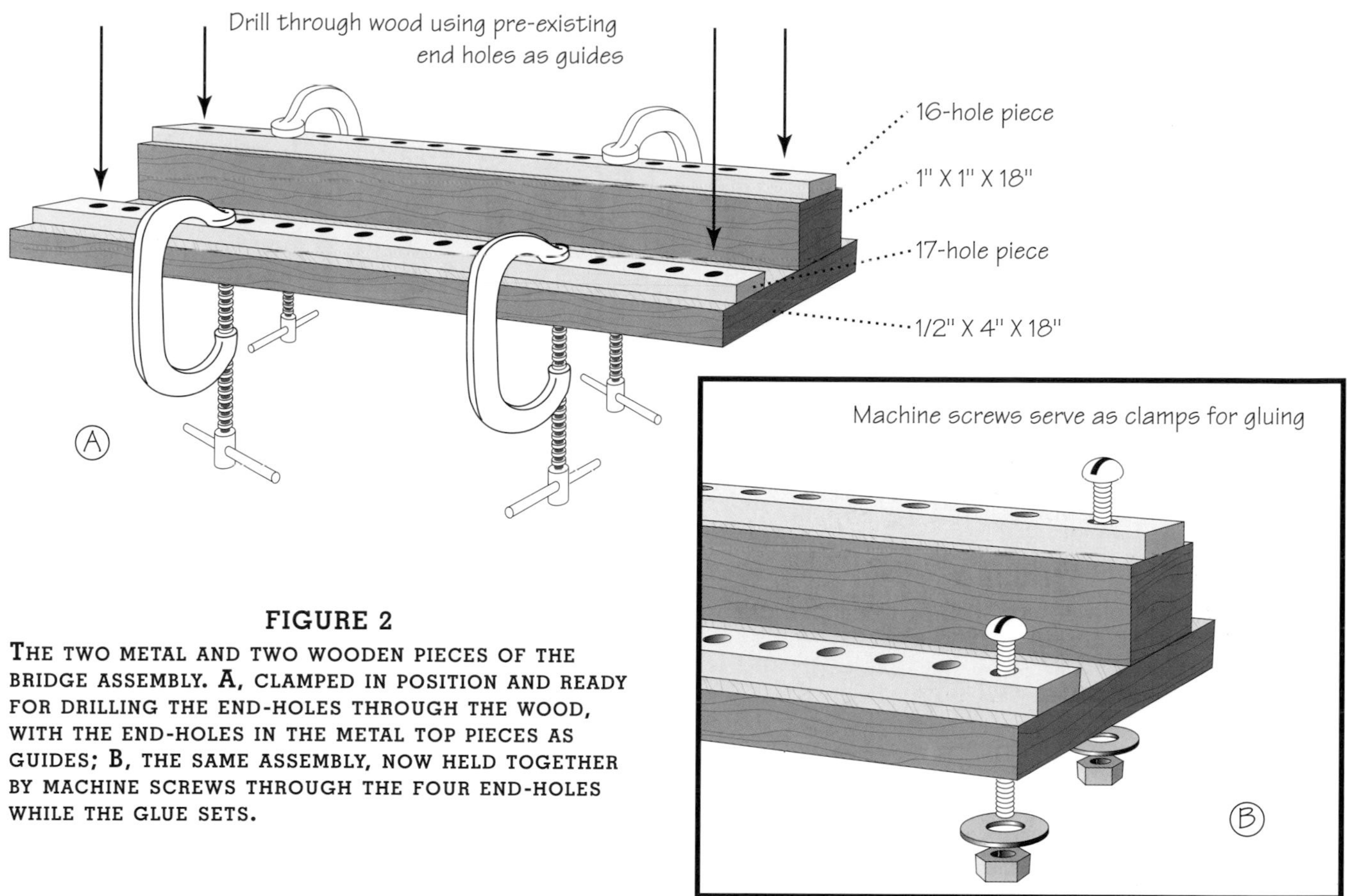

FIGURE 2

THE TWO METAL AND TWO WOODEN PIECES OF THE BRIDGE ASSEMBLY. A, CLAMPED IN POSITION AND READY FOR DRILLING THE END-HOLES THROUGH THE WOOD, WITH THE END-HOLES IN THE METAL TOP PIECES AS GUIDES; B, THE SAME ASSEMBLY, NOW HELD TOGETHER BY MACHINE SCREWS THROUGH THE FOUR END-HOLES WHILE THE GLUE SETS.

INSTRUCTIONS

1. Cut two bridge top pieces from the steel bar, both 18" long. Drill the 7/32" holes—33 of them all together—in the two pieces, as shown in Figure 1.
2. Cut the two wood pieces for the bridge. Clamp them together with the metal top pieces (Figure 2A), and drill through the four indicated end holes already in the metal, right through the wood. Remove the clamps. Mix some epoxy, and spread it on all the surfaces where the three pieces contact one another. Avoid spreading excess glue near the four screw holes. Take four #10 machine screws and tightly screw the whole thing together (Figure 2B). Use alcohol to clean up any epoxy that squeezes out around the edges. The screws are used temporarily for gluing purposes; the reason to avoid getting glue around the screw holes is to avoid gluing them in place.
3. While the epoxy dries on the bridge assembly, you can build the sound box as shown in Figure 3, page 36. If you are an experienced woodworker, make it beautiful in all the ways you know how. If not, you can (as I did) use simple butt joints, held together with wood glue and finishing nails.
4. Mark the outline of the soundboard on the 1/8" plywood at 26" x 26". Then cut it about 1/8" oversized in each dimension (this will ensure a generous fit; it will be trimmed later).
5. With a jigsaw or coping saw, cut a sound hole in the upper left portion of the board (Figure 4, page 36). The hole can be a 5" diameter circle, or you can make it a more decorative shape of about the same total area. The hole (and later the bridge assembly) should be located in such a way that the grain of the wood will run vertically on the assembled instrument.

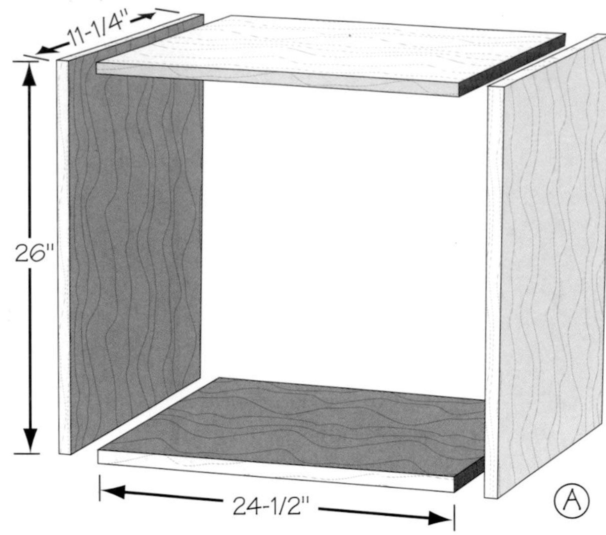

FIGURE 3

The assembly of the sound box. A, the sides can be assembled with simple butt joints, glued and nailed with finishing nails; B, the back of the box is ready to be glued and nailed in place.

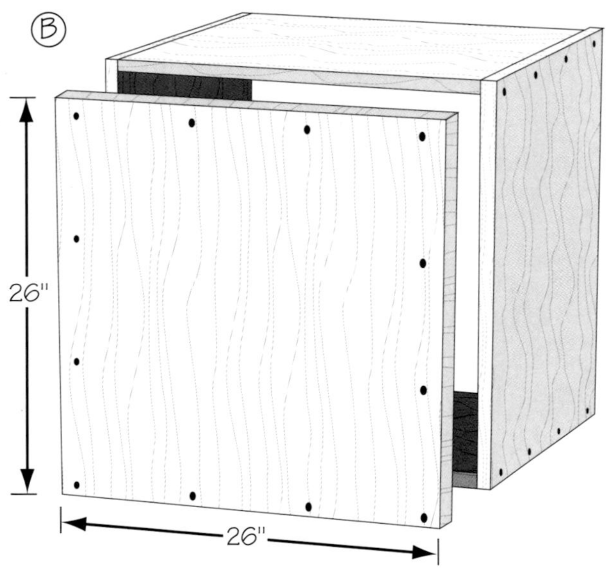

6. Cut the five 1/2" x 1" struts to lengths of 16", 15", 14", 13", and 12". Place the soundboard face down on a flat clean surface, and mark the locations for the struts on the back of the board (Figure 4). Glue the struts in place using epoxy. Find some very heavy objects to weigh them down as they dry (got any cinder blocks around the house?). Make sure they don't slip out of position as you place the weights.
7. While the struts dry, you can return to the bridge assembly. Assuming the glue is dry, use the 7/32"

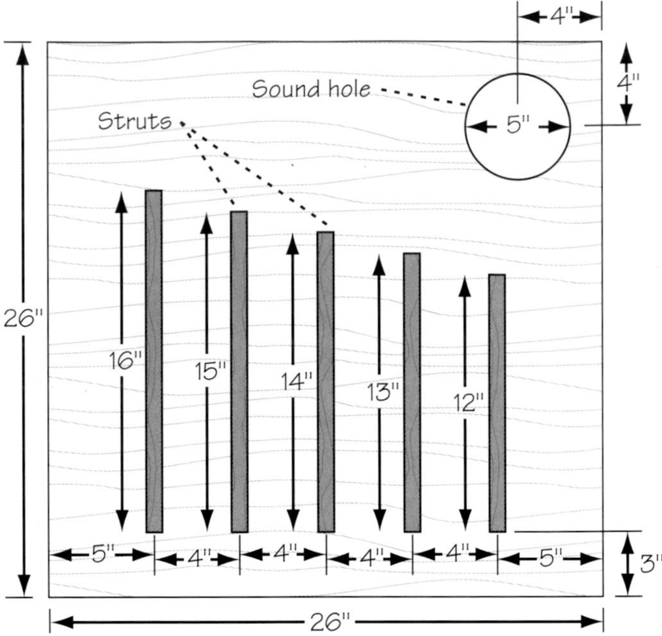

FIGURE 4

The back side of the soundboard. Shows the location of the struts and the sound hole.

bit to drill through the remaining 29 holes already in the metal top piece, going all the way through the wood. Then use the 1/4" x 20 tap and the tap wrench to thread those 25 holes. Run the threads through the metal and 1/2" or so into the wood. If you have never done this before, drill a hole in a scrap piece of metal and experiment. The trick is, once you've got the tap started in the hole, turn it clockwise just a bit at a time—an eighth or a quarter of a turn—then back it up a half turn or more, continue forward another eighth or quarter past the previous stopping point, then back up again, and so forth. When you are doing it right, you will hear and feel the tiny bits of metal breaking off and dropping out as you go.

8. When the soundboard struts are dry, you can glue and screw the bridge assembly to the board. Mark the bridge location on the front of the soundboard (Figure 5). Remove the four #10 machine screws from the bridge assembly. Place the bridge on the board, holding it carefully in place. Put the machine screws back in their holes, so that they drop against the soundboard beneath, and tap them with the hammer. This will mark the location for drilling the screw holes in the soundboard. Remove the bridge and drill with the 7/32" bit at the points

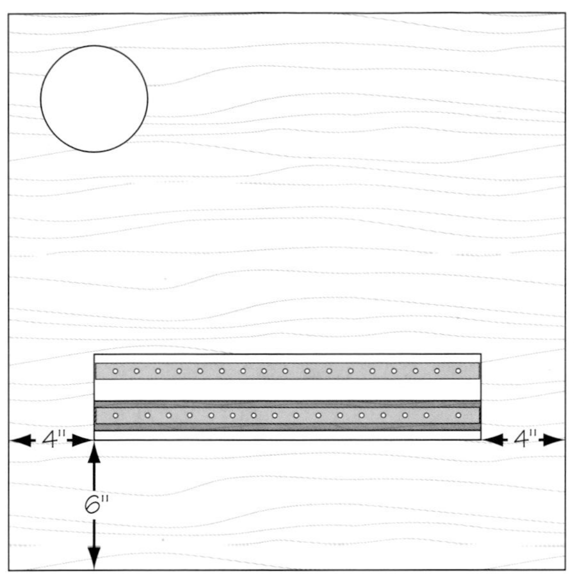

FIGURE 5

THE FRONT OF THE SOUNDBOARD. SHOWS THE LOCATION OF THE BRIDGE ASSEMBLY.

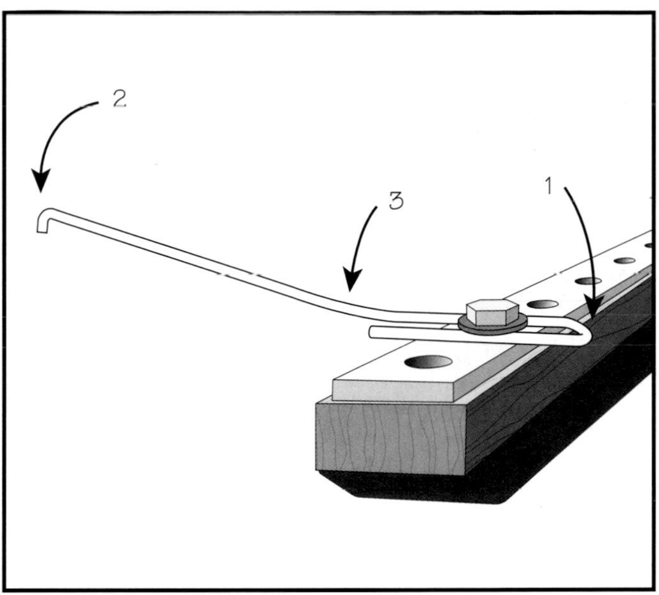

FIGURE 6

MOUNTING SYSTEM FOR THE PRONGS. SHOWS THE THREE BENDS IN THE PRONG.

the screws marked. The holes should pass through the two side struts. Mix some epoxy and spread it on the underside of the bridge assembly. Place the bridge in position on the soundboard, line up the holes in the bridge and board, put the screws through and tighten. The screws will hold the ends. To ensure good bonding at the middle, clamp or weight the center of the bridge against the soundboard. Clean up extra epoxy with alcohol.

9. When the epoxy is dry, attach the soundboard to the box with wood glue and finishing nails. Trim and sand away any overhang. Now you can do any finish work that you want to do: sand all the joints flush, ease the edges by sanding, and sand any of the flat surfaces that need it. Apply whatever wood finish you wish.
10. Time now to cut and bend the tongues, mount them on the box and tune them. The following procedure applies to all 25 tongues. Figure 6 shows the tongue mounting system, and Figure 7 is a chart indicating rod diameters and providing some sense of what lengths to expect across the range. The lengths you cut need not be precise, because the mounting system allows for later tuning adjustments. In any case, after cutting and

PRONG #	PITCH	THICKNESS	APPROX. LENGTH
1	A_1	1/8"	8"
2	Bb_1	1/8"	7-3/4"
3	B_1	1/8"	7-1/2"
—	—	—	—
—	—	—	—
9	F_2	1/8"	6"
—	—	—	—
—	—	—	—
16	C_3	1/8"	5-1/4"
17	Db_3	3/32"	4-1/2"
—	—	—	—
—	—	—	—
25	A_3	3/32"	3-1/2"

FIGURE 7

PRONG PITCHES, THICKNESSES, AND APPROXIMATE LENGTHS. THE DATA IS GIVEN FOR SEVERAL REPRESENTATIVE PRONGS; THESE WILL ALLOW YOU TO MAKE REASONABLE ESTIMATES FOR THOSE IN BETWEEN. THE GIVEN LENGTHS ARE ACTIVE LENGTHS, INCLUDING THE LENGTH OF THE BENT TIP BUT NOT INCLUDING THE U-BEND SECTION THAT DOES NOT VIBRATE. WHEN CUTTING THE PRONGS, ADD ABOUT 3" TO THE GIVEN LENGTH TO ALLOW FOR THE U-BEND.

mounting the first few tongues, you will be able to gauge about how much shorter to cut each subsequent rod as you go along. Start with the longest tongue, which goes on the side of the bridge farthest from the sound hole. The bilevel bridge configuration allows for many possible pitch layouts; you may want to use a keyboardlike arrangement with the naturals in the lower row and the sharps and flats arrayed like the piano's black keys in twos and threes above. Here is the procedure that you will follow for each tongue:

A. Cut the section of spring-tempered rod to the expected overall rod length. Do this by grinding through the rod. (Wear safety goggles!) For safety, carefully round off the ends of the rods immediately after cutting. The points that remain after grinding through are viciously sharp.

B. Figure 6 shows the mounting system for the tongues and the bends in the prong. There are three bends: 1) The *U*-bend at the base allows the tongue to stay in place around the hold-down bolt, yet to slide for tunability. The parallel sections should be just far enough apart to fit around the bolt—that is, 1/4" apart. 2) A length of about 3/8" should be bent down 90 degrees at the opposite end, to round the playing end. 3) The shaft of the tongue should be bent so that it curves slightly upward away from the soundboard, to give it playing room. The short leg of the *U* should end up on the left relative to the upward curve of the shaft for all prongs (or always on the right—just be consistent). You will be able to do the bending without too much difficulty using gloved hands and a bench vise.

C. After the bending is done, take one of the 1/4" x 1/2" hex head screws and matching washers, and put the tongue in place on the bridge (Figure 6). As a starting position, place the prong so that the screw will tighten down over a point near the middle of the *U*-section of the rod. Tighten the screw down and pluck the prong. If the pitch is higher than the intended pitch for that prong, loosen the screw and slide the prong farther out, so as to effectively lengthen it. If the pitch is too low, slide it in. Tighten the screw down again, and test the pitch. Repeat until you get the pitch right. If necessary, put that prong aside and make a new prong of better length to achieve the intended pitch. Follow the above steps for all 25 prongs. With all the prongs in place, the rumba box is complete.

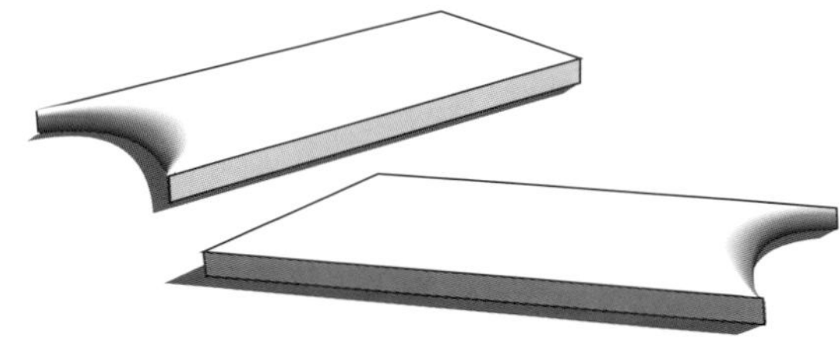

FIGURE 8

Wooden rumba box picks about 1/2" x 2". The curvature at the picking end keeps the pick from sliding sideways off the prong.

Playing Technique

Play by plucking the prongs. You must pluck them forcefully for good volume: the rumba box is not a delicate instrument. This is not traditional, but I have found that using wooden picks like those shown in Figure 8 is a great help in developing a good, strong sound and clear tone quality.

In the traditional playing position for rumba boxes, the player actually sits on the box as if it is a bench, reaching down with the hands between the legs to pluck the prongs. The box we've built here is so big that this position is awkward. An alternative is to kneel behind the box. Pull it down so that it rests in your lap, or tip it over all the way so that it lies on its back. For all of these positions, the visual impression created in performance is not what one might call elegant, but that's the spirit of the rumba box. What works, works.

Variations

With no alteration to the basic box, you can substitute shorter and/or thinner prongs to give the instrument a higher range.

For a simpler instrument, eliminate the dual-tier bridge and give your rumba box just one row of 15 prongs. This will restrict you to a diatonic scale, but that's still more than traditional rumba boxes have. For the single wooden bridge piece, use a piece of 1" x 3" board (or, for convenience, use a piece of finished nominal 1 x 4).

A Word About Relative Masses and Rigidities

The sounding elements of the rumba box are fairly heavy and rigid. They drive the soundboard forcefully when they vibrate. If the mountings were not strong and heavy enough, the prongs would not have sufficient counterpoise, causing the vibration to die out rapidly without producing a good tone. That is why the bridge assembly on this rumba box is made very heavy. Yet I have designed the soundboard to be fairly light (many such instruments have soundboards 3/16" or 1/4" thick). The intent is that the prongs will drive the board hard, making for a rapid transmission of energy resulting in a relatively loud sound of brief duration (suitable for a nice, oomphy bass line). Were the board made much lighter or less rigid, however, the problem of insufficient counterpoise would arise.

Small Percussion Instruments

EASY

Here are plans for several simple instruments from the percussionist's kit bag.

Clavès

Clavès consist of a pair of cylindrical hardwood sticks that produce the penetrating click once associated with popular Latin music (they are now more widely used). The trick to playing clavès is to cup one of the sticks loosely in one hand in a way that allows it to vibrate in its fundamental free-bar mode, and to strike it at the center with the other stick. In other words, one stick acts like a hand-held xylophone bar, and the other as the beater. Either stick can serve in either role.

High quality clavès are usually made from rosewood. With temperate hardwoods like maple the tone is quieter and not as sharp, but effective enough still. Even fir can produce a recognizable clavè sound, though duller.

Instructions

Cut two sections of dowel about 8" or 9" long each, unequal in length, to yield different pitches for each clavè. If more wood is available, cut extra clavès to varying lengths for a wider range of pitches.

Playing Technique

See photo above.

Materials List

Lumber

1 1" x 18" hardwood dowel (Note)

Suggested Tools

Saw

Note

A slightly larger diameter is preferable, but the widely available 1" dowel will suffice.

Slapstick

A slapstick is two small pieces of board, hinged together at one end. When the two halves slap together, they make a loud, dry slap-sound. You can make a louder slapstick, with a darker tone quality which you may or may not prefer, by carving a small air cavity within the slapping surface of each stick.

Instructions

1. Cut the two boards to size as shown in Figure 1A.
2. Optional: use a router or chisels to carve out matching hollows in the two sticks. Typical dimensions for the cavities: 1-1/2" wide x 1/2" deep x 5" long.
3. Cut the leather for two straps, each 1" x 5".
4. Use small nails or tacks to tack the straps in place on each board (Figure 1B).
5. Attach the hinge to join the two sticks (Figure 1B). A metal hinge will assure that the sticks remain aligned when they slap, but you also can use a leather or canvas hinge for more rustic appeal (inset).

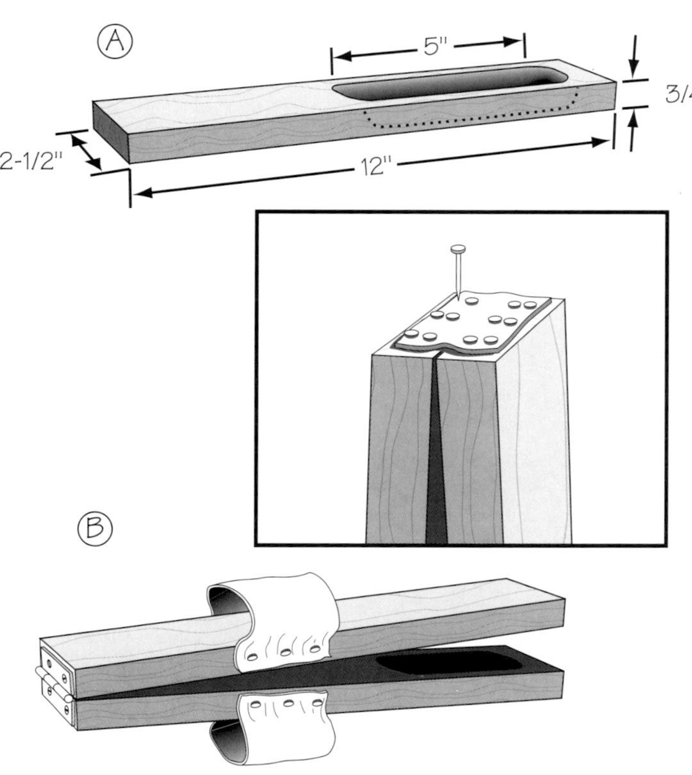

FIGURE 1

The slapstick. A, one of the two matching pieces that make the slapstick, (the cavity carved into each stick shown is optional); B, the completed slapstick with metal hinge or (in inset) cloth hinge.

Playing Technique

Insert three fingers from each hand under the straps, with the palms near the base of the sticks. Slap the two sticks together. No need to be subtle: a hard slap will produce the best tone.

Materials List

Lumber

1 3/4" x 2-1/2" x 2' board of your choice ***Sticks***

Hardware & Supplies

1 5" x 5" leather or canvas ***Straps***

1 3/4" x 2-1/2" hinge, with wood screws

Small nails or tacks

Suggested Tools

Saw

Hammer

Screwdriver

Scissors

Optional: router or chisel

Scrapers #1: Guiro

Guiro is the name most commonly used for a hollowed wood or gourd instrument with a ridged back, scraped with a short stick. Many manufactured materials have ridged surfaces and can be played in a similar manner. Among them are gas heater hose, the flexible pipe used to connect water lines under sinks, and various larger diameter plastic flex-pipes. You can easily create your own scraper from other materials, such as PVC or ABS plastic tubing, by filing or grinding ridges into the surface. The best sounds will come from hollow materials, such as tubings of at least one or two inches in diameter.

For the guirolike instrument described below we will use bamboo, because it combines a sharp surface tone with the air resonance of the hollow, as well as an attractive look and feel. Each piece of bamboo has its own personality, and if you make several of these guiros, each will sound and feel different. So do that—make a set of them. Then you can choose the best of the lot to keep, or keep them all and enjoy the variety.

Instructions

1. Cut one section of bamboo just beyond the nodes, so that the ends are stopped by the natural blockages (but see alternatives under "Variations" below). Sand and round the edges of the newly cut ends to reduce splintering.
2. Use a grinder or a narrow rat-tail file to make a series of grooves along the surface of the bamboo (Figure 2A). The grooves should be about 1/4" or 3/8" apart on center, but they need not be perfectly regular.
3. In the opposite side of the bamboo, drill two 1/2" holes (Figure 2B). Place them about one-fifth of the bamboo section's full length from each end (but again, see "Variations").
4. Bamboo is very prone to splitting due to changes in moisture content. Treat the ridged section with tung oil or a similar penetrating finish to control moisture loss. Coat the newly cut ends of the bamboo with varnish, verathane, wax, or anything else that will serve as a moisture barrier.

Playing Technique

Hold the bamboo in one hand and use the other to scrape lengthwise with a scraper (hardwood stick or screwdriver shaft). Scraping at different speeds and pressures and at different points along the scraper's shaft will bring out different sounds. When you get good at it, you will be able to make the thing talk.

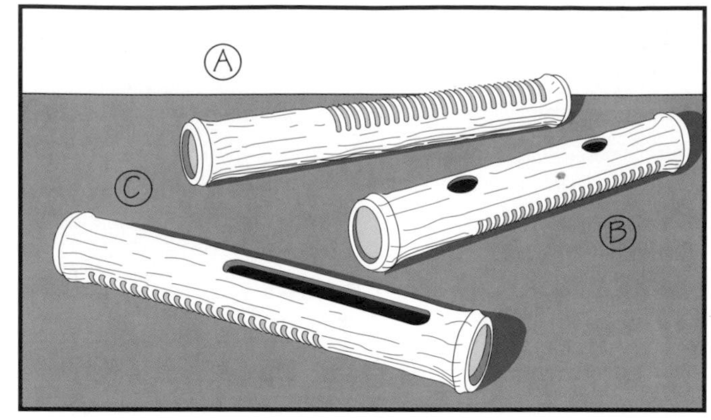

FIGURE 2

Bamboo guiro. A, ridges in the surface of the bamboo guiro (the bamboo can be held at the end that has no ridges); B, the underside of the same bamboo, showing the air resonance holes; C, optional variation: a long open slit in place of air resonance holes.

Materials List

Hardware & Supplies

1 1" - 2" x 4' bamboo pole (Notes-1)
1 1/2" x 6" hardwood stick (Notes-2)
Tung oil and varnish - See step 4

Suggested Tools

Saw
Bench grinder or rat-tail file
Drill with 1/2" bit
Sandpaper

Notes

1. Bamboo poles in this diameter often are sold at nurseries and garden supply centers.
2. The shaft of a medium-large screwdriver can work as a scraper, producing a pleasing, heavy tone. A hardwood stick about 6" long, 1/2" thick at one end and half that at the other, will yield a lighter, brighter tone (scrape with the thin end).

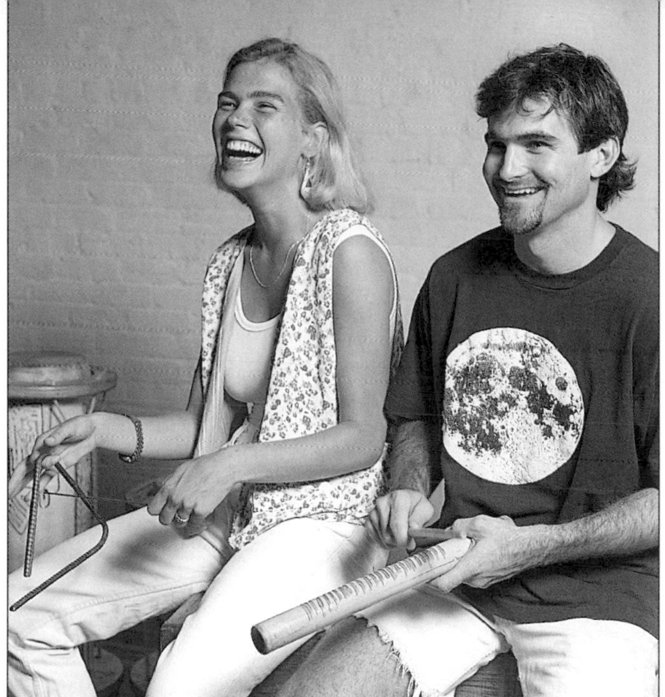

Variations

The best sound usually will come out when the enclosed air within the bamboo can communicate with the outer air through a hole somewhere. As an alternative to drilling the holes in the back, you can cut the bamboo section short of the node, so as to leave one or both ends naturally open. Another option is to replace the holes with an open slot along the back, 3/8" wide and anywhere from a few inches to most of the length of the bamboo (Figure 2C). If you do not have an electric router to do this job, drill a series of closely spaced 3/8" holes and carefully break out the material between them. In playing, use the hand that holds the bamboo to cover and uncover this slot to vary the tone quality. Master this technique, and the bamboo will *really* talk.

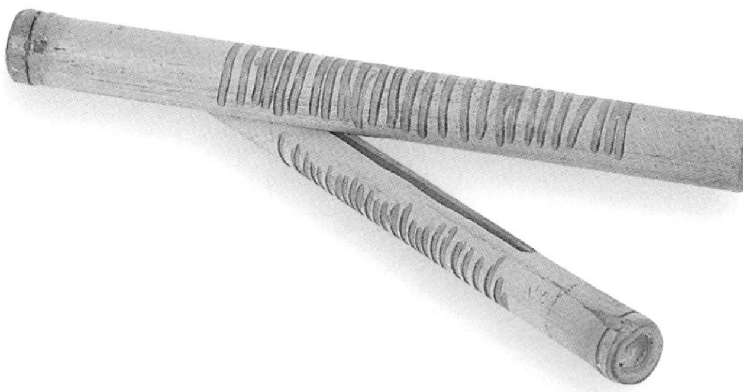

One of these guiros shows the long slot cut in the back, which allows a wider variety of timbral effects, as describe under "Variations." The other has the standard two holes drilled in the back, not visible in the photo.

Scrapers #2: Sandpaper

Sand blocks are a standard feature in books about easy-to-make children's musical instruments. The scraping sound can lend a nice rhythmic feel in adult music as well, having that insinuating, gets-under-the-skin quality. But I disagree with the sand block approach: backing the sandpaper with wood and giving it a handle makes it a little easier to play, but it dulls the tone quality, diminishes volume, and causes the sandpaper to wear out faster. My suggestion is, use the sandpaper free, without backing.

Materials List

Hardware & Supplies

2 12" x 12" sandpaper (Note)

Suggested Tools

Scissors or snips

Note

Different grits produce different tone qualities. A medium-fine grit is good for starters.

Instructions

Cut the sandpaper into two pieces, in sizes that you find you can handle comfortably. I have found that an uneven pair with one piece about 6" x 9" and the other about 4" x 6" works well. Alternatively, take two full-sized pieces, roll them up to form cylinders about 1" in diameter, and tape the ends to keep them from unraveling. The cylinders don't sound quite as appealingly gritty, but they're a little easier to play.

Playing Technique

For flat pieces: hold the larger piece more or less steady and use the smaller piece to scrape it. Experiment with different ways of holding and flexing the paper in search of the most facile technique and the best sound. With rolled cylinders: scrape in whatever way feels natural.

Triangle

The percussionist's triangle is a suspended metal rod with two sharp bends in it, struck with a narrow metal beater. An ideal triangle sound is a sizzling jangle of high overtones, with a minimum of lower-frequency bong. Any long, narrow steel rod will do fairly well on this score because such rods are rich in nonharmonic upper partials, and the hard, small beater will bring those out most strongly. In addition, the fundamental and other lower partials (the unwanted bong-tone) are scarcely heard because the rod does a very poor job of projecting lower frequencies (being so skinny, it lacks the radiating surface area required to push the longer wavelengths of lower tones). The sharp bends in the triangle have the effect of partially subdividing it into subsidiary segments, each with its own complement of partials contributing to the dissonant jangle.

Triangles normally are suspended at one corner by cords. But to bring out an astonishing rainbow of tones in your triangle, I suggest an alternative mounting which, although awkward, is justified by the resulting sound: rest the triangle on three balloons. The balloons support the triangle with the minimum possible damping, allowing it to ring to its fullest capability. In addition, the triangle transmits its vibration to the balloons. Because they have far more surface area, the balloons radiate more effectively, making the sound louder and clearer. They also radiate lower frequencies more effectively, which for traditional triangle tone can be regarded as a disadvantage. Try it anyway.

Materials List

Hardware & Supplies

1 3/8" x 20' steel reinforcement rod (rebar) (Note)

1 3/16" x 8" or 10" metal rod

A bit of cord and something to hang it from (or)

Several long, thin, sausage-shaped balloons (optional)

Suggested Tools

Hacksaw

Bench grinder or file

Vise

4' section of 1/2" interior diameter steel pipe

Note

Rebar is inexpensive, widely available at hardware stores, easy to work, and will make a triangle with decent sound. (Harder steels will produce a brighter sound.) A 20' length will allow you to make several triangles and choose the best, or keep them all and enjoy the variety.

Instructions

1. Cut a section of rebar to the desired length. Anywhere from 20" to 60" will produce good results; try 36" to start. De-burr the cut ends with a file or grinder.
2. Put two bends in the rebar to form the triangle shape. Make the sides unequal in length. The bends should be sharp, not gradual curves. When the bending is done, the two ends should be close but not touching. To make the bends: secure the rebar in the vise with the end to be bent overhanging. Place a 1/2" interior diameter steel pipe roughly 4' long over the overhanging section of rebar, and use the pipe's leverage to make the bend.

3A. Blow up three balloons. Place the balloons on a flat surface. Place the triangle on top, with a balloon under each corner. (or)

3B. Tie a suspension cord at one corner of the triangle to hold or hang it.

Playing Technique

Use the metal rod beater to strike the triangle near the corners.

Variations

A straight rod placed over two balloons has a slightly different musical character that you might enjoy. There are not quite as many conflicting overtones, and this allows you to play with more control. Strike at selected points to bring out specific overtones; damp at selected points by pinching lightly with your free hand to inhibit others. You can even play melodies this way (albeit very strange ones). It's great fun to explore. A 30" length of the 3/8" rebar is a good place to start. To prevent the two balloons from rolling, place objects alongside them to serve as blocks.

Acknowledgments: The idea of balloon mounting comes from Prent Rodgers via Tom Nunn.

Cowbell

For musical purposes, a cowbell is a heavily damped metal bell. The damping comes about because the rim is not circular but rectangular in shape and does not support sustained vibration. In addition, the player often deliberately holds the bell in such a way as to damp it further. In a good cowbell, air resonance from within the enclosure adds to the richness of the tone. The result at its best is a loud, short, not-too-clangy metal tone. We will make a cowbell of excellent tone by squashing a circular bell.

Instructions

Place the bell in a strong bench vise and gradually crank the jaws together, squashing the sides toward one another. When the formerly circular opening has narrowed to an oval a little over 1" wide, remove the bell, hold it, and strike it as described under "Playing Technique" below. You are listening for a clear, penetrating *chok!* If you hear what you want to hear, the bell is ready. If not, try putting it in the vise and narrowing a bit more.

One trick: while some bells will sound great even without this, you will get the best sound when the resonant frequency of the air enclosed in the bell is just a trifle below the frequency of the bell itself. To hear the air resonance frequency, blow over the rim of the mouth of the bell and listen for the pitch of the breathy tone that results. Then strike the bell to hear the pitch of the metal. If the air tone is higher than the metal tone, you can bring the two into better agreement by squashing further to narrow the mouth, which lowers the air resonance tone. If the air tone is too low, try rewidening the mouth a bit.

Materials List

Hardware & Supplies

3" steel fence pole caps (Note) ***Bell***

Suggested Tools

Vise

Note

These are the caps for fence poles used in cyclone fences (mentioned earlier as a possible source of bells in the bell tree plan). Used ones in a variety of sizes can often be found in scrap yards. New ones are sold at modest cost from places supplying fencing materials. The 3" diameter size seems to work particularly well as a cowbell; larger might be even better. My recommendation once again: get several caps and make several cowbells, then choose the best or enjoy them all.

Playing Technique

For most musical purposes, the preferred cowbell tone is heavily damped. Allow the fleshy part of your hand to rest on the metal as you hold it, and strike at the rim with the butt end of a drumstick or a medium hard beater (I suggest the wooden-headed mallet padded with moleskin described on page 53). Experiment with different amounts of flesh contact until you find the point where you get the maximum fullness of tone with the minimum clang.

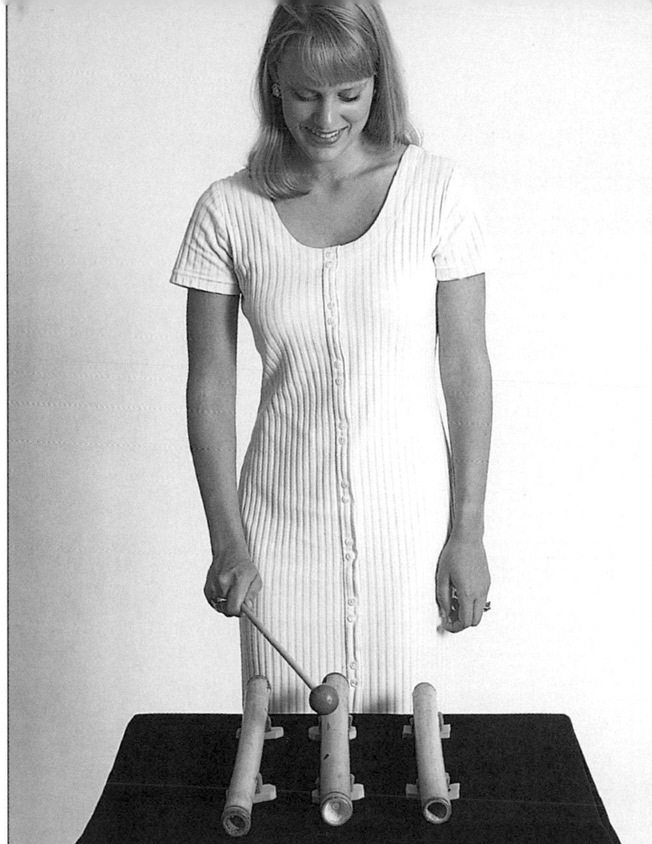

THE BAMBOO SECTION FOR THE WOODBLOCK ON THE FAR RIGHT HAS BEEN CUT SHORT OF THE NODES, LEAVING OPEN ENDS. THE OTHER TWO HAVE THEIR ENDS NATURALLY STOPPED BY THE NODES. THOSE WITH STOPPED ENDS HAVE AIR HOLES ALONG THE SIDES.

Materials List

HARDWARE & SUPPLIES

1 1" or 2" x 4' bamboo pole

1 3/4" x 1/2" x 10' roll of lightweight foam rubber weather strip

1 3/8" x 12" x 12" moderately dense foam rubber pad (Notes-1)

Adhesive for rubber or flexible plastics

Tung oil or varnish (Notes-2)

SUGGESTED TOOLS

Saw

Drill with 1/2" bit

Scissors

Sandpaper

NOTES

1. The exact size and shape of the 3/8" thick foam rubber pad is not important. It just needs to be enough to cut into 1" wide strips, 5" long for each bamboo block.
2. For notes on finishing bamboo, see step 4 in the Guiro plan on page 43.

BAMBOO WOODBLOCK

The woodblock, in its standard orchestral form, is a block of hardwood with flat, narrow cavities hollowed out from opposite sides beneath the top and bottom surfaces. Striking either surface with a drumstick or mallet produces a sharp *thok!* that is a mixture of woody percussion sound and air resonance from the cavity. You can get a similar sound less laboriously using bamboo.

There are many ways you can get a bright, woody sound from sections of bamboo. If you purchase a generous supply of bamboo, you can experiment with several approaches. If you make enough bamboo blocks at different pitches, you will have created something like a bamboo xylophone—a great-sounding instrument.

INSTRUCTIONS

1. One possible form for the bamboo woodblock uses a section of bamboo cut to include the nodes, so that the ends are stopped. Half-inch holes are drilled one-fifth of the section's length from each end. This is identical to the bamboo guiro described on page 43 and shown in Figure 2, but without the ridges. Other forms can have one or both ends open. For a particularly rich sound, review the metallophone plan. Use the side-hole drilling technique described under "Variations" in that plan (page 20) to tune the air resonance within the bamboo.
2. The bamboo blocks will need padded footings to sound well. Use the same padded footings described in steps 2A - 2D for the metallophone, page 19. Before putting on the footings, tap the bamboo at its center all the way around, listening for the striking point that produces the best tone. Place the footings on the opposite side, so that the preferred striking point faces up.

PLAYING TECHNIQUE

Strike the bamboo at the center with a moderately hard mallet. There are lots of possibilities for beaters. From among the mallets described on pages 50–53, I suggest the rubber-coated wooden-headed mallet.

Cymbals

Making a good cymbal requires specialized know-how, materials, and manufacturing techniques. You can get some very good cymbal-like sounds, however, from metal plates vibrating as gongs rather than cymbals. See the gongs plan on page 24–27, and in particular the "Variations" section at the end, for how-to information.

Shakers

You can make maraca-like instruments using almost any small, thin-walled, rigid container with hard pellets enclosed within. Likely materials for containers include food tins, plastic pill boxes, and other small metal, glass or hard plastic vessels. For the pellets, try unpopped popcorn or other dry grains, beans, peas, or seeds; BBs or small ball bearings; or pebbles. Playing handles look nice and make the playing marginally easier, but they are not essential. For a more varied sound, use a container whose lid is of a different material than the rest, for instance, a small glass jar with a metal lid. For a particularly nice drumming maraca effect, use a small can with a balloon rubber membrane stretched over the top and held in place with a rubber band.

Playing Technique

Maracas are among the most difficult of the percussionist's instruments to play well because of their inclination to produce an unwanted double beat. To avoid this, maraca players learn to play with a rolling motion. In addition to eliminating the after-beat, this opens up an additional vocabulary of sensuous swish-swish sounds.

Balloon Pellet Drum

For a very different shaker sound, place a handful of unpopped popcorn in a large balloon, then blow it up and tie it (the size that blows up to 16" works well). When you shake it, the balloon will produce an evocative low rumble-thunder sound. You can see the silhouettes of the kernels dancing energetically within, and the balloon bounces and sails erratically to the accompaniment of its own sounds when you bat it around the room. Great sport.

Acknowledgment: This idea comes from Robin Goodfellow.

Mallets

EASY

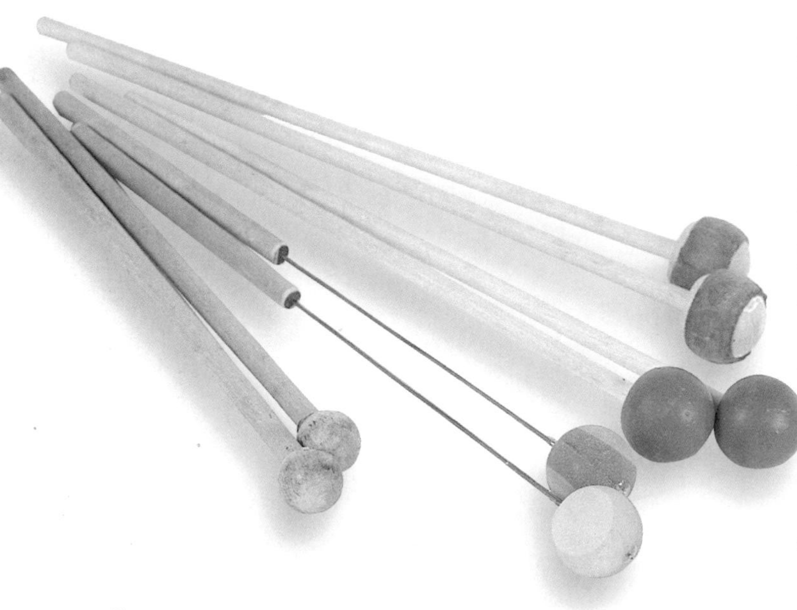

Several of the instruments in this book call for beaters of some sort. Beyond the covers of this book, too, is a world full of resonant objects just waiting for someone to come along with the right sort of percussion mallet. But an instrument that sounds delicious with a well-chosen beater is likely to be disappointing with an ill-suited one. To find the best beater for a given application, nothing is better than trial and error. Here are some general guidelines to keep in mind as you go.

Percussion mallets with small and hard mallet heads tend to bring out high frequencies that produce a bright, brittle, or clanging sound with prominent overtones. They usually work well on small, high-pitched sound sources, and do poorly in situations calling for a sound that is rich in the bass. Heavier and softer mallet heads are the reverse. Mallet heads with fuzzy surfaces tend to damp high frequencies.

The handle of the mallet makes a difference as well. With the most massive mallet heads, the handle needs to be suitably heavy and strong. But with lighter mallets it helps to have an element of springiness in the handle that allows the mallet head to bounce after striking. Springy materials don't always make the most comfortable handles—they tend to be too thin—so it often helps to have a thicker handle leading to a shaft made of a thinner and springier rod or stick, with the mallet head attached at the end.

Some mallet heads are made of a solid piece of single material, such as a sphere of wood or hard rubber, attached to the end of a stick. Others are compound, having layers of two or more materials. Compound mallet heads usually have a harder and more massive core, overlaid with a softer material. Here are some proven mallet-making materials.

Mallet handles

—For strong, rigid handles: wooden dowel, rigid metal or plastic rod, not-too-thin bamboo.

—For springy handles: smaller diameter bamboo, spring-tempered steel rod ("music wire") in diameters between 3/32" and 3/16"; some plastics.

Simple (noncompound) mallet heads

—Soft: high-bounce hard rubber balls; windings of yarn, felt, rubber bands or strips of inner tube rubber.

—Hard: spherical wooden or ceramic drawer pulls, gear-shift knobs, etc.; softballs and hardballs.

Compound mallet head cores

—Spherical drawer pulls, thread spools (the cylindrical shape makes overwrapping of other materials easier). For extra weight—large bolt heads or nuts.

Compound mallet outer layers

—Windings of yarn, rubber bands, strips of felt or inner tube; wrappings of felt or other clothlike materials including cloth adhesive tapes (duct tape); liquid plastic coating (sold as an easy-grip insulating coating for hand tools); moleskin (an adhesive-backed feltlike cloth sold as a foot care product).

Some instruments do not need mallets with separate heads; they do just as well with simple sticks. The drumsticks that are used with a drum set are specially shaped sticks of hardwood with a taper leading to a tiny head at the end. In other cases a simple metal rod works best.

At various points in this book, commonplace materials (metal rods, screwdriver handles or shafts) are suggested as suitable mallets for particular applications. Here now are plans for two more specialized mallet types, one fairly soft, the other fairly hard.

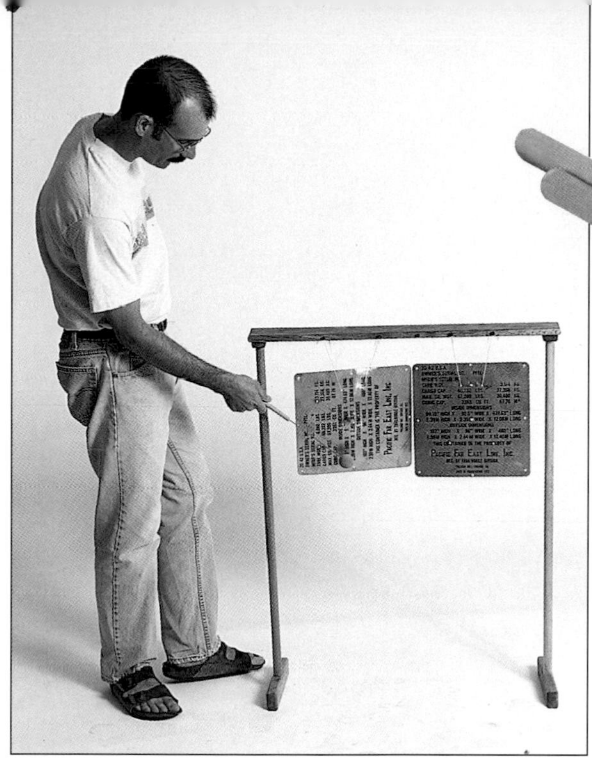

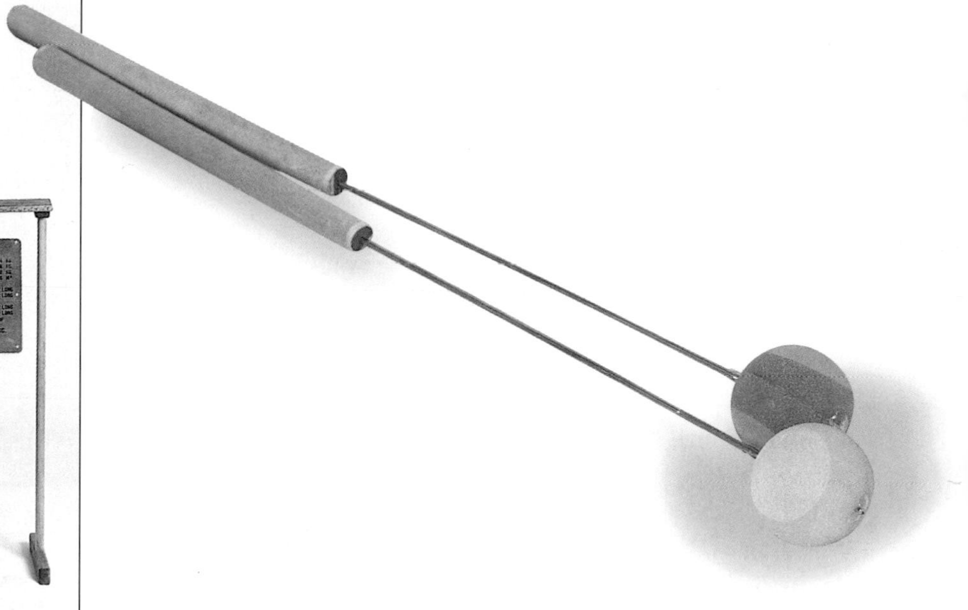

High-Bounce Ball Mallet

The high-bounce ball mallet is the greatest all-around soft mallet. It can coax good sounds out of things you might never have imagined had good sounds in them. Other sorts of rubber balls tend to be too soft for most applications.

Instructions

1. Cut two 6" lengths of 1/2" wooden dowel.
2. Cut two 10" lengths of 3/32" spring-tempered steel. See the notes on cutting spring-tempered steel rod at step 10A and at Note 5 under the Suggested Tools list in the rumba box plan on page 32.
3. Drill 5/64" holes directly into one end of each dowel, and through each ball (Figure 1). The holes in the balls will close in on themselves after the bit is removed, and that's o.k.
4. Assemble the two mallets (Figure 1). Drive the steel shafts into the holes in the handles with a hammer or rubber mallet. Force the other ends of the shafts into the balls.

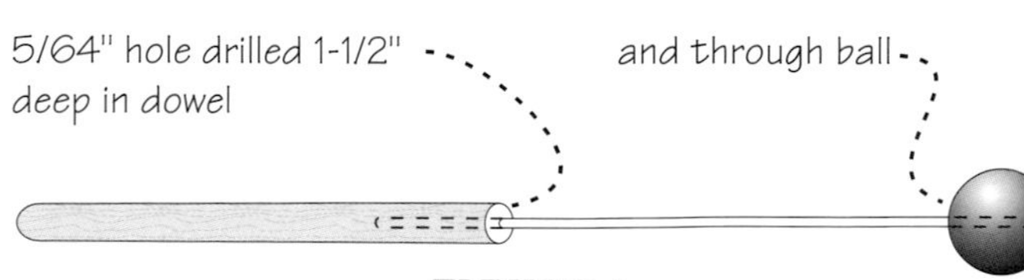

FIGURE 1
HIGH-BOUNCE BALL MALLET WITH WOODEN HANDLE AND SPRING-TEMPERED STEEL SHAFT

Materials List

Lumber

1 1/2" x 1' wooden dowel *Handles*

Hardware & Supplies

1 3/32" x 20" spring-tempered steel rod (Notes-1) *Shafts*

2 high-bounce balls (for two mallets) (Notes-2) *Mallet heads*

Suggested Tools

Hacksaw
Grinder or file
Drill and 5/64" bit

Notes

1. Sold as "music wire" at hobby shops.
2. High-bounce balls come in various sizes; your choice will depend on your purpose. You may find it valuable to make two or more pairs of mallets in different sizes.

Covered Wooden Mallet

You can make this mallet very hard or moderately hard, depending upon how you coat the surface. Make several in different sizes and with different surfaces to provide a choice of mallet types.

Instructions

1. The wooden spheres come predrilled for a metal screw. Drill these holes out larger with a 23/64" bit, stopping just short of drilling all the way through the sphere (Figure 2A).
2. Cut the 3/8" dowel to form two mallet handles, each 14" long. By sanding, make a slight taper about 3/8" long at one end of each handle.
3. Drip a bit of wood glue into the hole in the wooden sphere. Use a hammer or rubber mallet to tap the handle into the sphere, leading with the tapered end.

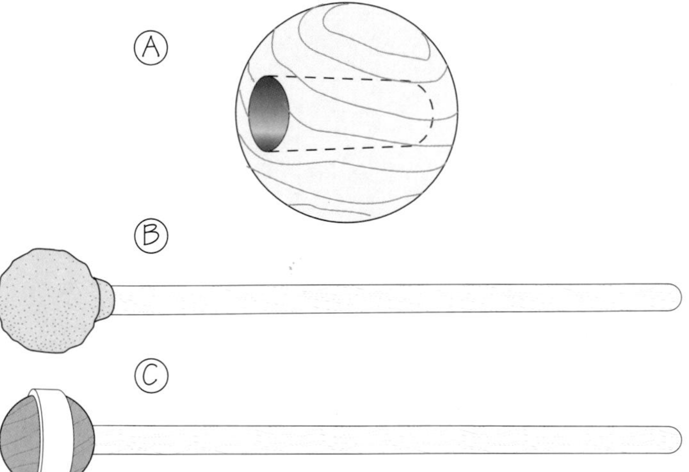

FIGURE 2

Mallets with wooden dowel handles and wooden drawer-pull heads. A, the head with the screw hole drilled out larger to accommodate the dowel; B, completed mallet with head coated in liquid plastic coating; C, mallet head wrapped with moleskin.

4. Covering the head:
   A. If you want to leave the head very hard, the pair of mallets is now finished.
   B. If you want a fairly hard head, dip the mallet heads in liquid plastic coating, following the instructions on the label. One or two coats will leave the head still quite hard; three or four coats will make it just a little softer.
   C. For a somewhat softer head, cover the playing surface with moleskin. Moleskin is slightly stretchy, allowing it to accommodate topographies such as the curved surface of the mallet head. Don't try to cover the entire surface of the head: cut a strip of moleskin between 1/2" and 1" wide (depending on the size of the head), and run it around the equator. Stretch it tight so that the edges pull down over the surface of the sphere. For a softer head, add another layer of moleskin.

Materials List

Lumber

1 3/8" x 28" hardwood dowel *Handles*

Hardware & Supplies

2 spherical hardwood drawer pulls (Notes-1) *Mallet heads*

Moleskin or liquid plastic coating (Notes-2) *Head covering/coating*

Wood glue

Suggested Tools

Hacksaw

Drill with 23/64" bit

Hammer or rubber mallet

Sandpaper

Notes

1. These are available at hardware stores in diameters ranging from 2" down to 1". Each size works well in different applications.
2. See steps 4A-C, and "Compound mallet outer layers" on page 50 for more information.

Drums

A scholarly term for drums is *membranophones*. It was coined to reflect the idea that the essential element in this class of instruments is a vibrating membrane. Typically, the membrane is a thin, flexible material such as animal skin, made rigid by stretching it over some sort of a frame. You can think of drums in terms of three main elements:

1. The membrane itself. The membrane provides the primary vibration. The player excites it by percussion or, more rarely, by friction.

2. The drum body, over which the membrane is stretched. The body may be nothing more than a shallow frame, as with a *bodhrán* or a tambourine. Or it may take the form of a deeper shell enclosing a body of air beneath the membrane, as with a conga drum. The air below deepens and enriches the drum tone.

3. The mechanism for attaching the membrane to the body. The method of attachment may be nothing more than tacking or gluing, or it may be something elaborate like the tension-control machinery on modern orchestral kettle drums.

I emphasize this last factor—the method of attachment—because it highlights one of the central considerations in drum design: the interaction between the membrane and the body of air. When the two work well together, the drum speaks with a satisfying fullness. When they do

not, the tone seems lifeless.

Worldwide you can find a great variety of drum shapes and forms. The different forms bring out the acoustic coupling between membrane and air in a number of ways and to varying degrees. But on any given drum, the degree of tension on the drumhead is an essential factor. Some drums have mechanisms for adjusting head tension, either through lacing or hardware, so that the player can tighten or loosen the membrane to get a particular pitch or to find the point at which the voice of the drum is at its fullest. Other drums have no such ready adjustment mechanisms, and then it is the maker's job to attach the head at a good tension. This is not always easy to do, and even when it is well done, that tension is likely to slip over time. In drum design, there is always this trade-off between the attractive simplicity of a directly attached head and the practical advantages of adjustable head-tuning mechanisms.

There is one last point to convey, a point I will not try to explain because I don't understand it. Drums seem to have a profound effect on people: This comes out particularly, I find, in the playing of a hand drum that you have made yourself—or better, a set of two or three drums, as that seems to considerably open up the musical possibilities. You can test this hypothesis by trying the drum plans that follow.

Hand Drum

MODERATELY DIFFICULT

The hand drum in this plan is cylindrical in shape, eight inches in diameter and 20 inches deep: large enough for a nice, full bottom tone, as well as for a variety of slap and rim tones. The plan uses lacings and a drum hoop to attach the head and make it tunable. The tension-adjusting system is not standard or traditional but is easy to make. It has a nice soft-technology quality to it, and it does the job well.

For the drum body, the plans call for heavy cardboard tubing of the sort sold at building supply centers as forms for pouring concrete pillars. This material has some advantages and some disadvantages. It is inexpensive, widely available, easy to work, and environmentally benign. But it is not as strong as other materials used for drums and—potential disaster!—it turns to mush if it gets wet. It is unattractive in itself, but easy to decorate, as it takes paint well. The body's light weight is convenient but may be responsible for some loss in tone quality, because it does not provide good counterpoise for the movement of a hard-hit drumhead. For thoughts on alternative drum body materials, see "Variations" below. In the meantime, don't disdain this drum for the impermanence of its materials. It has a good sound.

For the drums shown here, the cardboard bodies were given a light, translucent spray of white paint, creating a cloudy effect. They were then decorated with the glue-like fabric paint now widely available. Patterns were carved in the upper and lower hoops using a router.

Instructions

1. Place the goatskin drumhead in water to soak.
2. Cut the cardboard tube to 20" long. Make the top and bottom rims as uniform, smooth, and level as possible; if necessary, level them after cutting by sanding or trimming with a sharp utility knife. Keep the leftover tubing.
3. Decorate the tube. Painting or otherwise coating the surface will provide some protection against moisture.
4. This drum will use two plywood rings: one for the drum hoop and one for the base. Cut the two rings out of 1" plywood to the dimensions shown in Figures 1A and 1B. To make the inner cut, drill a hole somewhere within the portion to be removed, and start the cut from there. A jigsaw will make the work go quickly; if you are working by hand with a coping saw, it will take some

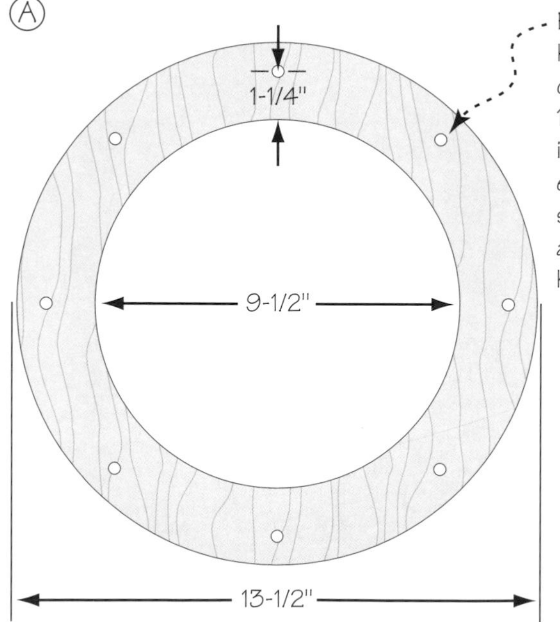

FIGURE 1

The plywood rings. A, one of two plywood rings to be cut from 1" plywood; B, the base.

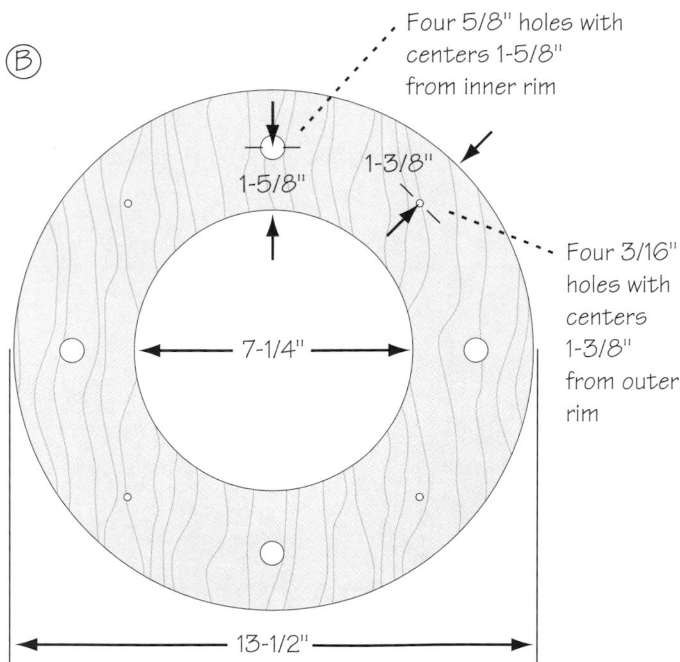

Materials List

Lumber

1 1" x 14" x 28" plywood ***Hoop & base***
1 2" x 2" x 24" wood of your choice

Hardware & Supplies

1 8" diameter x 24" heavy cardboard tubing (Notes-1) ***Body***
1 16" unmounted goatskin drumhead (Notes-2) ***Head***
1 1/2" outer diameter x 28" clear, flexible plastic tubing ***Rim***
1/4" x 12' nonstretchy rope, such as natural sisal ***Lacing***
1 6" x 6" scrap of heavy carpeting ***Foot pads***
4 20d (4") nails
4 2" #10 wood screws
4 2" outer diameter x 3/4" inner diameter large steel washers
Duct tape
Wood finish of your choice
Paint to decorate the cardboard tube
Mink oil or mineral oil

Suggested Tools

Carpenter's handsaw or circular saw
Jigsaw or coping saw
Drill with these bits: 5/8", 5/16", 3/16", 5/32", and countersink bit
Utility knife
Sander or sandpaper
Heavy scissors or snips
Staple gun (Notes-3)

Notes

1. This tubing, sometimes known as sonotube, is sold under various manufacturer's names at building supply centers.
2. Available from the source listed in the Appendix on page 140. For alternative materials, see the sidebar following this plan.
3. A hammer and large headed short nails (roofing nails) will work too.

patience. Do not throw away the cut away portions. Round over the edges of the rings (top and bottom; inner and outer), and clean up all around by sanding.

5. Drill the eight 5/16" holes in the hoop (Figure 1A). Drill the four 5/8" holes and the four 3/16" holes in the base (Figure 1B). Slightly bevel the edges of the 5/16" and 5/8" holes with a countersink bit.

6. Apply wood finish to the two hoops and allow to dry.

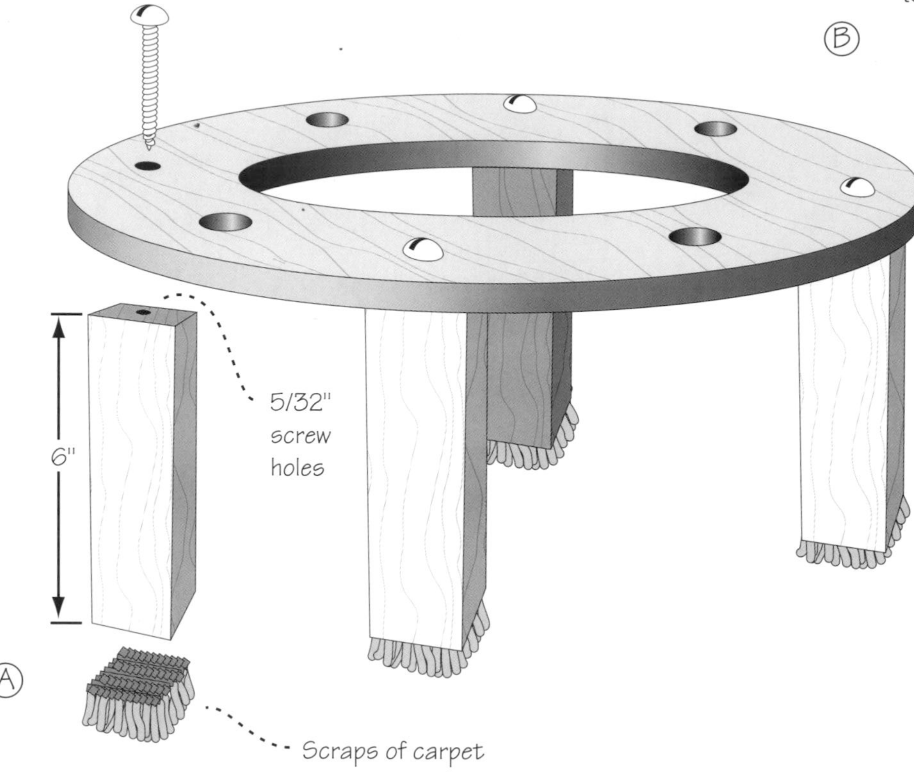

FIGURE 2

The legs for the base. A, dimensions and screw hole locations; B, the assembled base, including foot pads of scrap carpet.

7. From the 2" x 2" wood, cut the legs, and predrill a 5/32" screw hole centered in the top of each leg as shown in Figure 2A. Apply wood finish to the four legs.

8. Attach the legs to the base using the four 2" #10 wood screws through the four 3/16" holes in the base (Figure 2B).

9. Cut four 2" squares of heavy carpeting scrap, and tack them to the bottom of the feet with small nails or tacks.

10. Cut a 28" length of the 1/2" plastic flexible tubing. Using a sharp utility knife, slice the tubing over its entire length. Place it over the upper rim of the cardboard tube (Figure 3A). Run it all the way around, and cut off the extra tube where it overlaps so that the plastic tube

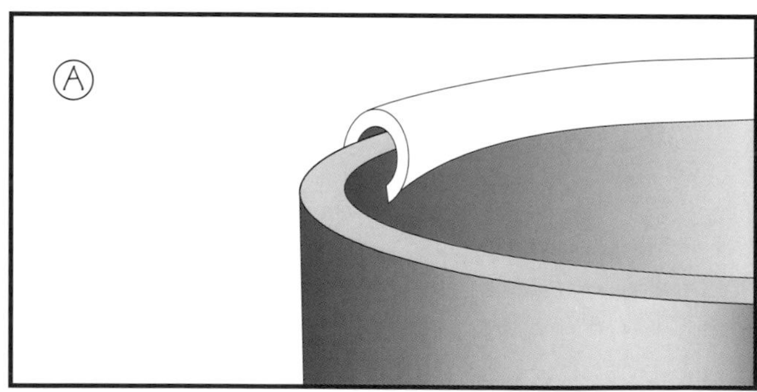

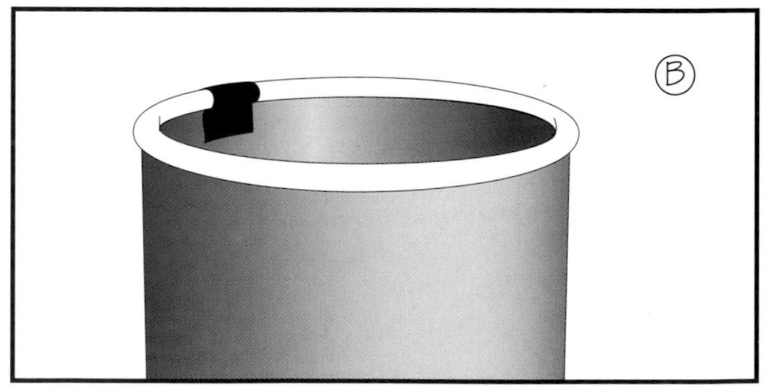

FIGURE 3

Flexible plastic tubing for rim. A, the tubing, sliced longitudinally, placed over the rim of the cardboard drum body; B, the tubing circling the rim, with duct tape over the point where the ends meet.

ends meet snugly. To secure them there, run a piece of duct tape over the place where the plastic tube ends meet (Figure 3B).

11. For a hand drum such as this, the position of the hoop should be an inch or more below the rim on the finished drum, as in Figure 5A. To accomplish this, follow this procedure in attaching the head: As illustrated in Figure 4, place the hoop on a flat work surface with spacers around the outer edges beneath, holding it an inch or so above the work surface. The cut away scraps left over from when you made the hoop will work perfectly as spacers, without blocking space in the center of the hoop. Remove the goatskin head from its bath and place it over the hoop. Take a leftover section of 8" cardboard tubing, preferably not more than about 8" long, and use it to press the skin down through the middle of the hoop, so that the center of the skin rests flat against the work surface

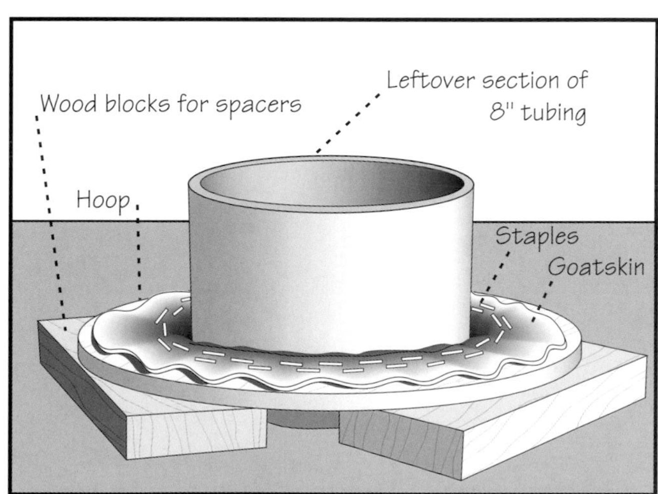

FIGURE 4
STAPLING THE GOATSKIN HEAD TO THE PLYWOOD HOOP

below. The periphery of the skin will still extend out over the hoop. Make sure all is well centered and there are no wrinkles in the part of the skin pressed against the work surface.

Then begin stapling the skin to the hoop. Place the staples about 3/4" from the inner rim of the hoop. Put them at opposite sides of the hoop initially, then gradually fill in the gaps. Keep stapling until you have a continuous ring of overlapping staples. If necessary, go back and firmly tap in the staples with a hammer.

12. Place the drum body on the base assembly, and place the hoop and skin on the top of the drum, as shown in Figure 5A. Each of the 5/8" holes in the base should be centered between a pair of holes in the hoop above.

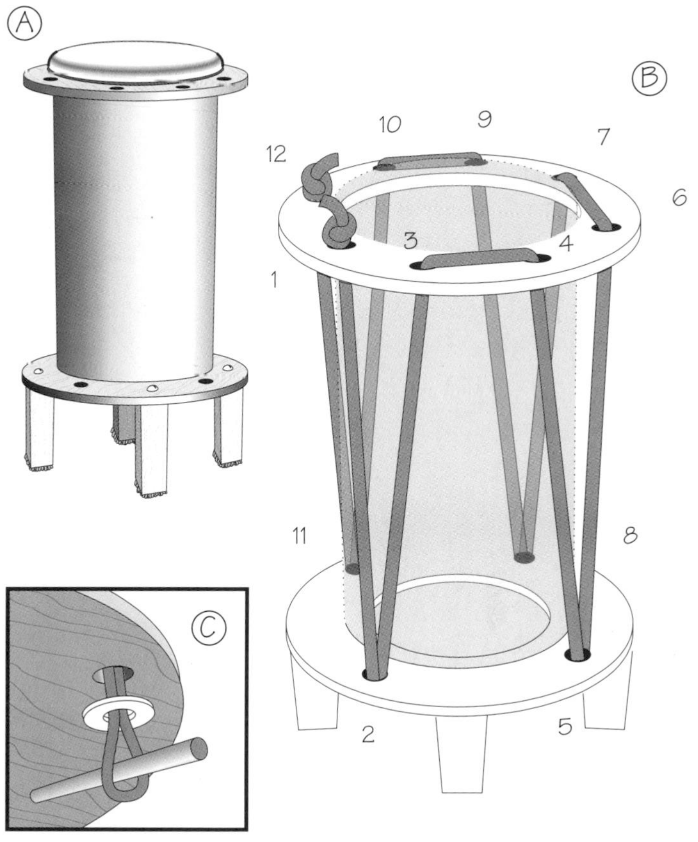

FIGURE 5
THE DRUM BEFORE AND AFTER LACING. A, THE CARDBOARD BODY IN PLACE ON THE BASE AND THE HEAD AND HOOP IN PLACE ON THE BODY; B, THE LACING PATTERN; C, THE RODS PASSING THROUGH THE LOOPED ROPE ON THE UNDERSIDE OF THE BASE.

13. Find four 4" nails, and cut the head off each, leaving a steel rod of just under 4". Use a file, grinder or sandpaper to round and de-burr where the cut was made and to blunt the point.

14. Figure 5B illustrates the lacing procedure described in the following. Cut the lacing rope to 12'. Tie a knot at one end. Pull the rope down through a hole in the upper hoop, marked 1 in Figure 5B, so that the knot pulls down against the top of the hoop. At the hole in the base below, marked 2, push a loop of rope through from above. Below the hole, push the loop through one

of the large washers, and place one of the 4" nails through the loop, as shown in Figure 5C. With the rope pulled tight, the nail will pull up against the washer and the underside of the base. Run the free end of the rope back up and through the next hole in the upper hoop, marked 3. From there, run it over the top of the hoop and down through the hole marked 4. Bring it down to the hole in the base marked 5, push a loop through the hole and a washer below, place the nail in the loop, and run the rope up through the hole in the upper hoop marked 6. Continue this way through all eight hoop holes and all four holes in the base. When you come up through the last hole in the hoop, marked 12, pull the rope tight all around, and then tie the rope off with another knot.

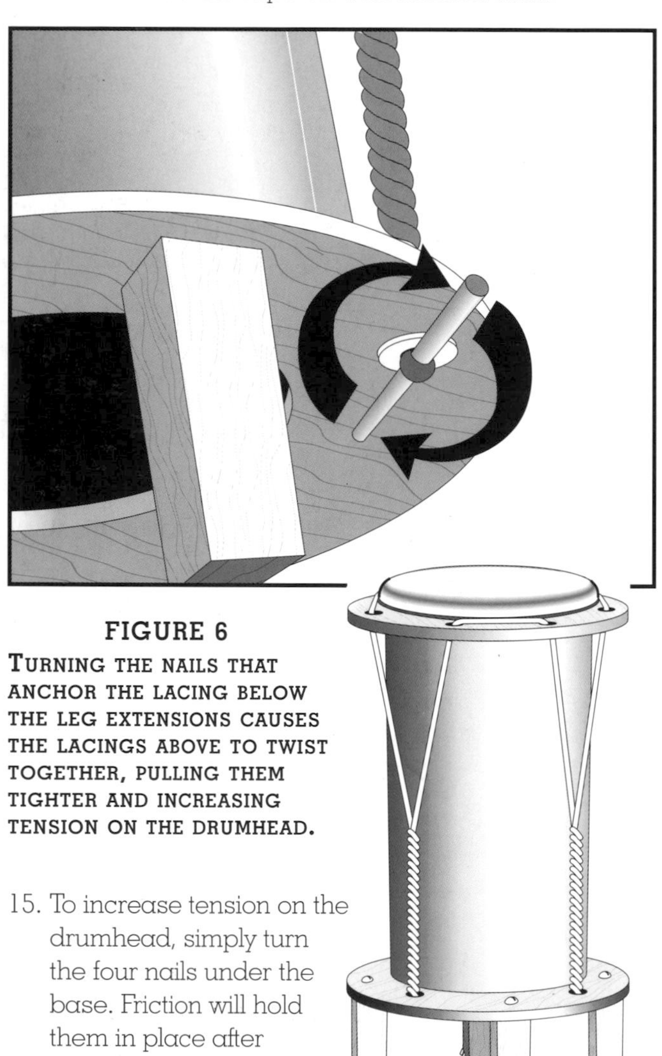

FIGURE 6

TURNING THE NAILS THAT ANCHOR THE LACING BELOW THE LEG EXTENSIONS CAUSES THE LACINGS ABOVE TO TWIST TOGETHER, PULLING THEM TIGHTER AND INCREASING TENSION ON THE DRUMHEAD.

15. To increase tension on the drumhead, simply turn the four nails under the base. Friction will hold them in place after turning. As shown in Figure 6, turning the nails twists the ropes together. The more they twist, the tighter they get, and the harder they pull down on the hoop that holds the head. Because the drumhead is wet now and will contract as it dries, you want a moderately low tension on the head at this time. Give the nails just enough turns to take any slack out of the ropes.
16. Let the drumhead dry for a day or so. When it is dry, give it an oil treatment. Drumheads made of skin need to be oiled to keep them supple; it really makes a difference in tone. The traditional oil for the purpose—don't ask me why—is mink oil. I use mineral oil—it's much easier to find at the local pharmacy and it works fine. Rub a generous amount into the playing surface of the skin, and give it time to soak in.
17. Bring the drum up to playing tension by turning the nails The right playing tension is whatever brings out a good tone. Typically this is a moderately high tension. Be aware that the same drum may sound very different in different rooms, and even in different locations within a room, as well as outdoors, and on different playing surfaces—carpets versus hard floors, or held up off the floor. As you do your initial tuning, move about and find a place where the drum likes to be.

PLAYING TECHNIQUE

Strike the drum with your bare hands. Except when you want a slap tone, you will get the best sound when the stroke is short and sharp—get your hand off the drum even as you hit it, so you don't damp the vibration. A heavy stroke near the center will bring out the drum's bottom tone; lighter strokes near the edge will bring out various rim tones.

VARIATIONS

A set of two or three drums will present a richer musical potential than a single drum. You can make companion drums following this plan but varying them in length from, say, 14" to 36", and using tubing of different diameters. Consider more durable materials for the drum body, such as large diameter plastic tubing (sold in construction yards as culverts). With a little more ambition you can work in wood, either hollowing out larger logs or practicing the art of cooperage. If you do work in wood, consider this important option: a drum that tapers to a narrower opening at the base will usually possess better air resonance and produce a richer tone than a straight cylinder.

Drumheads and Drum Hoops

The most common traditional material for drumheads is animal skin. Goatskin most often serves for smaller drums and cowhide for larger, but many other types have been used. More than any other material, skin offers the right balance between a satisfyingly full fundamental tone and enough upper partials to lend excitement and definition. Animal skin has another advantage: it expands greatly when wet. The maker can soak a skin and attach it wet to the drum. It naturally contracts as it dries, tightening to a far greater tension than would be possible otherwise. This is how sufficiently high tensions have been achieved through most of humankind's history of drum making. But the blessing is mixed. Drumheads made of skin tend to go slack in humid weather. Heating or drying can improve the situation within limits, but at some inconvenience.

Drumheads also are made of synthetics, primarily fiberglass or polyester films, such as Mylar™, which have no humidity problems. Nowadays, such heads are used routinely on stick-played drums. They generally have more ring in the upper partials and less fullness in the bottom—good for certain kinds of music. A ready alternative material for homemade instruments is rubberized cloth, such as that used to make the yellow raincoats known as slickers. It will make a fair drumhead, with a reasonably nice bottom but disappointing rim tones. Stretchy materials like inner tube rubber make tempting candidates for drumheads because they are easy to apply under tension, but except in special cases (as we shall see in the following plan), they generally yield poor results.

In the simplest drums, the heads are simply tacked or glued directly on to the drum body. Most adjustable tension drums have the head attached to a drum hoop, which holds the skin securely, distributes tension evenly, and gives tension mechanisms such as lacing or hardware something strong on which to hold. Some drums, like the hand drum in the preceeding plan, have just one hoop, called a *flesh hoop*. It is a ring of wood or metal, large enough to fit over the top of the drum and pull the skin down over the rim. Most tunable drums have a second hoop, called the *counter hoop*, which rests on top of the flesh hoop. Whatever it is that applies the tension—lacings or hardware—pulls down on the counter hoop.

The plywood drum hoop used in the hand drum plan is unusual. Most drum hoops are

made of metal or thin strips of wood laminated in several layers to form a sturdy wooden ring. Making the hoops and attaching the skin to the flesh hoop by traditional means are tricky operations requiring a bit of explaining. That is why I have substituted the alternative, but perfectly functional, plywood ring for the hand drum described here.

Balloon Drums

MODERATE

In the previous plan, I mentioned that you can do a lot more musically with two or three drums than with a single drum. Why not, then, bring together still more drums, all with their different pitches and tone qualities, for a sound that much richer? The problem is that individual drums usually are often difficult and costly to make. Assembling a large set of them becomes quite a job. The balloon-headed tube drums described here, on the other hand, are easy and inexpensive to make. They are small enough that you can bring a complete set of them together without demanding too much space, and a single player can manage them comfortably.

This design allows for 12 drums, with tubes of varying lengths producing a range of pitches, all mounted in a small tablelike frame. Each drum is nothing more than a long, narrow tube with a portion of a balloon stretched over the top. The tone is rather like tom-toms, although much quieter. The interaction between the membrane and the air column varies from one drum to the next, so that each one in the set has its own individual tone quality. Therein lies much of the charm of the instrument.

The defining pitch in each balloon drum is that of the tube's air resonance fundamental, with the membrane tone adding color and distinctive character above. The air resonance fundamental pitch depends upon both tube length and membrane tension. Stretching the balloon membrane tighter raises the pitch. With great diligence and patience, you could create a tube drum set tuned to a particular scale as follows: Chose a series of tube lengths that are about right to bring each drum into the general range of its intended pitch, then painstakingly adjust the balloon membrane tension to achieve that pitch. Then you could play "When the Saints Go Marching In" on the balloon drums. But the process of fine-tuning the membrane tensions is pretty iffy, and once you've got the tunings set, they don't hold very well. More importantly—this is the other side of the same coin—balloon drums have a peculiar knack for producing lovely random tunings. Because of that, my preference is to throw to the wind any prescriptive ideas about tuning and to enjoy whatever collection

of pitches and tone qualities the drums happen to yield on their own.

Soft, stretchy membranes such as balloon latex usually are not good candidates for drumheads, for reasons having to do with internal damping and the poor spreading of the impulse. But in this special case, where we want the air column to dominate the sound, the light, stretchy membranes do nicely. The not-so-great volume of the balloon drums is a price we pay for using something so insubstantial and compliant.

Instructions

1. To make the top of the stand, cut a 20" x 12" rectangle of 3/4" plywood. For the base, cut a 12" x 12" plywood square. Clean up the sides and round all edges by sanding.
2. Using a hole cutter or circle cutter, cut 12 holes in the plywood top in the locations indicated in Figure 1.
3. If you intend to paint or otherwise finish the wood, now is the time.
4. Attach the four furniture glides near the corners on the underside of the base. Use 3/4" wood screws to attach the pipe mounting brackets to the center of the top of the base and the center of the underside of the top. Thread the steel pipe into each, and the stand is complete.
5. It is time now to cut the tubes, apply the balloon heads, and set the tubes in the holes in the top. The longest tube can be 32", the shortest 8", and the others varying lengths in between. Start with the longest

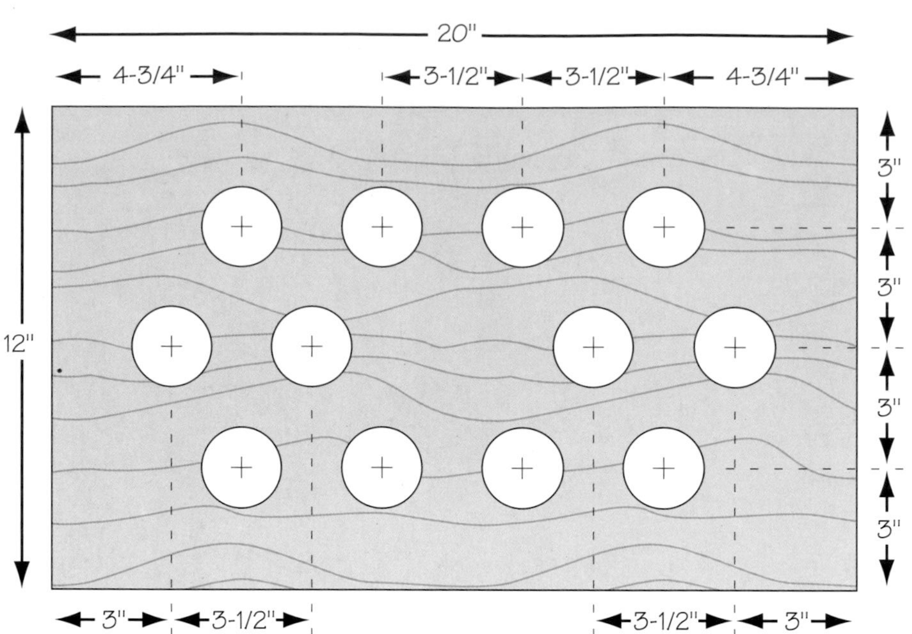

FIGURE 1
LOCATIONS FOR THE 12 HOLES IN THE TOP OF THE STAND. HOLE DIAMETERS SHOULD BE JUST BARELY LARGER THAN THE OUTSIDE DIAMETER OF THE DRUM TUBES.

Materials List

LUMBER

1 3/4" x 12" x 20" plywood *Top of stand*
1 3/4" x 12" x 12" plywood *Base*

HARDWARE & SUPPLIES

1 2" internal dia. x 20' plastic tubing (Notes-1) *Body*
1 1/2" x 30" steel pipe, threaded at both ends *Upright for stand*
2 floor flanges (mounting brackets for threaded pipe) threaded to hold 1/2" pipe
3/4" wood screws
15 or more 16" latex balloons (16" diameter is the size they blow up to) *Drumheads*
30 or more 1/4" x 2-1/2" rubber bands (designated as size #62)
4 small furniture glides
Electrician's tape
Wood finish of your choice

SUGGESTED TOOLS

Carpenter's saw or circular saw
Optional: Large tubing cutter
Circle cutter or hole saw (Notes-2)
Scissors
Screwdriver
Electric sander, sandpaper, or files
Paintbrush or rag
Air-filtration mask (Notes-3)

NOTES

1. White PVC tubing is inexpensive and widely available. It is made in two thicknesses; the thinner schedule 125 will do for the current purpose. PVC is unattractive and produces toxic fumes when heated (as with cutting or sanding), so you might consider the more expensive black ABS plastic. Alternatively, heavy cardboard tubes or other workable tubing materials may serve as well, with some modifications to the construction procedures given here.
2. These are available at reasonable cost as electric drill attachments. You will need a size just barely larger than your tube's outside diameter, probably 2-3/8" or 2-1/2".
3. If you use PVC tubing, you will want to wear a breather (air-filtration mask) while doing any cutting and sanding.

tube. The procedure for each one is as follows:

A. Cut the tube to length using a handsaw, a circular saw, or large tubing cutter. Do this work in a location with good circulation, and wear a breather.

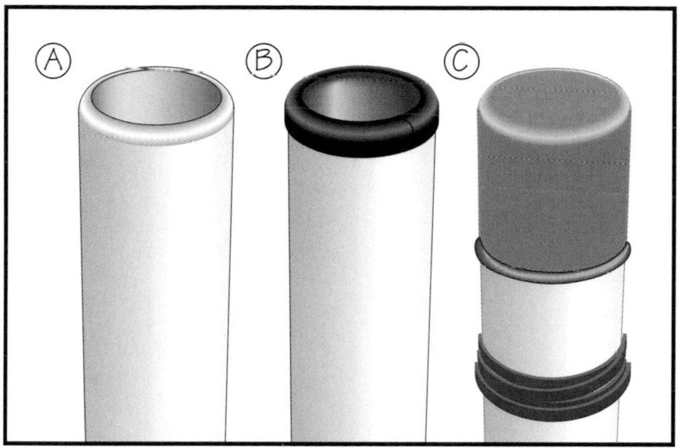

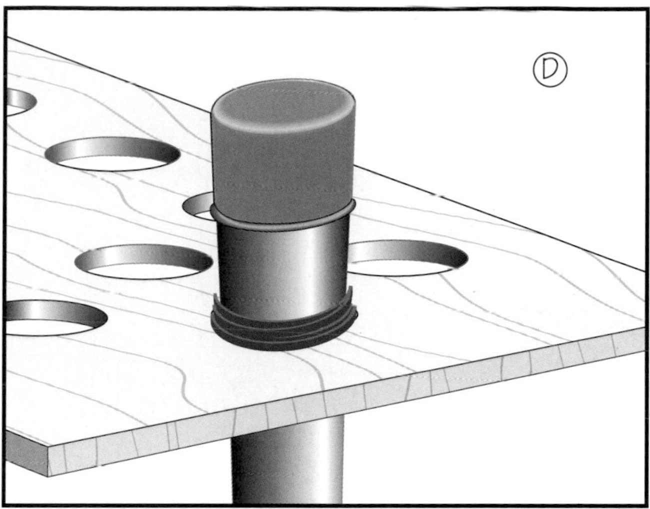

FIGURE 2

The tube end. A, with rounded edges; B, with the electrician's tape stretched tight around the top; C, with the balloon membrane in place on top and the rubber band collar 4 inches below; D, (above right) in place in the stand.

B. Round the upper edge of the tube (where the balloon membrane is to pass over) as smoothly and gradually as the thickness of the material will permit (Figure 2A). Membrane breakage is a potential problem, and this step is essential to help reduce it. Use a belt sander, or do the rounding by hand with sandpaper or files. Don't forget the breather.

C. If you want to do anything to alleviate the ugliness of the plastic tube, it will be best to do it before going on to the next step. But what to do? I have yet to find a paint or finish that will bond adequately to these plastics. My suggestion regarding the decorating process: have fun; don't worry too much about permanence; don't worry too much about timeless craftsmanship. This is the nice thing about working with materials that have no class: you can decorate them in any manner you choose, no matter how poor your taste may be, without ever feeling that you have committed a serious faux pas.

D. Cut a strip of electrician's tape slightly longer than the tube circumference. Stretch it very tight around the perimeter at the top, positioned so that the upper edge of the tape is on a level with the top of the rounded edge. Due to the stretching, the upper edge of the tape will pull in and down over the rounded edge (Figure 2B). This will provide a smooth surface for the balloon to pass over.

E. Take a balloon, stretch it over the top of the tube, and pull it all the way down so that the top of the balloon pulls flat over the top (but no need to stretch tight at this time). Some balloons have wide enough necks that you can do this step with the balloon left whole, though it takes some effort. Narrow-necked balloons will need to have their necks snipped off in order to fit over the tube. Don't snip off more than necessary.

F. Roll the sides of the balloon back up along the side of the tube (Figure 2C). Take it off, and then put it back on again, with the sides still rolled up, this time stretched tight (this requires strong fingers). The tighter you stretch the membrane, the higher will be the drum's pitch. Tap it lightly with your fingers to see how it sounds. If you wish, you may tighten or loosen the membrane a bit to improve the sound or change the pitch.

One of the nice things about this instrument is that, because it is played very lightly, there's no need for heavy hardware. With the membrane, for instance, the traction of the latex against the side of the tube holds well enough that no more attachment is needed. We'll use a similar soft-technology approach to hold the tube in position in the top of the stand, and prevent it from slipping through the hole.

The PVC tubing used for the balloon drum tubes is one of the most naturally ugly materials known, and it takes paints and other finishes poorly. For the balloon drums shown here, I attempted to improve the situation with a combination of spray paint and random scraping.

G. Take one of the #62 rubber bands and place it around the tube at the point where the tube is to be supported (Figure 2C). A typical support point might be 3" to 4" below the top of the tube. The longest tubes may require a lower support point to keep the openings at the lower end at least 2" from the floor.

With the rubber band in place, slip the tube through its hole in the top of the stand. (Which hole? Whichever you like. You can place the tubes of different lengths in the tabletop in whatever pattern you choose.) If the hole size is very close to the tube's outside diameter size, the tube will catch at the rubber band and stay there. If not, add another rubber band, or two or three, until the cumulative rubber band diameter is enough to prevent the tube from slipping through (Figure 2D).

When you have completed steps A through G for all the tubes, and the 12 drums are in their places in the stand, the instrument is finished.

Playing Technique

Tap the drumheads with your fingertips or with very light beaters. I have found that the eraser ends of new, unsharpened pencils work nicely. As with all drums, allow the playing hand or beater to bounce off the head immediately after striking; don't let it linger on the head unless you wish to damp it.

Variations

You could extend the range of the instrument using more tubes and a greater range of lengths. Larger diameter tubes will produce a slightly louder or fuller tone. Louder and more dependably tunable tube drums are made with goatskin or heavier plastic heads and much more elaborate head-mounting hardware, as well as stronger stands for holding the drums.

Acknowledgments: Many makers have experimented with balloon drums. The design given here is loosely based upon drums made by Tom Nunn. Tom, in turn, gives credit to an earlier master of balloon sonics, Prent Rodgers.

Coffee Cuica

EASY

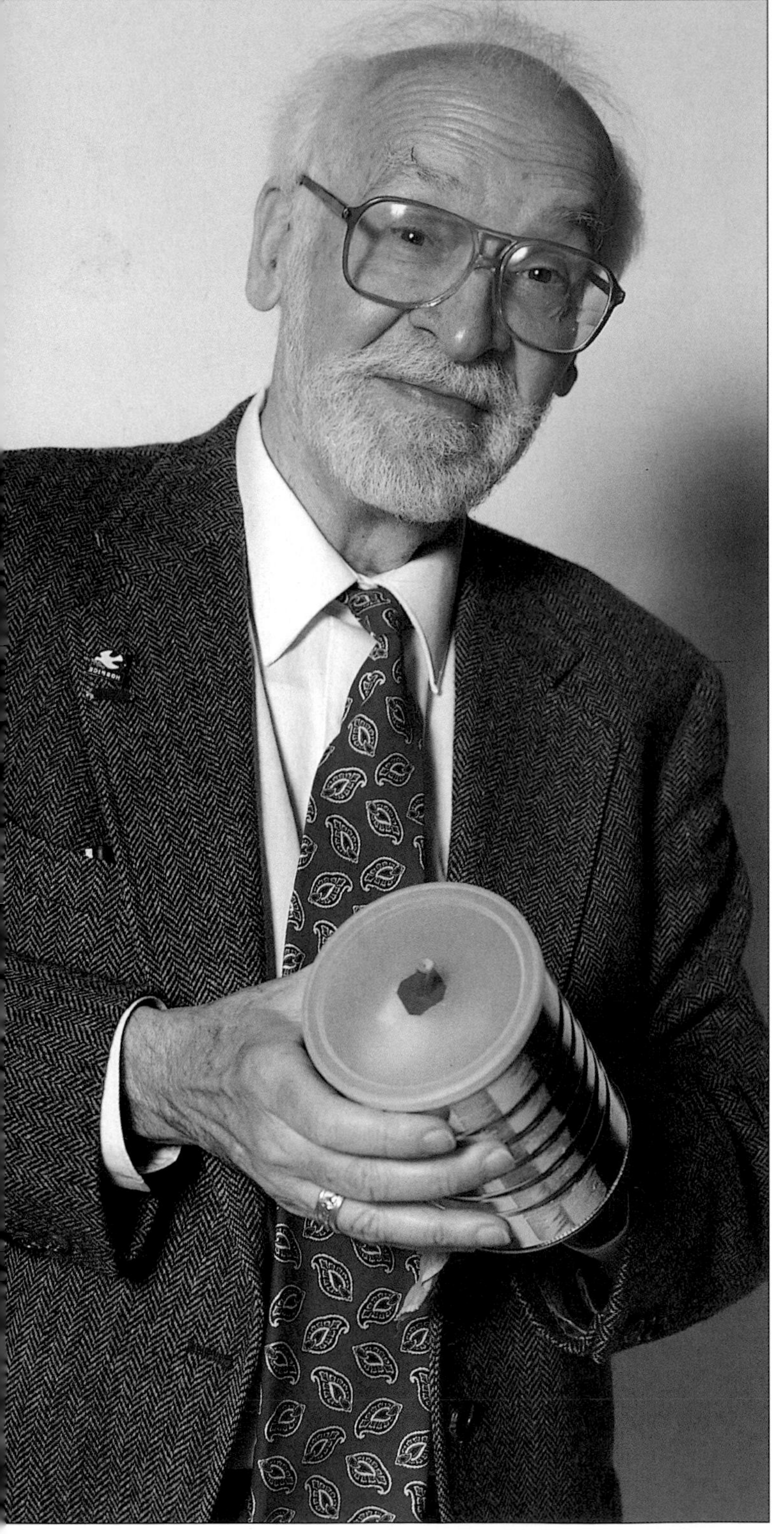

Not all drums are sounded by percussion; you can also create a vibration in a membrane by friction. The friction may take place directly against the membrane of a conventional drum (try drawing a high-bounce ball mallet across a tom-tom head). But with drums designed specifically as friction drums, the friction usually takes place against a cord or stick that is attached to the center of a drumhead. The player rubs the cord or stick with fingers or a small piece of wet cloth, and the stick-slip movement of the friction is transmitted to the drumhead. The resulting sound—a sighing, grunting, moaning sort of sound—may have a bestial or anatomical quality, or it may seem conversational, even lyrical. Friction drums are not the most common of instruments, but they can be found in diverse forms the world over.

The *cuica* is a Brazilian friction drum, known outside of Brazil through its association with popular music styles like samba and bossa nova. Here are plans for a surprisingly effective cuicalike instrument that you can make in a matter of minutes from commonly available materials.

Materials List

Hardware & Supplies

1 24-ounce metal coffee can with plastic lid for resealing (Note) ***Drumhead and body***

1 1/8" diameter x 10" bamboo skewer or similar light stick

Duct tape

A scrap of chamois or cotton rag, a few inches square

Suggested Tools

Drill with 1/16" bit

Can opener

Scissors

Note

24-ounce cans are best, but a 12-ounce can will do. You may also find similar cans made for hot chocolate or iced tea mix, equipped with the plastic lid but with a body of cardboard. The cardboard cans also work but not as well.

Instructions

1. Remove both ends of the coffee can with a can opener.
2. Place 1" squares of duct tape at the center of the plastic lid on each side, and press them firmly in place.
3. Drill a 1/16" hole through the very center of the plastic top, passing through the duct tape (Figure 1).

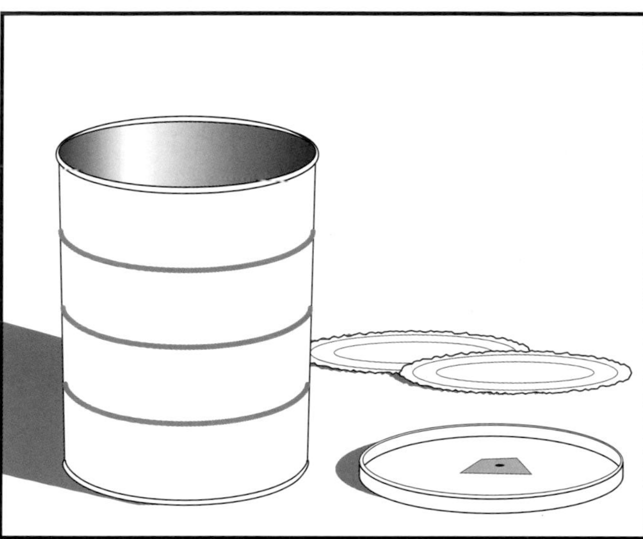

FIGURE 1

Coffee can with top and bottom removed. Shows plastic lid with small squares of duct tape in place and 1/16" hole drilled at the center.

4. One end of the stick will go through the hole in the lid. There are lots of ways to secure it in position. Here's a very easy method. Narrow one end of the stick to a point by sanding or whittling (if you use a bamboo skewer, it will already have a sharpened end). Cut two strips of duct tape, 1/2" wide and 3" long. Wrap one of them around and around the stick at a point 1" from the pointed end (Figure 2A). Poke the pointed end through the hole in the lid from the underside to where the tape wrap butts up against the plastic. Wrap the second duct tape strip around the part of the stick that protrudes through the lid, making the wrap sit as snugly as possible against the top surface (Figure 2B). Snip off the pointed end that extends beyond the wrap (Figure 2C).
5. Put the plastic top on the can, so that the stick extends through the interior of the can and out the opposite end.

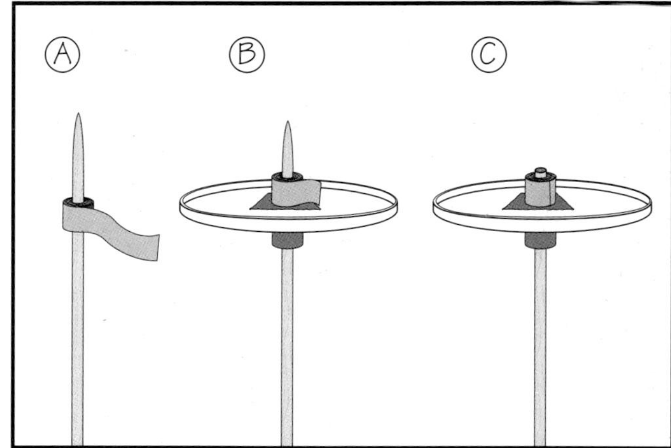

FIGURE 2

The stick. A, pointed end and duct tape; B, poked through the plastic lid to where the tape wrap is flush; C, second duct tape wrap in place, with the pointed end of the stick snipped off.

Playing Technique

Wet the scrap of rag. Hold the can with one hand. With the other, reach into the can and lightly pinch the stick with the wet rag between thumb and forefinger. The membrane, in the form of the plastic lid, moans and groans and burbles when you rub the rag up and down the stick. Vary the pitch, volume, and sound quality by altering the pressure or speed of your rubbing. You can also vary the pitch by pressing firmly against the lid with the fingers of the hand that holds the can.

Acknowledgment: I first saw this wonderfully simple instrument in the hands of Mary Buchen.

Winds

To make a workable musical instrument, you must find a way to create a vibration. With many musical instruments the player excites a vibration in some sort of solid object—by plucking a string for instance, or striking a drumhead, or tapping a marimba bar. The vibration is transmitted to the surrounding air and through the air to people's ears. Wind instruments don't work this way. Winds are those instruments in which the sound begins with a vibration in the air itself.

For most familiar wind instruments, the heart of the instrument is some sort of chamber that encloses a body of air. The air chamber may take the form of a long and narrow tube, as with a flute or clarinet, or it may be more globular in shape, as with an ocarina or wine jug. The purpose of the chamber is to allow for the creation of a controlled vibration. The air in an enclosed chamber typically vibrates readily at certain frequencies and not others. These preferred frequencies are determined primarily by the size and shape of the chamber, and by the size and location of any openings in the chamber. By controlling these features, you can control which pitches the chamber naturally resonates.

An air chamber remains silent unless something happens to get it vibrating. There are many ways to start an air chamber vibration. One is to blow through a reed or through buzzing lips, as in clarinets, oboes, or trumpets. The reed or lips act as a gateway to the airflow from the player's lungs, allowing the air to pass into the tube in a series of rapid bursts rather than in a continuous stream. Another way to set up the vibration is to direct an airstream over the edge of an opening in the chamber, to produce an *edge tone*, as with flutes and recorders. Edge tone mechanics are more complex than reed mechanics, but the effect once again is that an airflow enters the tube in a rapid series of pulses.

In either case, if the frequency of those bursts agrees with one of the preferred frequencies of the air chamber, the chamber will respond with a strong resonance. Most wind instruments are designed so that the pulsing frequency of the reed or edge tone will tend naturally to accommodate itself to the preferred frequency of the chamber. This allows the instrument to produce a strong, sustained tone at that frequency. Then, if you can control and vary the preferred frequency of the chamber, you can control the pitch of the coupled system and...play a tune! There are many ways to alter the preferred frequency of an air chamber. Perhaps the simplest approach of all is to have many individual air chambers of different sizes, as on an organ with its many pipes of different lengths. The trumpet's valves and the trombone's slide represent another approach. These mechanisms do what they do by altering the effective length of an air column. For the wind instruments in this book, we will work mostly with finger holes, which allow the player to vary the size and location of openings in the chamber. We will learn more about how finger holes work as we proceed through the plans that follow.

Side-Blown Flute

MODERATELY EASY

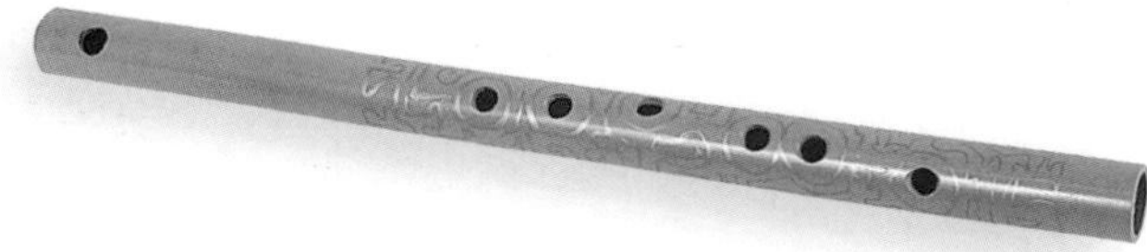

In flutes a vibration is set up when a narrow stream of air strikes the edge of an opening in the body of the instrument. In some flutes the player blows through a windway that directs the air over the edge, while in others the player blows directly over the open end of a tube, or over the edge of a hole in the side of a tube. Side-blown flutes, like the one in this plan, are of the latter sort: the body is a narrow tube, and the player excites the sound by blowing over a hole in the side near one end. The classical silver flute is the most familiar of side-blown flutes, but the basic form can be found, in many variants, the world over.

The plan here calls for six finger holes. Uncovering them in sequence will yield the tones of a major scale in G. Through cross-fingerings (fingerings having one or two additional covered holes below the highest open tone hole), the player can fill in all of the chromatics except the low G#. Including its upper register, the flute yields a range of an octave and a half and more in the hands of a skilled player.

The dimensions and hole spacings here are taken from Mark Shepard's excellent booklet, *Simple Flutes: Play Them, Make Them.* I have found his suggested dimensions to be quite accurate, yielding a well-tuned instrument requiring a minimum of after-the-fact fine-tuning.

The fipple flute plan that follows this one will use the same tone hole layout, so the instructions for making the tone holes and the fingering chart given here will serve for both instruments.

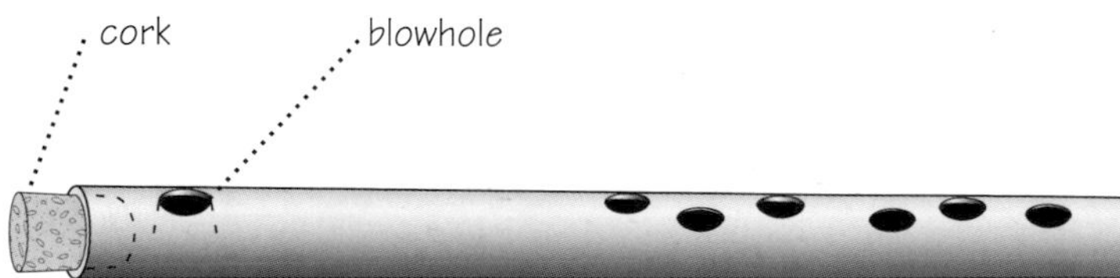

FIGURE 1

COMPLETED INSTRUMENT. SHOWS THE POSITION OF THE CORK STOPPER AND THE BLOWHOLE.

Playing a side-blown flute takes some practice. If you have never done it before, you will probably find it difficult at first to get a clear tone. Instructions to get you started appear under "Playing Technique" below.

INSTRUCTIONS

1. Cut the 3/4" tube to 16-7/16" length.
2. Tap the cork into one end to a depth of 1/2" (Figure 1).
3. To form the blowhole, drill a 3/8" hole in the side of the tube, 1" from the corked end. Ream out the hole slightly so that you end up with an oval shape, about 1/2" in the long dimension, with the long dimension along the line of the tube. Using a rat-tail file or a craft knife, angle very slightly inward the playing edge of the blowhole—that's the side that will be opposite the player's lips—as shown in Figure 2. Make sure the hole is smooth and free of splinters or burrs all around.

FIGURE 2

A CUTAWAY END-ON VIEW. SHOWS THE SLIGHT INWARD BEVEL OF THE BLOWHOLE ON THE SIDE OPPOSITE THE PLAYER'S LIPS WHERE THE AIRSTREAM WILL STRIKE.

4. Drill the finger holes, starting with #6 (farthest down the tube). All holes will be 3/8" in diameter, spaced as indicated in Figure 3. The location values represent the distance from the center of each tone hole to the center of the blowhole. Remember that the holes need not be in a straight line down the tube; it makes fingering easier if some are offset to one side or the other to accommodate the natural fall of the fingers.
5. Clean up the holes with the craft knife and/or rat-tail file, removing any clinging bits of plastic left over from the drilling. Very slightly bevel the rims of the holes with a countersink bit.
6. The flute is now essentially complete. But you may find that it will benefit from some fine-tuning of the tone holes. Or you may prefer to do a fine-tuning later, after you have developed some facility with the instrument. To do the fine-tuning, play through the natural, lower register scale on the flute, listening for the pitch produced

FIGURE 3

Finger hole positions for both the side-blown flute and the fipple flute, given as a distance from the center of the blowhole. (For the fipple flute, the distances will be from a point inside the aperture, or about 1/16" from the vertical cut.) All holes are 3/8" diameter.

Hole Number	Hole Location	Sounding Pitch
1	6-3/8"	F#
2	7-17/32"	E
3	8-25/32"	D
4	10-7/16"	C
5	11-3/16"	B
6	12-25/32"	A
Open end	15-7/16"	G

at each hole (basic playing technique is described below). If at any given hole the pitch is too low, raise it by enlarging a tiny bit. If it is too high, reduce the hole size by back-filling with epoxy gel. Start this fine-tuning process with the lowest hole and proceed through the remaining holes in sequence. During this pitch-testing and tuning process, strive for the most consistent blowing position and wind pressure you can. Otherwise, you will unconsciously tend to alter your playing technique to bend the sounding pitch to match what you want to hear. For more on the broad principles behind this tone-hole tuning process, see the "Air Column Resonances" sidebar on page 77.

One more optional fine-tuning adjustment: the stopper position recommended above is probably optimal. But you can try altering its position relative to the blowhole to improve the tone, make it easier to sound the upper octave, or improve the tuning in the upper octave. If you are satisfied with the cork positioning, for the sake of appearance you may choose to cut off the protruding part and sand the corked end smooth.

Playing Technique

Getting a good, clear tone from a side-blown flute takes practice. Hold the flute sideways in front of you, nonblowhole end to the right, with the fingers of the right hand positioned to cover the lower three tone holes, and the fingers of the left positioned to cover the upper three, thumbs supporting the flute from below. The blowhole should face up, directly in front of your mouth, with the side of the flute resting against the flesh just below your lower lip. Purse your lips so as to make a very narrow airstream, and blow toward the far edge of the blowhole. Adjust the positioning of the blowhole, and the angle, speed, and narrowness of the airstream, until you find a good tone. As you develop some skill, you will learn to fine-tune the pitch as you play by controlling these parameters.

Opening the holes in sequence will yield a G major scale. The fingering chart in Figure 4 will help you find chromatic pitches outside that scale. This flute will also play through a second register. That means that you can play a scale over one octave through the standard fingerings, then cause the flute tone to jump up to the upper register and continue the scale for most of another octave through a repeat of the same or similar fingerings. To throw the tone into the second register, do these things: 1) Uncover or partly uncover the uppermost hole (#6) while leaving the holes below it covered as needed for the

Materials List

Hardware & Supplies

1 3/4" internal diameter x 17" plastic tubing, wall thickness approx. 1/8" (Note) ***Tube***

1 3/4" cork (wine-bottle size) ***Stopper***

Epoxy gel (nonrunny epoxy glue)

Suggested Tools

Hacksaw

Drill with complete fractional drill bit set and countersink bit

Craft knife

Rat-tail file

Note

Plastic tubings work well, are inexpensive, widely available, and dependably free of dimensional irregularities. ABS plastic is good. PVC will work just as well but is unattractive and considered mildly toxic in oral contact by people who are sensitive to such things. Bamboo is most beautiful but less regular in shape, making the tuning of the tone holes less predictable.

FIGURE 4

Fingering chart for both the side-blown flute and the fipple flute. Darkened circles represent holes covered with a finger; hollow circles represent open holes. The pitches given in bold print above comprise the G major scale, which is the easiest and most natural for these flutes. Notes in the upper register are obtained by half-covering the uppermost hole (indicated by the half-darkened circle), increasing air velocity, and, for the side-blown flute, directing the airstream more into the flute. Skilled players will be able to work out fingerings to extend the given range upward to two full octaves and more.

G	G#/A♭	**A**	A#/B♭	**B**	**C**	C#/D♭	**D**	D#/E♭	**E**	F	**F#**	**G**	G#/A♭	**A**	A#/B♭	**B**	**C**	C#/D♭	**D**
●	NOT AVAILABLE	●	●	●	●	●	●	●	●	○	○	◒	◒	◒	◒	◒	◒	◒	◒
●		●	●	●	●	●	●	○	○	●	○	●	●	●	●	●	●	●	●
●		●	●	●	●	○	○	●	○	●	○	●	●	●	●	●	●	○	●
●		●	●	●	○	●	○	●	○	○	○	●	●	●	●	●	○	●	○
●		●	○	○	○	●	○	○	○	○	○	●	●	●	○	○	○	○	○
●		○	●	○	○	○	○	○	○	○	○	●	◒	○	●	○	○	○	○
LOWER REGISTER												UPPER REGISTER							

desired pitch; 2) increase airstream velocity; 3) direct the airstream more downward and into the flute. Chances are that the intonation in the upper register will be less than ideal, with the pitches tending toward flatness. That is a natural characteristic of simple cylindrical flutes such as this. Compensate to the extent that you can by adjusting the airstream as you play.

Variations

Make lower- or higher-pitched flutes by starting with longer or shorter tubes. Hole spacings will be roughly proportional to those given here (after-the-fact fine-tuning usually will be called for). Alternatively, explore other hole sizings and spacings to yield different scales. See the "Air Column Resonances" sidebar on the following page for more on this.

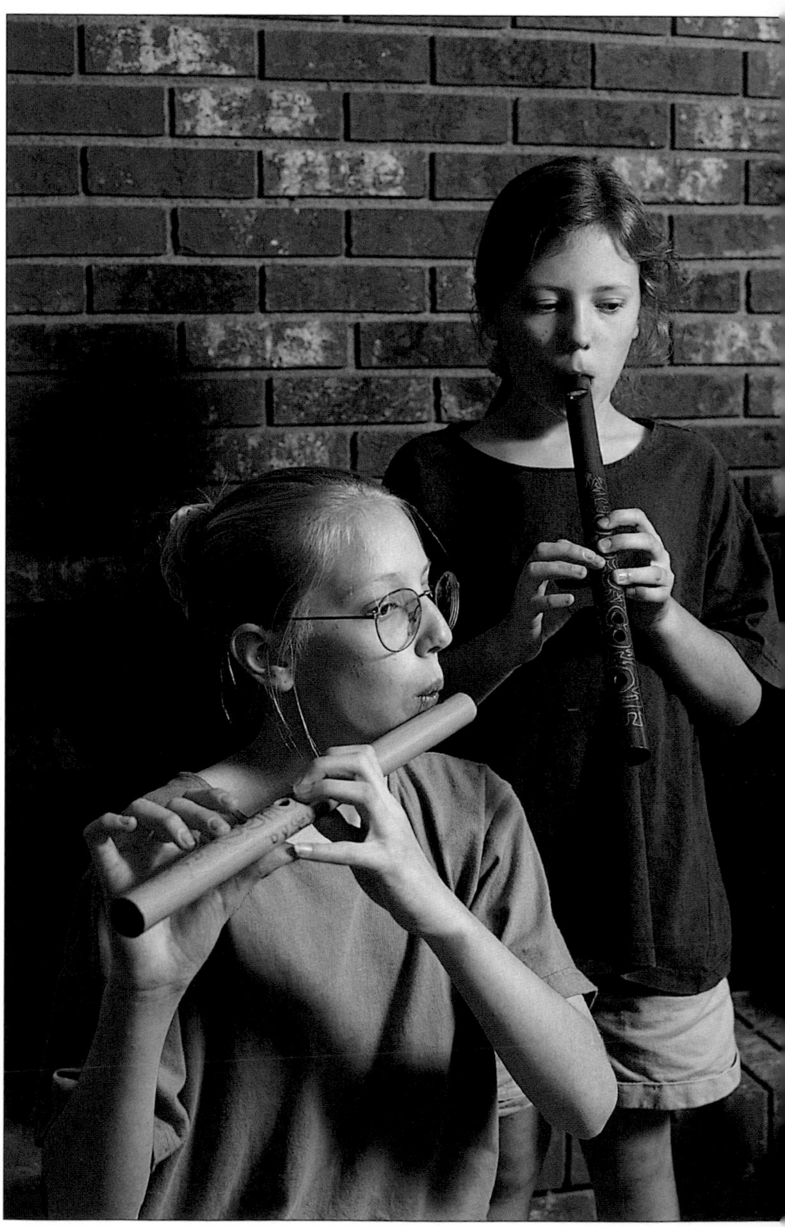

The plastic used for the fipple flute and side-blown flute bodies is unattractive in itself. The instruments shown here were given a little more elegance by decoration with metallic markers followed by several coats of clear spray-on acrylic finish.

Air Column Resonances

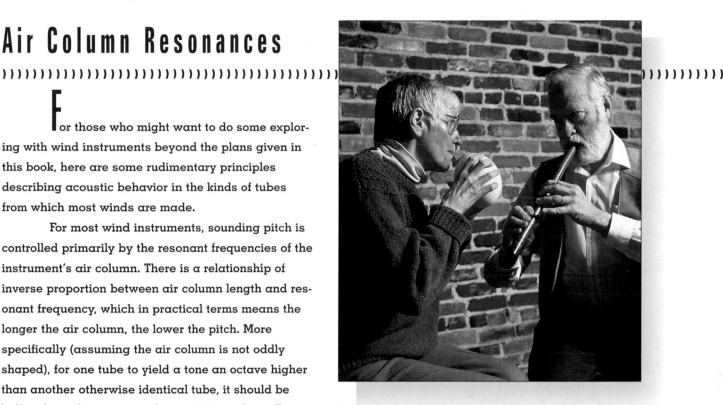

For those who might want to do some exploring with wind instruments beyond the plans given in this book, here are some rudimentary principles describing acoustic behavior in the kinds of tubes from which most winds are made.

For most wind instruments, sounding pitch is controlled primarily by the resonant frequencies of the instrument's air column. There is a relationship of inverse proportion between air column length and resonant frequency, which in practical terms means the longer the air column, the lower the pitch. More specifically (assuming the air column is not oddly shaped), for one tube to yield a tone an octave higher than another otherwise identical tube, it should be half as long; for an octave lower, twice as long. For a tone a semitone higher in 12-tone equal temperament it should be 0.94 times as long; for a semitone lower, 1.06 times as long. There are, however, offsetting factors that render these numbers imprecise. Use them only as rough guidelines.

Most flutelike instruments can be thought of as cylindrical tubes open at both ends. Clarinets for the most part are cylindrical too, but the reed covering the opening causes them to behave as a tube stopped at one end. It is the nature of the stopped cylindrical tube to produce a fundamental resonance approximately an octave below what an open cylindrical tube of the same length yields. Some wind instruments, including saxophones and oboes, have tube shapes more closely approaching conical—that is, stopped at the narrow end and uniformly increasing in diameter toward the other end. For practical purposes they behave similarly to open-ended flutes.

Placing tone holes along the side of a tube is one commonly used trick for varying the effective length of an air column, making it possible to get many notes from an instrument comprised of a single tube. An open tone hole causes the air in the tube to behave acoustically as if the tube were shorter than it actually is. The larger the hole, the greater the shortening effect—which is to say, the larger the hole, the higher the resulting pitch when that hole is open. By adjusting hole size, you can make accommodations in the location of tone holes to make them easy and comfortable for the player's fingers. And you can tune a wind instrument by modifying the hole sizes.

To make a wind instrument from scratch and tune it to produce the pitches you want, follow this procedure: Starting with the lowest tone hole, make a guess as to its best location to produce the pitch you want from it. Drill a small hole there. Due to its smallness, the resulting pitch should be low. Gradually enlarge the hole, testing frequently for pitch, until you arrive at the desired pitch. Go on to the next hole and the next and the next. When you are done, go over all the holes once more for fine-tuning.

Fipple Flute

MODERATE

With fipple flutes, the player does not blow directly over a sounding edge, as with the side-blown flute of the preceding plan. Rather, the player blows into a narrow passageway that concentrates the airstream and directs it over the edge. Recorders are the best known fipple flutes.

Fipple flutes are easier to play than side-blown flutes because the player need not master the subtleties of edge playing. Fipple flutes also are a little harder to make but, as you will see in the plan that follows, not all that much harder if the design is kept simple. Our plan features a wonderfully easy approach to making a windway: using a cork to make a beveled cylindrical stopper. This idea is not new; many makers have used it, and it has appeared previously in Dennis Waring's book, *Making Folk Instruments in Wood.*

The fipple flute described here is identical to the side-blown flute from the preceding pages except for the different blowing arrangement. You should read through the side-blown flute plan on pages 74–76 in preparation for making this instrument, even if you don't actually build the side-blown flute. The fipple flute plan occasionally will refer you to the earlier plan rather than repeat instructions.

Instructions

1. Cut the tube to the 16-1/2" length.
2. Cut the cork to 1" long. Flatten one side by sanding to create a sloped flat surface along one side (Figure 1). Be careful not to overdo the bevel; reduce the height at the upper end by only about 3/32".
3. Tap the cork into the tube so that the end is flush (Figure 2). This will leave a narrow windway between the tube and the flattened part of the cork.
4. Cut the angled opening in the tube to form the aperture and edge. Make the angle cut as shown in Figure 2, approximately 1/2" long and 1/4" deep, and end it with the vertical cut at 1" from the tube end. Carefully de-burr the edge and the windway outlet as needed, and smooth them with a flat file.
5. Blow through the windway to check for tone. If you don't get a clear tone, adjust the cork to shift the airstream angle. This is a subtle business and requires some patience. If the flute simply refuses to speak after several adjustments, start with a fresh cork, give it a slightly different bevel, and try again.
6. When you have a good tone and the cork position is set, make the curved undercut below the fipple (Figure 3). This makes the playing a bit more comfortable, and it looks nice. Make a straight rough cut first, then give it the curvature and clean it up by filing and/or sanding. The curved end of a belt sander will make quick, very neat work of this job. The precise shape is not critical. Be careful not to jar the cork out of position.
7. Finally, make the tone holes. The arrangement is exactly the same as that described for the side-blown flute. Follow steps 4, 5, and 6 from that plan (page 74), and follow the measurements given in that plan's Figure 3 (page 75).

Materials List

Hardware & Supplies

1 3/4" internal diameter x 16-1/2" plastic tubing (Notes-1) ***Tube***

1 3/4" diameter x 1" cork (wine bottle size) (Notes-2) ***Stopper***

Epoxy gel

Suggested Tools

Hacksaw

Drill; complete fractional drill bit set; countersink bit

Craft knife

Rat tail file and flat file

Optional: belt sander

Notes

1. For more on plastic tubings, see the note under the materials list for the side-blown flute on page 75).
2. Have two or three corks on hand in case you don't get the shape just right on the first try.

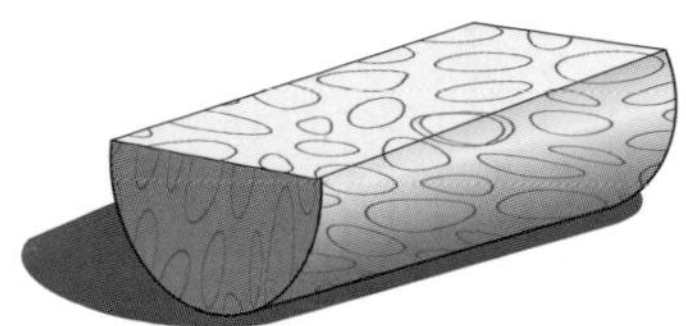

FIGURE 1
THE CORK WITH ITS BEVEL

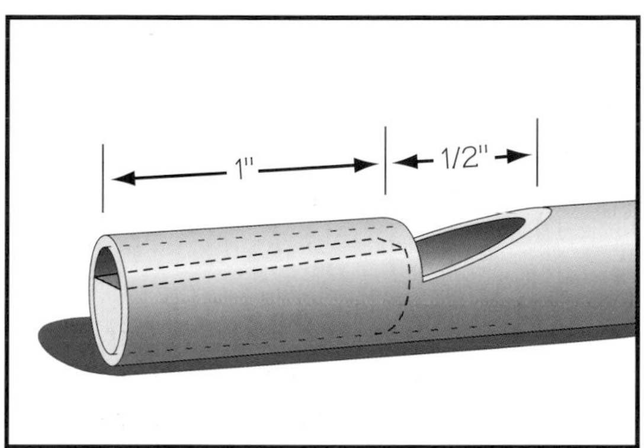

FIGURE 2
THE CORK POSITION AND THE EDGE-CUT

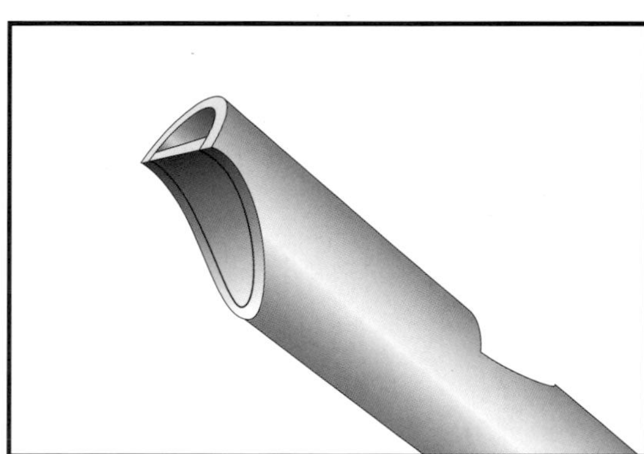

FIGURE 3
THE CURVED CUTAWAY AT THE WINDWAY END

PLAYING TECHNIQUE

Place the right hand fingers over the bottom three holes and the left hand fingers over the top three, with the thumbs underneath the body of the flute for support. Hold the flute directly in front of you, angled downward, and blow through the windway. The fingering chart given for the side-blown flute (Figure 4 for that plan, page 76) applies as well to this instrument. Use less wind pressure to bring out the lower notes, more for the higher.

Ostrich Egg Ocarina

DIFFICULT

Ocarina is the most common name in English for globular flutes—that is, flutes having a short, fat air chamber rather than a long, thin air column. There are many different sorts of globular flutes, and many different materials will do to form a globular air chamber. One of my favorites is eggshell. Chicken eggs can work, but they are small and rather fragile to work with. Goose eggs are a little better, and I imagine that emu eggs might do quite nicely. But I have most enjoyed working with ostrich eggshell. Ostrich eggs are large enough to produce a satisfyingly deep, hooting sort of tone. The shell is surprisingly strong—strong enough to make you wonder how those little ostriches ever manage to get out—and it is workable: you can drill and file it without fear of breakage. With their dimpled, cream-colored surface, the shells are beautiful to see. Ostrich eggshells are commercially available, and because the birds are widely domesticated, you needn't worry about diminishing a threatened population.

The ostrich egg ocarina described here, like most ocarinas, is a fipple flute. We will make the windway out of wood, and glue it to the shell in such a way that it directs the airflow over the edge of a blowhole at the top of the eggshell. Because eggs tend to roll whenever you set them down, the plans include a stand.

Globular flutes, like other flutes, can produce different pitches through the use of tone holes. But globular air chambers operate by their own rules. In globular chambers the locations of the tone holes are relatively unimportant. The essential factor in controlling pitch is the size of the holes or, to be precise, the cumulative size of all open holes at a given moment. This means that on an ostrich egg ocarina you can place the tone holes at whatever locations happen to be comfortable for your fingers and tune them by adjusting their sizes. The rule for tuning is simple: the larger the hole, the higher the resulting pitch. As with other tone hole instruments, you can make the holes small initially and tune by enlarging.

Instructions

1. We will start by constructing a too-long stretch of windway from which we will cut off a shorter section. It is easier to make this extra-long windway than to try to make one as small as is actually required. Also, this way you will have some leftover windway for your next ostrich egg ocarina.

   Cut the two pieces of hardwood to length as shown in Figure 1A (page 82). You can cut the smaller piece from the larger if need be. The surfaces that are to be joined should be as straight and level as can be. Level them by sanding or other means.
2. Down the center of the good edge on the larger piece, make a trough 3/4" wide and just 1/32" deep (Figure 1B, page 82). Make the trough as smooth and accurate as possible. An electric router with a 3/4" flat bottom bit, with fences care-

Materials List

Lumber

1 1" x 2" x 6" hardwood of your choice ***Windway***
1 1" x 3/8" x 6" hardwood of your choice ***Windway***
1 3/8" x 6" x 1' wood of your choice ***Stand***

Hardware & Supplies

Ostrich egg (Note) ***Sound chamber***
Epoxy glue (extra-strength variety, not quick-set)
Walnut oil or mineral oil

Suggested Tools

Band saw, jigsaw, or coping saw
Electric router with a 3/4" flat-bottom bit, or 3/4" flat chisel and hammer
Drill and full set of fractional drill bits
Small conical grinder bit or burr bit
1" drum sander bit with sanding sleeve
2 C-clamps
Craft knife
Flat file
Square or triangular file
Small rat-tail file or a round riffling file
Sandpaper

Note

Ostrich egg shells are available for $10–$20 from the source listed in Appendix 1, page 140.

fully set up to guide the router, will do very neat work here. If you don't have a router, you will need to do some careful chisel work.

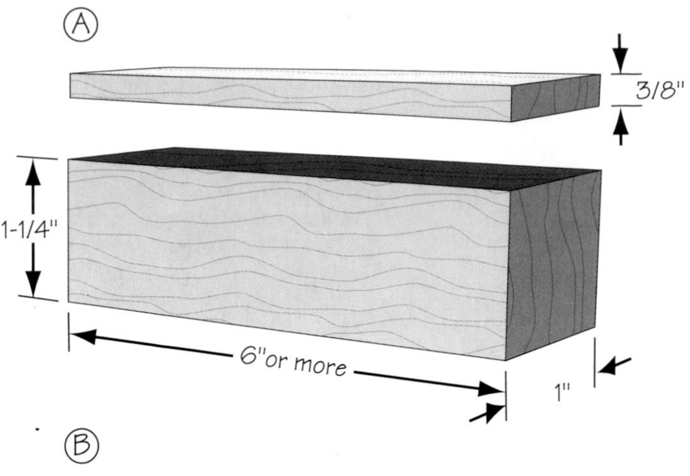

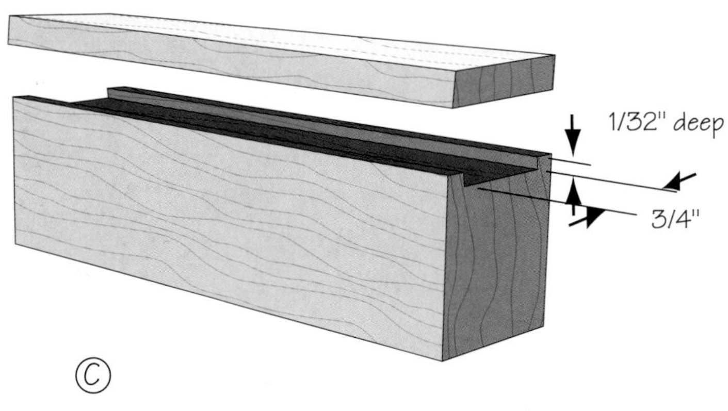

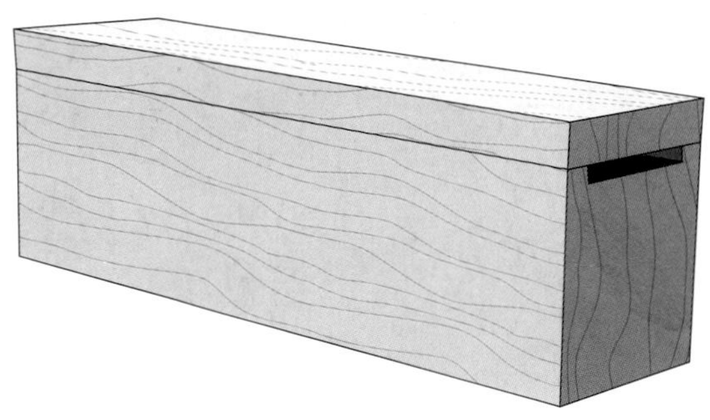

FIGURE 1

TWO WOODEN PIECES FROM WHICH THE WINDWAY OR MOUTHPIECE IS TO BE MADE. A, THE UNDERSURFACE OF THE SMALLER PIECE AND THE TOP SURFACE OF THE LARGER PIECE SHOULD BE MADE PERFECTLY FLAT AND SMOOTH; B, THE GROOVE CUT IN THE LARGER PIECE; C, THE TWO PIECES GLUED TOGETHER.

3. As shown in Figure 1C, you will glue the smaller piece with its true side down over the channeled edge of the larger piece, so that it forms the top of a narrow windway. Carefully and conservatively spread epoxy only on the ridges at the sides of the channel in the larger piece, so that the glue will not squeeze into the windway and block it. Position the smaller piece carefully over the larger and clamp with two C-clamps. Double-check the alignment before leaving it to dry.
4. Your ostrich egg will have come with a hole about the size of a dime in the top, through which the contents were removed (someone's breakfast?). That hole will serve as the opening in front of the windway, and the edge of the hole will serve as the edge against which the air is directed. Use a narrow square or triangular file to reshape the hole to provide a straighter edge on one side (Figure 2).

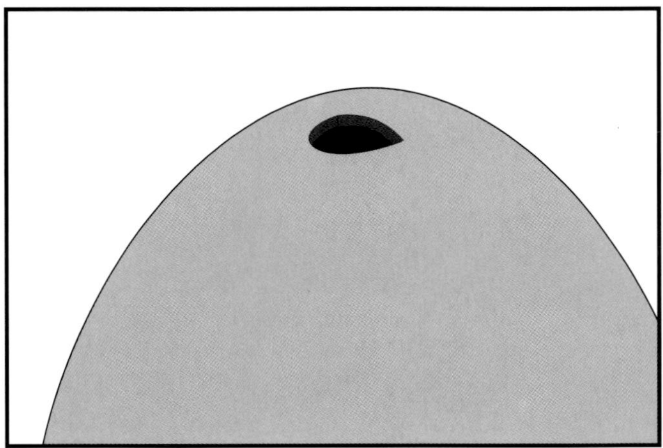

FIGURE 2

THE HOLE IN THE TOP OF THE EGG, RESHAPED TO GIVE A STRAIGHTER EDGE

5. Now is a good time to make the stand for the egg. Using a band saw, jigsaw, or coping saw, cut two pieces of 3/8"-thick wood to the shapes shown in Figure 3A or a similar design of your own. Redraw the deep curve in the top of each piece to more closely match the size of your egg (make the concavity just a little broader than the egg). After cutting the two pieces, try fitting them together as shown in Figure 3B. If they won't go together, sand or file the slots as necessary for a good fit. Then thoroughly sand both pieces and round all edges except the edges of the slots.

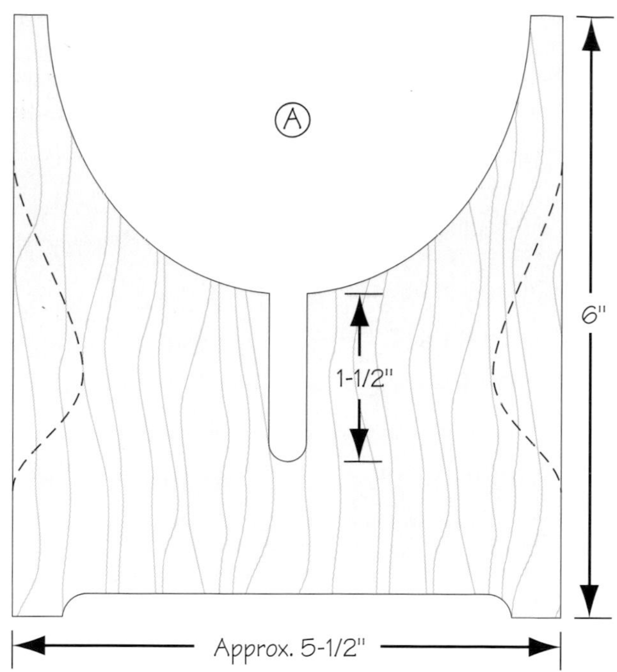

Ⓐ
1-1/2"
6"
Approx. 5-1/2"

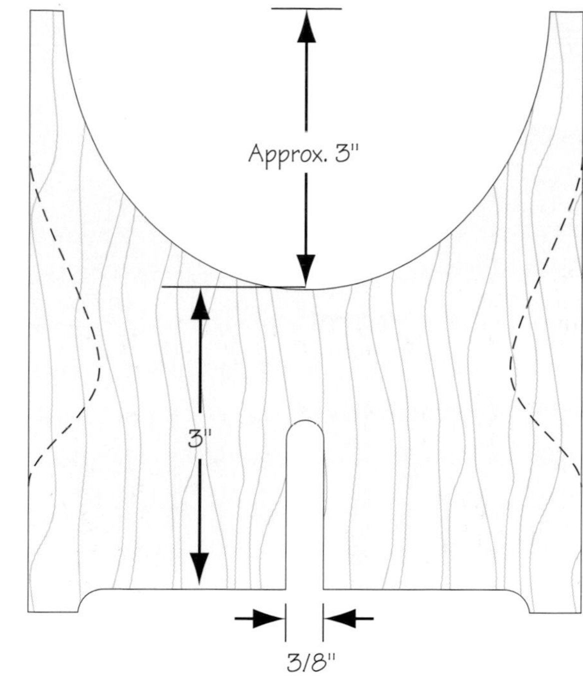

Approx. 3"
3"
3/8"

Ⓑ

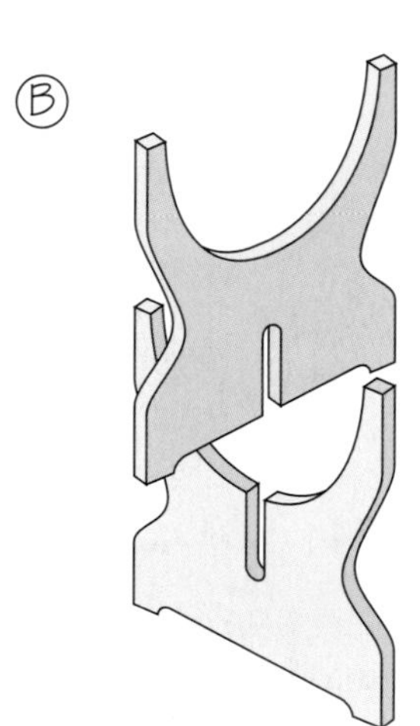

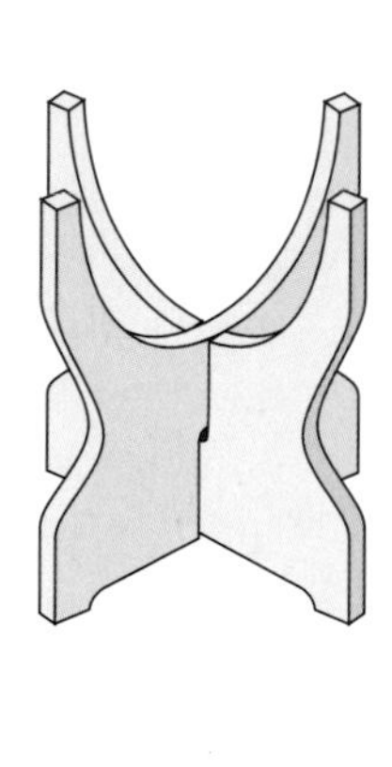

FIGURE 3

The two halves of the egg stand. A, the bold rectangular outlines show a simple, easy-to-make form for the stand; the dotted outlines show a more decorative shape; B, assemble the stand by sliding the two halves together.

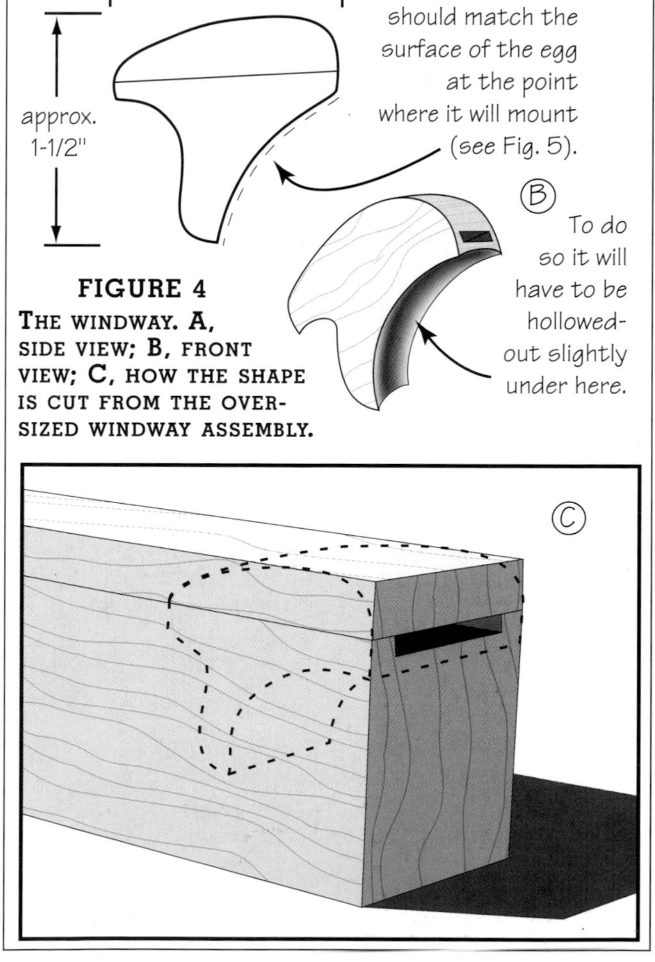

approx. 1-1/2"
Ⓐ The curvature should match the surface of the egg at the point where it will mount (see Fig. 5).
approx. 1-1/2"
Ⓑ To do so it will have to be hollowed-out slightly under here.
Ⓒ

FIGURE 4

The windway. A, side view; B, front view; C, how the shape is cut from the over-sized windway assembly.

6. When the glue on the windway is dry, cut a section of it to the size and shape shown in Figure 4. Approximate the shape with a band saw, jigsaw or coping saw, then refine it and pretty it up by sanding. The bottom surface of the windway will be glued to the egg (Figure

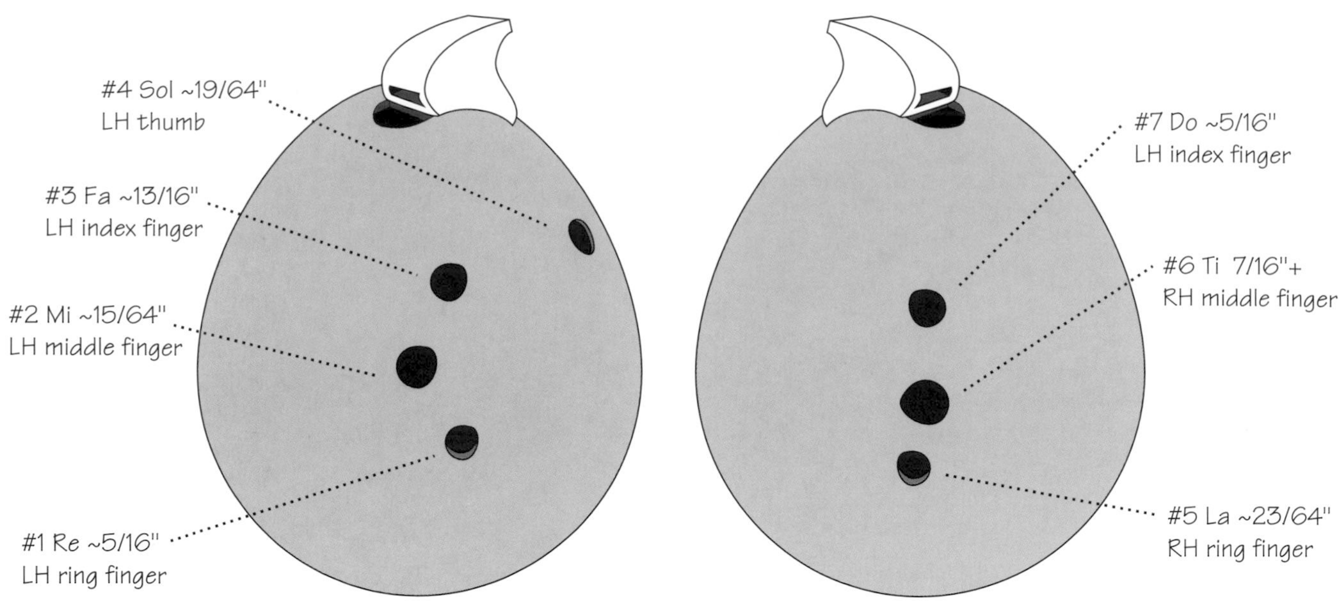

FIGURE 5

PITCHES AND TONE HOLE SIZES. THESE HOLE SIZES ARE SUITABLE FOR AN UNUSUALLY SMALL OSTRICH EGG. FOR A TYPICAL EGG, YOU CAN SAFELY DRILL AT THESE SIZES AND THEN ENLARGE THE HOLES TO TUNE TO PITCH. THE PITCH FOR THE ALL-HOLES-CLOSED FINGERING, WHICH WE CAN REFER TO AS HOLE NUMBER ZERO WITH PITCH *DO*, WILL DEPEND PRIMARILY ON THE SIZE OF THE EGG. THE OTHER PITCHES ARE TO BE TUNED RELATIVE TO THIS *DO*. HOLE #6 SHOULD BE DRILLED AT 7/16" AND ENLARGED INTO AN OVAL SHAPE; THAT'S WHY ITS SIZE IS GIVEN AS 7/16" +. IN THE FINGERINGS FOR THE DO-RE-MI SCALE, THE HOLES WILL BE OPENED CUMULATIVELY IN SEQUENCE, LEAVING THE PRECEDING HOLES OPEN—E.G., WHEN YOU TUNE HOLE #2 TO GET *MI*, LEAVE HOLE 1 OPEN AS WELL; FOR *FA* AT HOLE 3, LEAVE HOLES 2 AND 1 OPEN, ETC. (OTHER FINGERINGS, WHICH YOU CAN EXPLORE LATER, WILL YIELD PITCHES OUTSIDE THE SIMPLE MAJOR SCALE.) THE HOLE LOCATIONS SHOWN IN THE DRAWING ARE APPROXIMATE; YOU CAN SET THE LOCATIONS ACCORDING TO WHAT IS COMFORTABLE FOR THE PLAYER'S HANDS.

5). That undersurface must be made concave to accommodate the egg's convexity. I have found that a 1" drum sander, which can be mounted in a drill press or an electric hand drill, will do the job. You don't have to be particularly neat about it, except in trying to make the contour of the edges match reasonably closely that of the egg.

7. Place the windway piece roughly in position opposite the straight edge of the hole in the egg (Figure 5). Blow through it as you hold it there, listening for the tone. Move it about a bit, searching for the position at which it produces the clearest tone. When you've satisfied yourself that you've found that position, mark the location on the egg with a pencil.
8. To glue on the windway piece, position the egg upright in the stand you just made so that the windway, in its intended location, can rest centered and balanced at the highest point. Otherwise, it will slip out of position before the glue dries. Mix the epoxy, place it generously on the underside of the windway piece, and place it in its marked position on the egg. With a rag dipped in alcohol, wipe away any extra epoxy that squeezes out around the edges. Double-check it for correct placement, and then leave it to dry.
9. When the glue is dry, you can add the tone holes. Many ocarinas use a simple but effective four-hole fingering, but we can't use it here because the holes on the large egg would have to be too big to be covered by a finger. We'll use instead a seven-hole arrangement that allows you to play a major scale simply by uncovering all the holes in succession. It allows for many other scales as

well, including all the tones of the chromatic scale except the minor second. The range will be one octave, which is an acceptable maximum for an ocarina such as this. This one-octave major scale will be built over the pitch that your egg happens to produce with all holes closed, whatever that pitch may be.

Suggested hole sizes and locations are shown in Figure 5. The given sizes yield the desired pitches for a relatively small ostrich egg. That means that, unless you are working with an even smaller egg, you can safely start with the suggested sizes. Chances are that the holes will be a little too small, yielding pitches that are too low. You can bring them up to pitch by enlarging.

Here is a procedure for drilling and tuning the holes:

A. Start by grasping the egg in both hands, with the windway positioned for playing. Your fingers should be slightly spread, but not awkwardly splayed. With a pencil, mark the location where your left-hand ring finger falls. That is the location for the first hole.

B. Drill there, carefully and slowly, with the bit size suggested in Figure 5 for this first hole. After drilling, clean away any broken material, and round the edges of the hole—a round riffling file, a small rat-tail file and/or a craft knife are good for this.

C. Hold the ocarina to your lips and play, first with the new hole covered and then with it open. If you think of the closed hole note as *do*, then the open hole note should be *re*. Chances are it will initially be too low. To raise it to where it will sound as *re* relative to the egg's natural *do*, enlarge it one drill-bit size at a time, testing for pitch after each enlargement.

As you go through this tuning process you will find that wind pressure is an important element: the harder you blow, the higher the pitch. So you will need to keep the wind pressure steady for your test blows, at whatever pressure seems to bring out the best tone. Generally that pressure will increase as you go up the scale, so you can tune the higher holes at progressively higher wind pressures. Don't worry if at times the results seem a bit ambiguous or unstable. It's reassuring to know that during performance experienced players unconsciously adjust their tuning through wind pressure.

D. Proceed to drill and tune the second, third, and on up to the seventh hole, following the hole sizes suggested in Figure 5. Later, you can go back and adjust the sizes of previously tuned holes sizes if necessary. Keep in mind, however, that enlarging any hole will raise the pitch for all higher fingerings for which that hole is left open. For large holes, drill a smaller hole first, and then gradually enlarge it, rather then trying to drill the big hole all at once. Holes that are larger than about 7/16" will be hard to cover for people with average-sized fingers. For big holes, like the sixth hole, first make a hole of 7/16". Then, using a conical grinder bit or burr bit, tune by enlarging the hole into an oval shape, with the long dimension running in the direction from which the finger will approach. Don't widen beyond the original 7/16".

10. With the holes all in place, the instrument is done—except that we haven't put on any wood finish. For the mouthpiece, use something nontoxic like mineral oil or walnut oil. You can finish the stand the same way, or use a commercial wood finish. The egg needs no finish.

Playing Technique

Blow through the windway, covering and uncovering the tone holes to produce different pitches. Lifting the fingers in the sequence given in Figure 5 will produce a major scale. With a little experimentation, you will find fingerings for other tones of the chromatic scale, as well as other, more exotic scales. With practice you will learn to control wind pressure for fine-tuning.

Variations

Create different tunings by making instruments with different hole sizes. Make instruments in higher or lower ranges by using different sized eggs or eggs from different birds. If you have good flute-playing embouchure, you can make a nonfipple version of this instrument (easier to make, but harder to play). Then you will have something very much like the egg-shaped Chinese globular flute called *Xun*.

Natural Horn

DIFFICULT

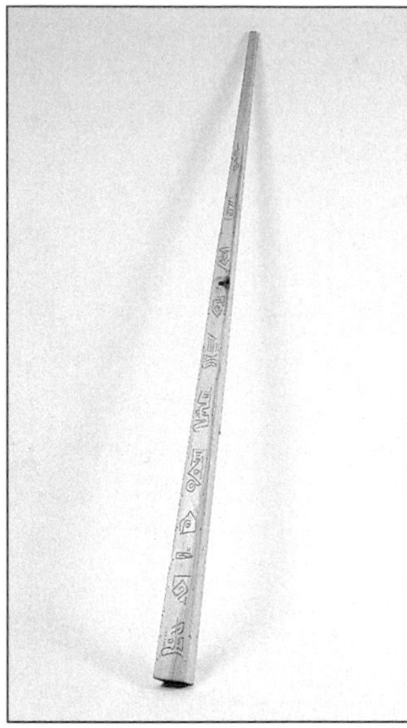

Trumpets, trombones, bugles, sousaphones, tubas, and an extended family of other modern and historical instruments are played by buzzing the lips into a mouthpiece attached to a long tube. The buzzing lips operate under the same principle as the reeds in reed instruments: they allow the air to enter the tube in a series of rapid pulses that stimulate the vibration. When the frequency of those pulses falls into agreement with one of the natural resonance frequencies of the tube, the result is a clear and stable tone.

Long tubes have not just one resonant frequency, but a series of them. By controlling lip tension, a skilled player can bring his or her buzzing frequency into line with different tube resonances, producing a range of tones from a single tube. But over the lower part of the range these playable pitches make up an incomplete scale, with the available notes too far apart to play familiar melodies. To fill in the gaps, many lip-buzzed instruments have valves, slides, or (now rare) side holes, making more notes available.

The term *natural horn* refers to lip-buzzed instruments having no valves or side holes. They are limited to playing the tones available through the natural tube resonances. Military bugles are the most familiar of natural horns, and recalling the sound of a bugle call will give you some sense of the set of pitches available on a natural horn. Yet skilled players, by playing in the upper registers where the pitches are not so widely spaced, can do things with a natural horn that bugle calls only hint at.

Our natural horn will be made of wood. It will have an expanding air column shape—an important feature in such instruments—made not by carving or hollowing, but by building a boxlike tube with four sides. (While the boxlike tube cannot properly be called conical, for acoustic purposes it functions much the same as a conical tube.) The mouthpiece will be integral rather than separate, carved directly into the opening of the tube. Despite the four-sided construction, our natural horn will most closely resemble an Alpine horn, the beautiful, extravagantly long, carved wooden pastoral horn of Switzerland, parts of the former Soviet Union, Germany, and other European territories.

Materials List

Lumber

2 1/2" x 6" x 8' hardwood (Notes-1) *Body*

Hardware & Supplies

1" finishing nails

Marine-grade wood glue

Waxed paper

Wood finish of your choice

Special finish for the mouthpiece area (Notes-2)

Suggested Tools

Circular saw or handsaws (ripsaw and crosscut saw)

Hand drill with countersink bit and a spherical burr bit, both 5/8" diameter

Plane, electric hand plane, or jointer

Rasp file

Electric sander or several grades of sandpaper

Paintbrush or rag

Notes

1. You probably won't find the 1/2" thickness ready-milled, so try for slightly thicker board and plane it down, or, alternatively, use it as is to make a correspondingly heavier instrument (see the caption for Figure 1 if you do this). You can use almost any wood species. The ideal is a close-grained hardwood such as maple. The disadvantage of soft wood is that the grain is coarse and rises when wet. This makes the mouthpiece uncomfortable on the lips and also has some acoustic disadvantages. But the cost of this quantity of hardwood may convince you to put up with these disadvantages.
2. Use mineral oil, walnut oil, beeswax, or a specially formulated beeswax salad bowl finish (available at upscale housewares stores).

To get a good tone through lip-buzzing takes a special knack. Some people seem to have it naturally; others must work to develop it. See "Playing Technique" below for a fuller description.

Instructions

1. Cut the four sides of the horn to the dimensions shown in Figure 1. After marking out the cuts on the wood, cut the two broader pieces just outside the lines, making them extra wide by about 1/16". These cuts need not be painstakingly accurate. The two narrower pieces, however, must be cut as accurately as possible, with the sides good and straight to ensure an airtight joint. A well-equipped woodworker might use a jointer to true the edge; short of that you might use a plane, or try to cut very accurately and clean it up by sanding.

   If your wood is over 1/2" thick, plane the surface to 1/2". Or, optionally, leave it thick and be content with a heavier instrument.
2. We're now ready to join the four sides. Here's how:
   A. Mix a batch of marine-grade adhesive, being sure to follow instructions on the label. Lay an 8' strip of waxed paper on a flat and solid floor. Place the two narrow wood pieces side by side on their edges on the waxed paper. Spread glue on the exposed edges and correspondingly along the sides of what is to be the inner face of one of the broader wood pieces. Avoid using an excessive amount of glue near the narrow end; we don't want glue to drip into the horn's interior there.
   B. Put the broad piece in place on the two side pieces (Figure 2A, page 88). Position the pieces carefully; in particular, make sure that the narrow end opening is 1/8". The edges of the broad piece can overhang the sides very slightly because you cut it slightly oversized. When you are sure everything is positioned right, drive finishing nails to secure the joint, positioning them at 6" intervals or less, 5/16" in from the edge, along both sides of the top piece. You will have to stop driving the nails 1' short of the narrow end (otherwise you will drive them right through into the floor). The greatest concern is to make a tight joint and get an airtight seal along both sides.

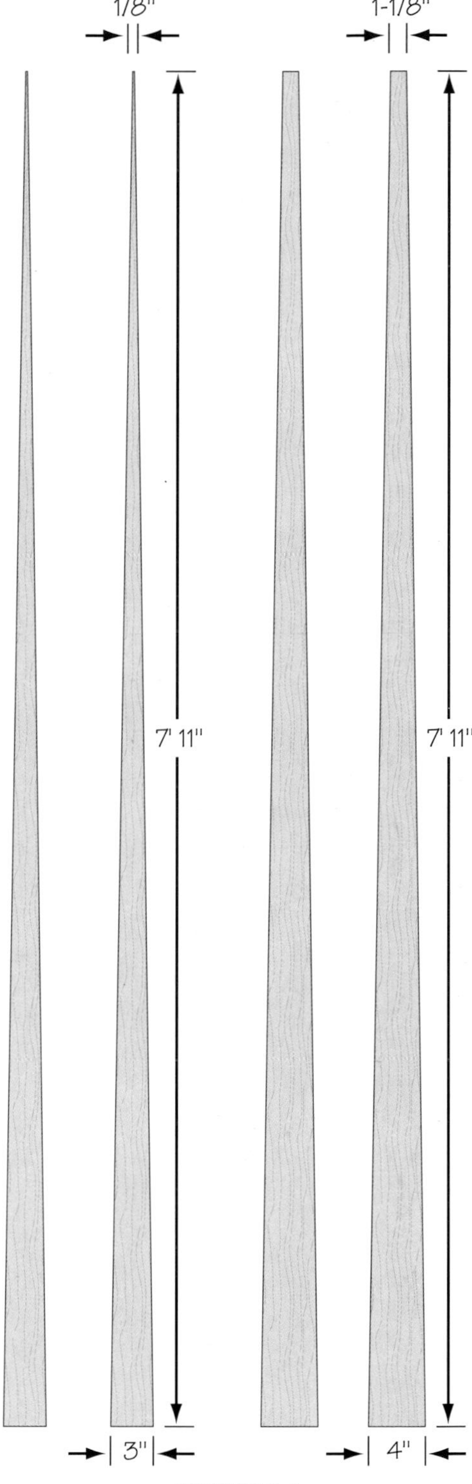

FIGURE 1

The four wood pieces for the sides of the horn. The boards should be 1/2" thick. If they are not, then the dimensions of the two broader pieces should be modified to [3" + 2T] at the wide end and [1/8" + 2T] at the narrow end, where T is the thickness of the wood. To get all four pieces out of two 6" x 8' boards, lay out the narrow end of one piece alongside the broad end of another on each board.

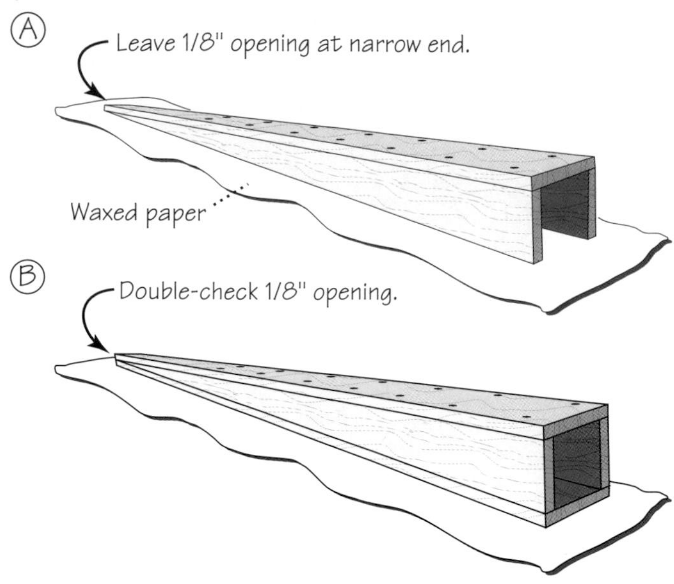
A
Leave 1/8" opening at narrow end.
Waxed paper
B
Double-check 1/8" opening.

FIGURE 2

Assembling the tube. A, attaching one of the broad pieces; B, attaching the other.

C. Turn the assembly over and repeat steps A and B to attach the remaining broad piece (Figure 2B). This time you can drive the nails all the way down to 2" from the narrow end (double-check again that the narrow-end gap is 1/8").

D. Weight or clamp the narrow end to ensure positive contact there, and let the assembly dry for a day.

3. When the assembly is dry, square the near end by sawing, planing, or sanding. Then trim and square the far end to leave an overall length of 7' 10-1/2".
4. Level the joints and clean up any glue drips. You can do this with a plane on the sides (eliminating the slight overhang of the broad pieces). On the top and bottom pieces, where the finishing nails are, clean up as necessary by sanding. Ease all the edges with sandpaper or a router with a rounding-over bit.
5. At the large end of the horn, round the inner edge of the opening as generously as the thickness of the wood allows, for an effect a little like a small bell (Figure 3). Use a coarse rasp file for the initial shaping, then smooth with finer files or sandpaper.
6. The mouthpiece will be carved directly into the narrow end, making a cavity that matches the shape of the cavity in a conventional brass instrument mouthpiece. Secure the instrument in a position where you have good access to the narrow end. Round, clear, and slightly enlarge the mouthpiece opening by drilling through with a 5/32" bit. Use the 5/8" countersink bit in an electric hand drill

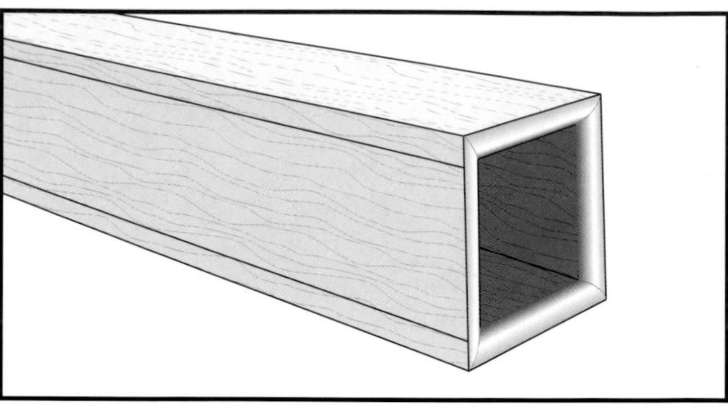

FIGURE 3

The rounded opening at the large end

to carve out the opening for the mouthpiece (Figure 4A). Be careful not to go too deep. Follow with the 5/8" spherical burr bit to round the cavity (Figure 4B). Tear off a small scrap of medium grit sandpaper and sand the cavity smooth, at the same time rounding the edges as in Figure 4C. Clear again with the 5/32" bit. Finish up with finer grades of sandpaper. Make sure no fraying or stray splinters are left in or around the opening.

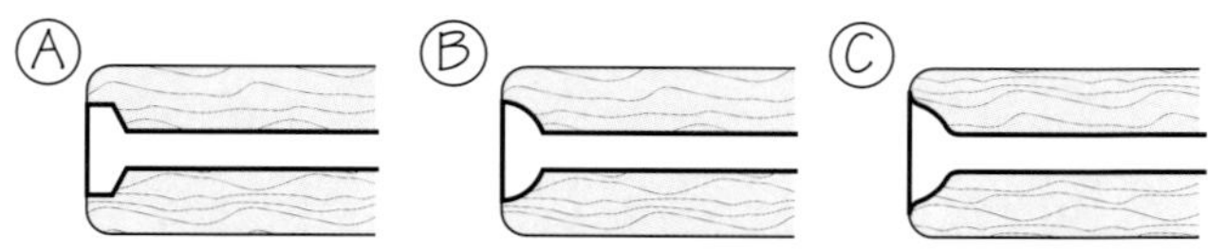
A
B
C

FIGURE 4

Stages in shaping the mouthpiece cup

7. Apply a wood finish of your choice on the exterior of the instrument, but do not use it on the mouthpiece cup or the surrounding area.
8. The mouthpiece area also needs some type of finish to make it smoother, harder, and more moisture-resistant, but it must be benign enough for prolonged skin and oral contact. The salad bowl finish suggested in the materials list works well because the wax tends to fill gaps and form a smooth surface. Afterwards, use the 5/32" bit by hand to clear out any finish that may clog the bore. Over time, as the instrument is played, the end-grain in and around the mouthpiece will tend to roughen up

This natural horn has decorative patterns carved in shallow relief in the sides using an electric router.

again. When that happens, sand it again and recoat with the nontoxic finish.

Playing Technique

The lip-buzzing technique is a little like a more controlled version of the sound sometimes called a raspberry or Bronx cheer, but with lips only—no protruding tongue. Press your lips firmly together and force air out between them at the middle for a buzzing sound. If you press your lips against the natural horn mouthpiece and buzz into the horn, you should begin to feel and hear the effect and can refine it from there. Tensing the lips more to produce a higher pitched lip-buzz will allow you to sound the horn's higher resonances; playing with looser lips will bring out the lower tones. A little coaching and encouragement from an experienced brass player will help. The preferred tone for a big expanding bore instrument like this is full and warm like a French horn, not bright like a trumpet.

Our natural horn can produce this series of tones: C_2, C_3, G_3, C_4, E_4, G_4, ↓Bb_4, C_5, D_5, E_5, ↓$F\#_5$, G_5, ↓A_5, ↓Bb_5, ↑B_5, C_6. The arrows before some notes indicate a tone somewhat above or below the indicated pitch. These tones comprise what is known as the harmonic series over the fundamental C2. In theory, the series continues upward indefinitely. Most players will not actually be able to get the lowest note or two to sound. The tones become increasingly difficult toward the top of the range as well, but a good player will be able to get all these and more.

Our horn's close relative, the Alpine horn, is beloved as an outdoor instrument. Similarly, the natural horn will sound well outdoors or in large interior spaces. Listeners standing some distance in front of the horn will hear the best sound. Ironically, what the player hears is not as rich.

Variations

You can make natural horns in other sizes to obtain the pitches of the harmonic series over other fundamentals.

You can modify the natural horn to accept a separate metal mouthpiece. This probably will improve the tone, both because of the more reflective metal and the more perfect shaping of the cup and the back-bore (the tubing section of the metal mouthpiece). Reconfiguring the natural horn for the separate mouthpiece may throw the harmonic series slightly out of tune. Alternatively, you can make a separate mouthpiece out of wood, especially if you can work at a lathe. Do your best to copy the form of a French horn or other brass instrument mouthpiece. You can then use inexpensive wood for the body of the instrument, and a close-grained hardwood for the mouthpiece. Boxwood for the mouthpiece is traditionally recommended, as its grain scarcely rises under moisture.

Chalumeau

MODERATE

We come now to the family of reed instruments. This next instrument employs what is known as a *single reed,* or *beating reed*—the same sort used on clarinets and saxophones. The idea behind a beating reed is this: an opening at the mouthpiece end of a wind instrument tube is covered by a thin, flat strip of cane. In its normal position, the cane reed is not actually fully closed over the opening, but stands slightly out and away, like a door ajar, leaving a small gap. When the player blows into the mouthpiece, the reed alternately slaps closed over the opening and then springs back open, letting the air through in a rapid series of puffs, thus setting up the vibration in the tube.

The *chalumeau* described here is really a simple clarinet. (Chalumeau is the name of a European ancestor of the modern clarinet.) Clarinets and chalumeaux can be known by two essential features: the single beating reed as described above and a cylindrical air column. (Saxophones, by contrast, have a conical, or expanding, air column, like the natural horn.)

The flutes that appeared earlier in this book likewise have cylindrical air columns, but the cylindrical column behaves differently when one end is blocked by a reed. Instead of overblowing the octave, clarinets overblow the interval of a 12th—a little over an octave and a half. With the flutes we were able to provide enough finger holes to cover a range of an octave, and then use the same finger holes in the upper register to extend the range further. But with clarinets you have to provide enough finger holes to fill in an octave and a half before jumping to the second register. That's a lot of finger holes. And that is why we are making a chalumeau and not a clarinet.

The basic difference between the chalumeau and the modern clarinet is that chalumeaux were made to play only in the lower register. Its makers contented themselves with a limited range rather than providing the elaborate key work by which clarinets fill in that octave and a half leading to the second register.

The plan that follows calls for eight finger holes, yielding a range of just over an octave. Like the

THE CHALMEAU'S UNATTRACTIVE PLASTIC BODY WAS MADE LESS UNATTRACTIVE BY A DAPPLING OF SPRAY PAINT FOLLOWED BY SEVERAL COATS OF A CLEAR ACRYLIC SPRAY-ON FINISH.

Materials List

Hardware & Supplies

1 1/2" internal diameter x 1/8" wall thickness x 14" plastic tubing (Notes-1) ***Body***

1 1/16" x 24" elastic cord (Notes-2)

1 #2 x 3/8" machine screw

1 Alto saxophone reed (Notes-3)

Suggested Tools

Hacksaw

Drill with fractional drill bit set and countersink bit

Craft knife

Small rat-tail file or round riffling file

Protractor

Small screwdriver

Medium-fine sandpaper

Notes

1. Plastic tubings sold as 1/2" internal diameter are often actually slightly larger. That's o.k. for this plan. See the materials list for the side-blown flute, page 75, for more on plastic tubings.
2. Available at variety stores or fabric stores.
3. Get a few; they don't last forever. Beginners will want a soft reed, designated as 1-1/2, 2, or 2-1/2.

flutes, this instrument is happiest playing in a particular key, but with cross-fingerings many of the tones of a chromatic scale become available. The instrument's diminutive size puts the finger holes close together, eliminating difficult stretches. But the range is an octave lower than what it would be for a comparably sized flute or saxophone; as discussed in the sidebar on page 77, that is another characteristic of the cylindrical air column stopped at one end.

Our little chalumeau will have an integral mouthpiece (i.e., the mouthpiece is not separate, but of a piece with the body of the instrument). The shaping of the single-reed mouthpiece is a rather subtle business, so I will make this suggestion: hold off on making this instrument unless you have experience playing single-reed instruments (saxophones or clarinets), or unless you can get an experienced single-reed player to assist you when time comes for mouthpiece shaping. You need someone who knows the feel and sound of a well-playing single reed to help determine when the mouthpiece is working properly.

Some of the early chalumeaux were things of great beauty, and purists might object to my applying the term to something made of plastic tubing. But you will be surprised at how nicely this little thing will play in the hands of someone experienced with single-reed instruments.

Instructions

1. Cut the plastic tube to 14" long.
2. Make the mouthpiece cut to form the 20° angle shown in Figures 1A and 1B. (This angle affects the sound significantly—see comments under "Variations" below.)
3. Note the point on the opposite side of the tube from where the oblique mouthpiece cut begins. At a location 1/4" closer to the tip from that point, predrill with a 1/16" bit. With a small screwdriver, screw the #2 x 3/8" machine screw part way in, to where the head stands 3/16" above the surface of the plastic (Figure 1C). The elastic cord that holds the reed in place will be hooked to this screw.
4. This is the time when some experience with single-reed instruments will be invaluable. If you don't have that experience, call a friend. The part of the mouthpiece over which the reed will lie (where you made the oblique cut in step 2) is called the *lay*. The shaping of the lay is crucial to the functioning of the reed. As shown in Figure 2, the last 3/4" or so of the tip must curve very slightly away from the reed, so that the reed can slap down over it under air pressure and then spring back up.

   To shape the lay, first, sand the oblique mouthpiece cut perfectly flat and smooth. To do this, lay a piece of fine sandpaper on a flat surface and carefully draw the chalumeau over it with the oblique cut down flat, as shown in Figure 3A. Then sand a bit more, but with a slight curving motion

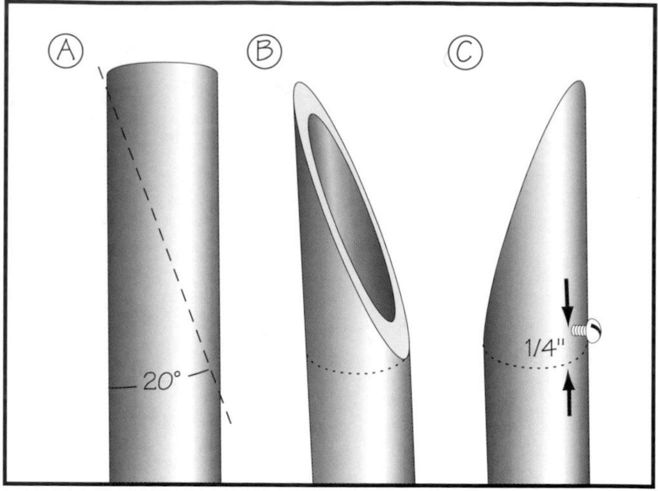

FIGURE 1

The mouthpiece. A, the angle of the mouthpiece cut; B, the finished cut; C, the small screw that holds the reed-binding cord.

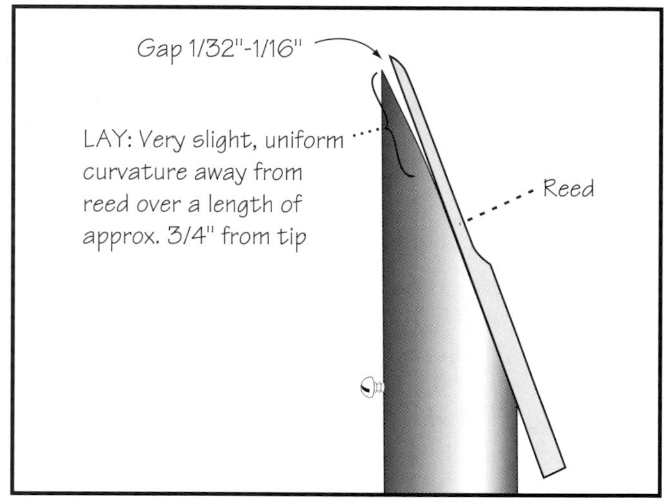

FIGURE 2

The mouthpiece lay. Shows the slight curvature of the mouthpiece facing and the gap at the tip of the reed.

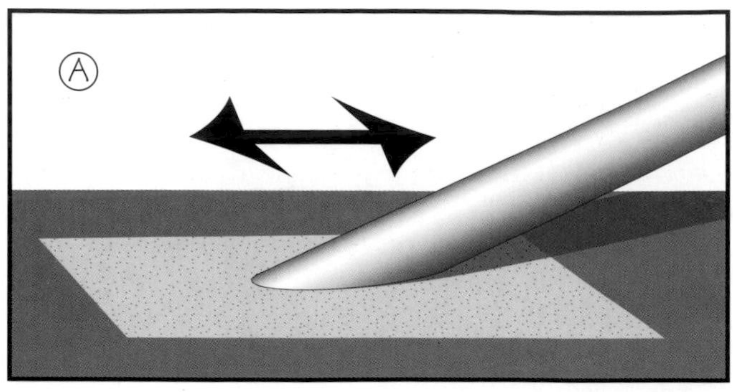

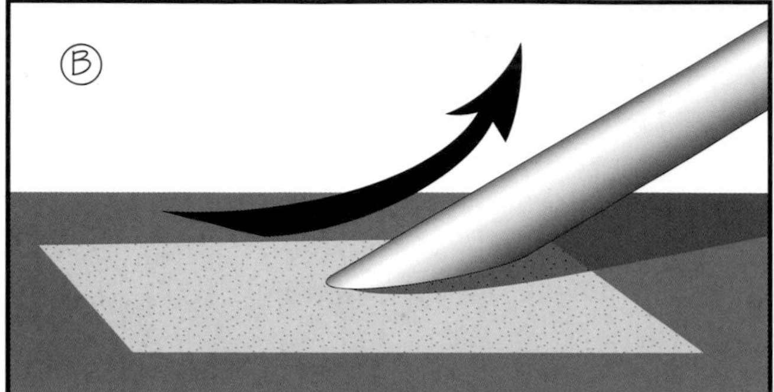

FIGURE 3

Sanding the mouthpiece lay. A, sanding with the surface perfectly flat with a level, side-to-side motion; B, sanding with a curved motion to impart a slight curvature to the lay.

as in Figure 3B. This will impart the desired curvature toward the tip. The upper part of the mouthpiece cut should remain flat to hold the base of the reed. Intermittently check your progress by holding the reed in place against the flat upper part of the cut and noting how large the gap between mouthpiece and reed is at the tip (look again at Figure 2).

The ideal size for the gap is somewhere between 1/32" and 1/16". When your sanding has created a gap in that range, with a very slight, very uniform curve leading up to it, wet the reed, strap it on, and give it a try. To strap on the reed: Tie a small loop at one end of the 24" elastic cord. Tie the other end to the small screw on top of the instrument. Hold the reed in place, and wrap around and around with the elastic under moderate tension (see Figure 4). Loop the end over the screw. Adjust the reed

FIGURE 4

The reed bound in place with elastic cord (two views)

position so that it just covers the opening of the mouthpiece cut.

Put the instrument to your lips and blow (for instructions on getting a sound out of a single reed, see "Playing Technique" below). If the reed slaps shut and stays closed, allowing no air to pass, then your curvature is too shallow; the gap is too small. If it doesn't close at all, and air simply rushes through the opening, the curvature is too deep and the opening is too large. If it produces a high squeal rather than a steady lower tone, the gap may be too small, the reed may be too dry, or there may be some unevenness somewhere. Remove the reed, go back to the sandpaper, and do some reshaping. When you have it right, the thing will play like a saxophone or clarinet. Very slight changes in the lay make a big difference in playability. It may take you several tries to get it right.

5. At this point you have a hole-less, one-note clarinet. We will now add eight finger holes of equal size. The chart in Figure 5 shows the hole locations as distances measured from the mid-point of the mouthpiece opening. It also shows expected overall tube length.

   Make a mark representing the midpoint of the mouthpiece opening on the side of the tube opposite the mouthpiece cut (the mark will be near the screw that holds the elastic, but closer to the tip). Measure and mark the cut-off point for the

FIGURE 5

Finger hole locations and pitches. Locations represent distances from the center of the mouthpiece opening to the center of the hole. Intended size refers to the expected ultimate size for the hole; the hole will initially be drilled slightly smaller and brought up to size in the fine-tuning process. Hole #0 represents the full tube length; its pitch is the pitch resulting when all holes are closed, and its location represents the tube end.

Hole #	Pitch	Intended Size	Location
0	C_4	--	11-7/8" (tube end)
1	D_4	11/32"	10-5/32"
2	E_4	11/32"	9-1/8"
3	F_4	11/32"	8-11/16"
4	G_4	11/32"	7-9/16"
5	A_4	11/32"	6-21/32"
6	B_4	11/32"	5-13/16"
7	C_5	11/32"	5-3/8"
8	D_5	11/32"	4-23/32"

expected tube length, as indicated in Figure 6. Cut off the tube 1/4" beyond that point. This leaves room for later shortening in the fine-tuning process.

6. Mark the eight hole locations on the tube, using the distances given in Figure 5 from the mouthpiece midpoint mark. The holes need not be set in a straight line along the top of the tube; as long as they are located at the given distance from the opening, you can shift lateral positioning for the comfort of the playing fingers. The photograph will give you some sense of typical hole positionings.
7. Drill the eight holes with a 1/4" bit. (The intended ultimate size is 11/32"; we are drilling small initially to allow fine-tuning later.) Slightly bevel the rim of each hole with a countersink bit. The drilling often leaves burrs or bits of plastic fuzz; clean these away with a craft knife and a rat-tail file or round riffling file.
8. Time for fine-tuning. The chart in Figure 6 gives intended pitch at each hole. Play the lowest tone (all holes closed). It is probably a little flat of the intended C_4. Shorten the tube in tiny increments, testing the pitch frequently, until the all-holes-closed pitch arrives at C_4. Next, play the tone with only the farthest hole open. It is probably just barely flat of the intended D_4. Enlarge the hole incrementally until it matches the intended pitch. Proceed this way through all the holes. If necessary, re-bevel with the countersink bit as the last stage in tuning each hole (this will further raise the pitch very slightly). Then go back and double-check your work with another round of fine-tuning (if you enlarged the upper holes a great deal, the lower holes may need a bit more enlarging at this point). Notice that the pitch for this small instrument is fairly flexible depending on your embouchure, especially in the high notes. Aim to bring the instrument in tune with the embouchure that feels most consistent and natural.

   With the tuning done, the instrument is finished.

Playing Technique

Wet the reed with water or saliva, then strap it on. Cover the four lower holes with the fingers of the right hand and the four upper with those of the left hand. The embouchure is similar to that of clarinet and saxophone: Place the tip of the mouthpiece in your mouth with the upper teeth resting directly on top of the tube, about 1/2" or 3/4" from the end. The lower lip should be pulled back and in, so that it covers the lower teeth. The reed then rests on the lower lip, with the lower teeth providing support and pressure from below. In this position, close the lips around the mouthpiece to form an air-tight seal, and blow. The amount of pressure on the reed from teeth and lips, the position of the lower lip on the reed, the moisture of the reed, and subtle aspects of the way in which the reed is cut, all affect the reed's performance. If these conditions are not right, the reed may squeal, or it may not speak at all.

Clarinet players will find the unfamiliar hole positionings on the little chalumeau disorienting at first, but it takes only a short time to get used to them.

Variations

The angle of the mouthpiece cut and the shaping of the lay affect the instrument's tone quality and its responsiveness. A less acute angle for the mouthpiece cut, up to about 28°, will bring out a warmer, mellower tone. This angle has the small and perhaps unimportant disadvantage that it provides a shorter flat facing for strapping on the reed and leaves the butt end of the reed protruding awkwardly. A more acute angle, down to about 16°, brings out a harsher and louder tone and, for what it's worth, provides a better facing for strapping on the reed.

You can extend the chalumeau's range if you are content with a *pentatonic* scale (five pitches per octave). This would allow you to cover an octave and a half with eight finger holes. Then you could consider adding a register hole, allowing the instrument to jump to its second register, at the interval of a 12th above the fundamental register. Make the register hole as a thumb hole on the back of the instrument, 3/32" in diameter, located at about 25% of the tube length from the mouthpiece end.

You can make a larger instrument, with correspondingly lower range. The finger holes for such an instrument will be farther apart and more difficult to cover. To remedy that, if you don't mind making life a lot more complicated, you can try your hand at the exacting art of woodwind keying systems.

Wooden Saxophone

DIFFICULT

The great majority of common musical instrument types have evolved incrementally and anonymously over the centuries. The saxophone, on the other hand, is one of the handful for which one can point to an individual inventor and a particular time of invention. The French instrument maker, Adolphe Sax created the first saxophones in a form scarcely different from the modern instrument, sometime around 1840.

Saxophones use a single beating reed, virtually identical to a clarinet reed. But unlike clarinets, the saxophone has an unusually broad conical bore. This has important acoustic consequences: it makes a saxophone louder than a clarinet; gives it a very different tone quality from the clarinet; puts the saxophone's range an octave higher than that of a clarinet of comparable size; and allows the sax, like the flute, to produce a second register at the octave (unlike the clarinet which over-blows the 12th), allowing for fewer holes and simpler fingerings. The saxophone design given here won't be nearly as elaborate as the commercially manufactured instrument. Our saxophone will be made of wood, with an integral mouthpiece. There will be no key work but instead a system of finger holes similar in layout to those of the two flutes in previous plans. This will allow it to play through a major scale in F, with most additional chromatic tones available through cross-fingerings. The simplicity of this wooden saxophone's design leads to one shortcoming: the upper register will tend to play sharp. See "Variations" below for notes on how to improve this.

As with the clarinet, I will make this suggestion: hold off on making this instrument unless you have experience playing single-reed instruments (saxophones or clarinets) or unless you can get an experienced single-reed player to assist you when time comes for mouthpiece shaping.

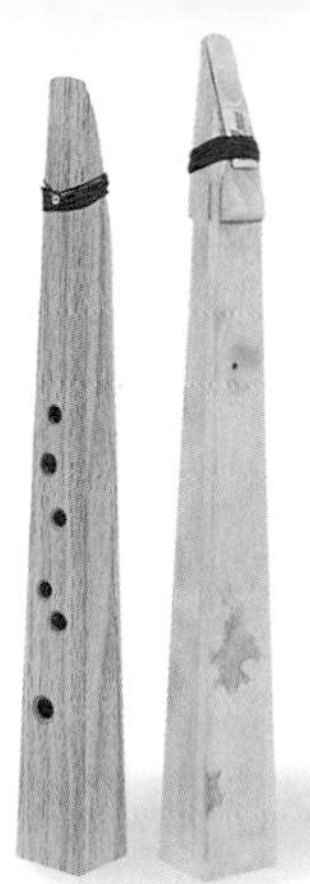

THE DARKER OF THE TWO SAXOPHONES WAS MADE ACCORDING TO THE BASIC PLAN. FOR THE LIGHTER-COLORED ONE ON THE RIGHT, A MORE ELABORATE PROCEDURE WAS USED IN FORMING THE BODY AND SHAPING THE BORE WITHIN. THE PURPOSE WAS TO CREATE THE EXTRA SECTION OF CYLINDRICAL BORE AT THE MOUTHPIECE END AND IMPROVE UPPER REGISTER INTONATION, AS DISCUSSED UNDER "VARIATIONS."

Instructions

1. The body of the saxophone will be built up box-like from four pieces of wood, like the natural horn but much smaller. (The square cross-sectional shape, while unconventional, makes little difference acoustically.) Cut the four pieces to the shapes and dimensions shown in Figure 1. Make the edges of the two narrower pieces as perfectly straight and smooth as possible. Check them against a metal straightedge and sand, plane, or use a jointer to assure this.

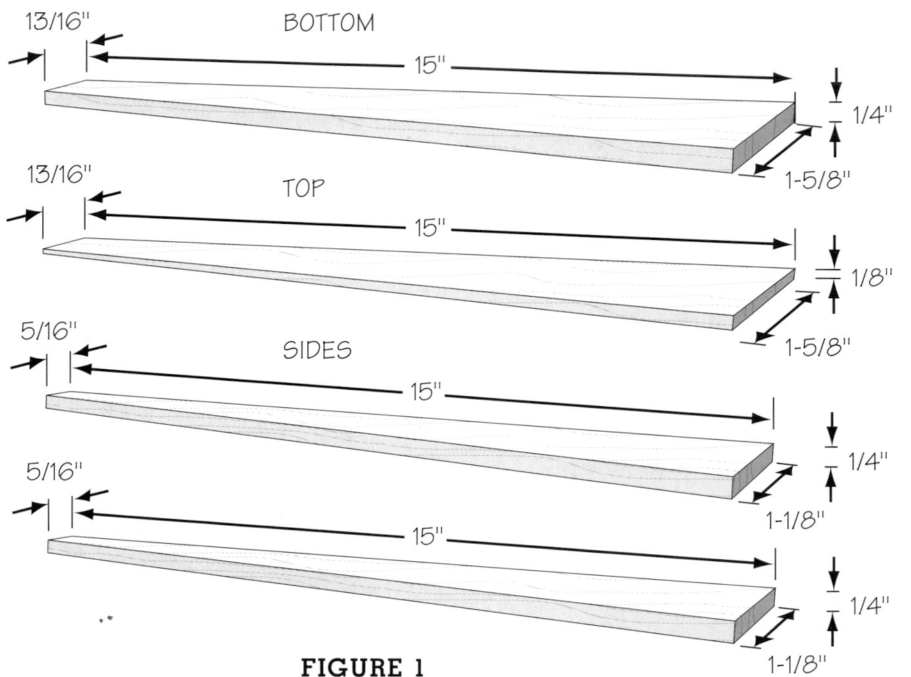

FIGURE 1

The four wood pieces that will form the tube. The two sides are identical. The top and bottom pieces are also identical, except that the top is 1/8" thick and the bottom is 1/4" thick.

2. As indicated in Figure 1, the two side pieces and the bottom piece are to be 1/4" thick. The top is to be 1/8" thick. Plane the wood as necessary to achieve these thicknesses.

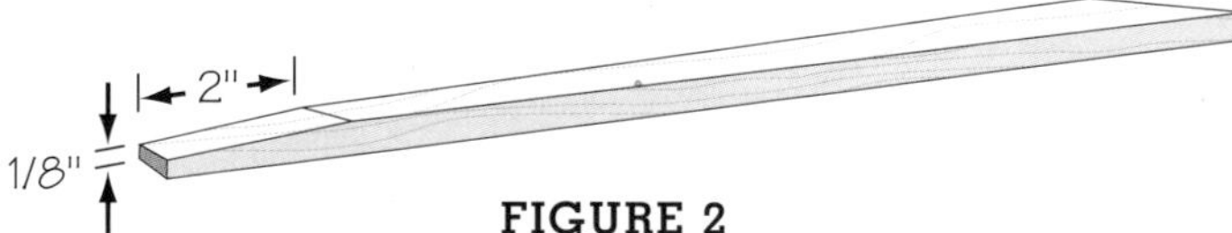

FIGURE 2

Narrow end of both side pieces thinned to 1/8" thick, through a gradual incline over the last 2 inches. The thinning is on what is to be the inside face of the side piece on the finished instrument.

3. By sanding or planing, reduce the thickness of the two side pieces toward the narrow end, as shown in Figure 2. This thinning will result in a slightly larger mouthpiece opening and cavity when the instrument is assembled.
4. Glue the four pieces together, positioned as shown in Figure 3, using a marine-grade wood glue. The thinned portions of the side pieces should be on the inside. The pieces must be leakproof and perfectly, permanently joined, so: follow the instructions for the adhesive carefully; make sure that the parts are lined up properly; clamp well; leave plenty of drying time. Hand-screws (the wooden clamps with two threaded operating screws) will serve well for clamping since they spread the pressure and can operate at nonsquare angles.
5. When the assembly has thoroughly dried, sand the exterior to remove excess glue and make the joints flush. Gently round the four long edges.
6. Make the oblique mouthpiece cut at 22° as shown in Figures 4A and 4B. Altering this angle affects the tone quality of the finished instrument—see the comments on this under "Variations" in the chalumeau plan, page 95.
7. Note the point on the opposite side of the instrument body from where the oblique mouthpiece cut begins. At a location 1/4" closer to the tip from that point, predrill with a 1/16" bit. With a small screwdriver, screw the #2 x 3/8" machine screw part way in, to where the head stands 3/16" above the surface of the plastic (Figure 4C). The elastic cord that holds the reed in place will be hooked to this screw.
8. With a rat-tail file, slightly hollow the last inch or so of the portion of the top piece just inside the mouthpiece cut, as shown in Figure 5. (See "Variations" below for some optional further improvements you can make in this area.) Then use sandpaper to round the very tip of the mouthpiece, so that it isn't quite as long and pointy. But don't overdo it: be sure to leave some flat surface at the end for the reed to slap shut against.

9. The part of the mouthpiece over which the reed lies (where you made the oblique cut in step 6 above) is called the *lay*. As discussed in the chalumeau plan preceding this one, the shaping

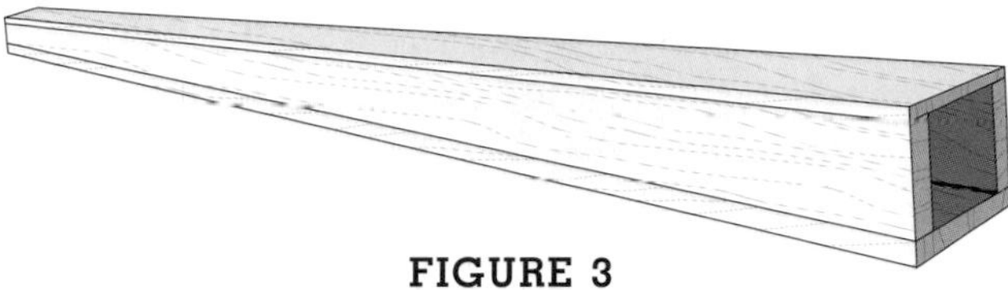

FIGURE 3
POSITIONING THE TOP, BOTTOM, AND SIDES FOR GLUING

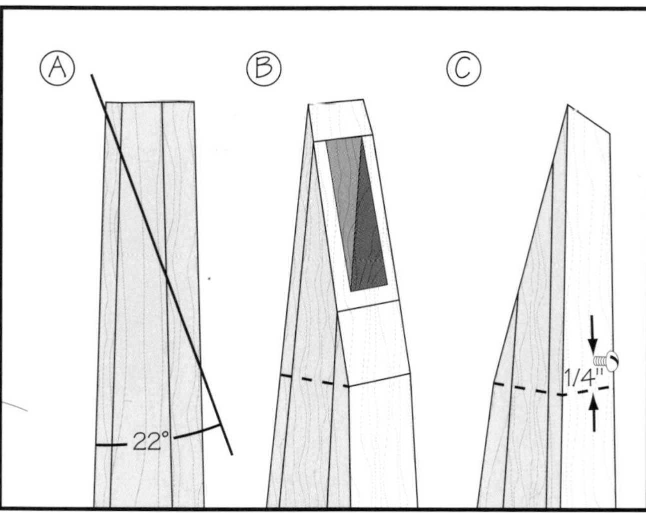

A
B
C
22°
1/4"

FIGURE 4
THE MOUTHPIECE. A, THE ANGLE CUT; B, THE APPEARANCE OF THE MOUTHPIECE END AFTER THE CUT IS MADE; C, THE SMALL SCREW THAT WILL ANCHOR THE ELASTIC CORD THAT HOLDS THE REED.

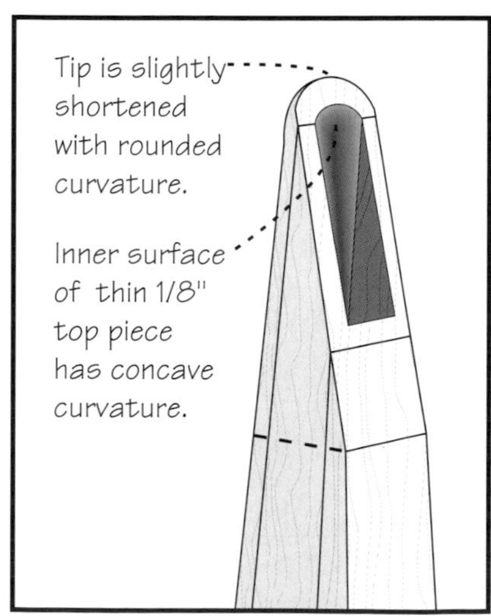

Tip is slightly shortened with rounded curvature.
Inner surface of thin 1/8" top piece has concave curvature.

FIGURE 5
THE SLIGHT CURVATURE, OR CONCAVITY, IN THE INNER SURFACE OF THE TOP PIECE AT THE MOUTHPIECE

Materials List

Lumber

3 1/4" x 2" x 15" hardwood (Notes-1) ***Body***
1 1/8" x 2" x 15" hardwood (Notes-2) ***Body***

Hardware & Supplies

1 soprano saxophone reed (Notes-3)
1 1/16" x 24" elastic cord
1 #2 x 3/8" machine screw
Marine-grade wood glue
Nontoxic wood finish (Notes-4)

Suggested Tools

Carpenter's saw, band saw or circular saw
Plane, electric hand plane, or electric surface planer
Rat-tail file and flat file
Electric sander or sandpaper
Drill with fractional drill bit set, spherical rotary burr bit, and 5/8" or larger countersink bit
Clamps: 3 or more wooden hand-screw type clamps will work best
Small screwdriver

Notes

1. The wood should be close-grained and of the sort where the grain will not rise too much when the wood gets wet. Boxwood is ideal; maple is good; many other woods will suffice.
2. This 1/8" piece can be planed down from the 1/4" stock.
3. Get several reeds; they don't last forever. If you are a beginner, use a soft reed, designated as 1-1/2, 2, or 2-1/2.
4. See the suggestions for nontoxic finishes in the materials list for the natural horn, page 86.

of the lay is crucial to the functioning of the reed. Step 4 in that plan, page 92, describes the process of shaping the lay. Though the mouthpiece looks a little different, the process is essentially the same for both instruments. The method for binding the reed in place is also essentially the same for both instruments, despite the differing mouthpiece shapes. Turn to those instructions and follow them now; then return for step 10 below.

10. When you have the lay set right and the saxophone is speaking well, you can drill the tone holes in the top piece. Figure 6 shows the hole locations. Drill the six holes initially with a 5/16" bit. (The intended ultimate size is 3/8"; we are drilling small initially to allow fine-tuning later.) Clean any splinters from the holes with a craft knife and/or a small rat-tail file or riffling file. Bevel the edges of the holes a little less than 1/16" with the countersink bit.

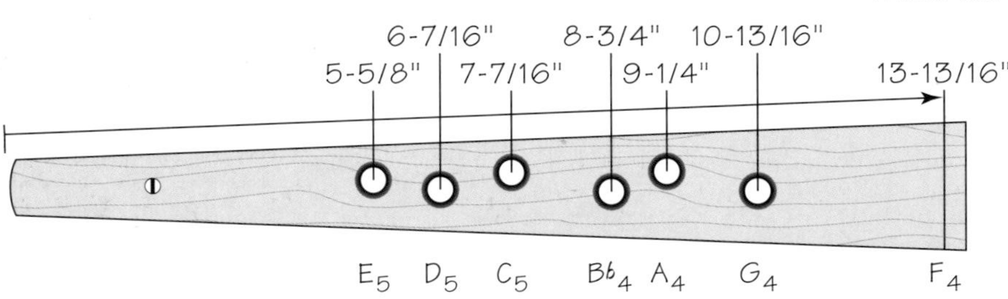

FIGURE 6

The top of the saxophone. Shows finger hole locations and intended lower register pitches at each hole. Distances represent distances from the tip of the narrow end of the instrument to the centers of the holes. All holes are initially drilled at 5/16" diameter. Hole centers should be at least 1/2" from the edge of the wooden piece. Their actual lateral positioning is a matter of finding comfortable positions for the playing fingers.

11. The register hole (a smaller finger hole that helps the saxophone to speak in its upper register) will take the form of a thumb hole located in the back piece. Drill the 1/8" register hole in the back piece at the location shown in Figure 7, and clean away any splinters around the hole edges. Carve out a concavity around the hole about 1/8" deep and 3/4" across, making a smoothly rounded hollow in which a thumb will fit comfortably. An easy way to make the hollow is to rough it out with a spherical rotary burr bit, then smooth it by sanding.

12. Now for the fine-tuning. Figure 6 gives the intended pitch at each hole, as well as the full tube length (all-holes-closed) pitch. Start by covering all the holes, including the register hole, and play that lowest pitch. Chances are the instrument is a little too long, and the sounding pitch is slightly below the intended F4. Shorten the tube by cutting or sanding a tiny bit at a time from the large end, checking the sounding pitch after each shortening, until the pitch arrives at F4.

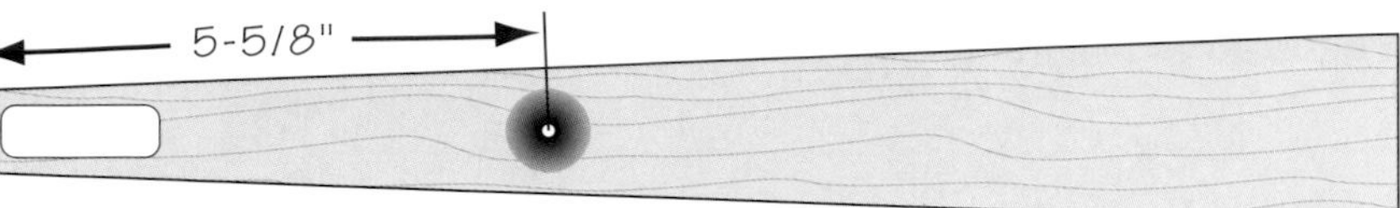

FIGURE 7

The bottom of the instrument. Shows location of the 1/8" register hole and the concavity around it.

When the all-holes-closed pitch is in line, turn to the tone holes, proceeding from the lowest to the highest. Once again their pitch should be low, since we deliberately drilled the holes a little small initially. Bring them up to their intended pitches, given in Figure 6, by enlarging incrementally. Rebevel the hole edges if necessary with the countersink bit as the final step (the beveling will raise the pitch slightly, just as further slightly enlarging the hole would). Once each hole is tuned, remove any splinters and take the sharp edge off the inner rim with the craft knife and/or file. If you are unsure of this hole-tuning process, review step 8 in the chalumeau plan, page 95, and step 6 in the side-blown flute plan, page 74.

Even more than with the chalumeau, the saxophone pitches in the upper parts of the range are highly flexible: by controlling lip pressure on the reed and other aspects of the embouchure, you can bend the pitch quite substantially up or down. Try to adjust the tone hole sizes so that the note is in tune when the embouchure feels consistent, comfortable, and natural. Be warned: given this flexibility and the resulting ambiguity, it is easy to unconsciously adjust your embouchure for the note you want to hear, tricking yourself into making mistakes. The hole-tuning process, as a result, can be exasperating. If you find that you have unintentionally made the pitch at a given hole too high by making the hole too large, you can reduce the hole size by partly recovering it using epoxy gel (the nonrunny version of epoxy glue).

13. When the tuning is set, clean up the large end (which probably was recut in the tuning process) with sandpaper. Round the inside edge of the opening as generously as the thickness of the wood allows.
14. Finish the wood with a nontoxic finish.

Playing Technique

The saxophone embouchure is similar to that described under "Playing Technique" for the chalumeau. But the fingerings are different. Cover the lower three holes with the fingers of the right hand and the upper three with the fingers of the left. Cover the register hole (the small hole on the back) with the left-hand thumb. Play an ascending diatonic scale by opening the holes in sequence. After all are open, continue into the next octave by opening the register hole, recovering the main tone holes, and beginning the sequence again (see "Variations" below for comments on intonation in the upper register). Many of the additional chromatic tones can be obtained through cross-fingerings (closing one or two additional holes below the first open hole). For an analogous situation, see the fingering chart in the side-blown flute plan, Figure 4, on page 76. The wooden saxophone's range extends to about an octave and a half, though an experienced reed player might be able to take it further after becoming familiar with the instrument.

Variations

The greatest weakness of this instrument is the intonation in the upper register. The pitches in the upper octave are likely to be seriously sharp. The reasons for this have to do with the fact that the mouthpiece cut foreshortens what would ideally be a "conical" bore shape (in quotes because, in our case, we have substituted a square cross-sectional shape for the true cone). Experienced players will be able to compensate, to some extent at least, by adjusting their embouchure. The best solution, however, is to

increase the air volume within the mouthpiece area of the tube, to make up for volume lost to the cut-off at the mouthpiece end. You can do this by inserting a 2" section of cylindrical bore between the mouthpiece and the start of the expanding section of the tube. This makes the job of fabricating the tube quite a bit more involved. A simpler action you can take is to use an electric hand drill with a tiny grinder bit to enlarge the inside of the existing mouthpiece area as much as possible, being careful in the process not to alter the lay or the surface on which the reed sits. This will improve the situation somewhat, though it falls well short of correcting the situation entirely.

More variations: You can design a wooden saxophone to play in different scales by altering the finger hole sizings and spacings. You can make a larger, lower-pitched saxophone, but to get a good saxophone tone you will find it necessary to make the holes large. To cover the large holes, it may be necessary to design keys with large key heads and pads, as on commercial saxophones.

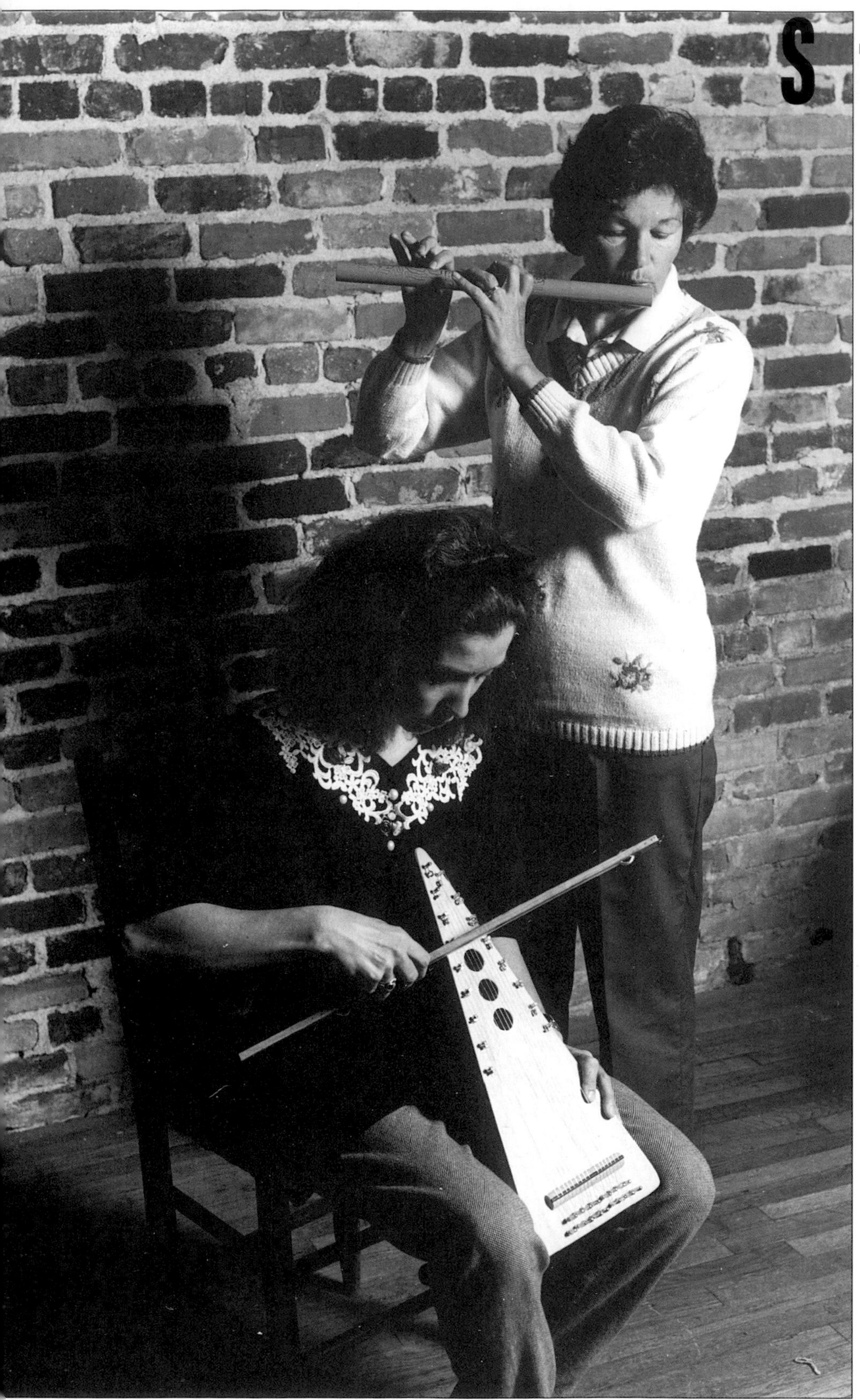

Strings

Here is an essential consideration in making stringed instruments: a vibrating string alone will scarcely move any air. As skinny as it is, it doesn't have any appreciable surface area to push the air. If the air doesn't move, no one will hear anything. In order to make more than a tiny sound, a string must be attached to something with greater surface area. That surface can pick up the vibration from the string and transmit it more effectively to the surrounding atmosphere. The heart of the art of string instrument-making lies in the creation of these sound-radiating bodies—the soundboards and sound boxes—to which strings are attached.

Most musical strings do not have much mass, and their vibrations do not carry much energy. For that reason, a string will not drive a soundboard very well if the soundboard is too heavy. To be responsive, the soundboard must be light, yet still reasonably rigid. Wooden soundboards for strings usually are made rather thin, using light and springy woods. To increase their rigidity, they may be formed into curving shapes, or they may have reinforcing struts along the back. Membrane soundboards (used in banjos and, more importantly, a host of Asian and African instruments) are even lighter and thinner. Stretching the membrane gives the soundboard the needed rigidity. With many string instruments, the soundboard covers a partially enclosed air chamber. This brings an element of air resonance to the tone, and is especially valuable in enriching the lower frequencies.

Everybody knows—it is part of our folklore—that to make the soundboard and chamber for a fine violin requires diligence, practice, and skill. But here is a little secret: it is not hard at all to make a sound box that will do a *reasonably* good job of projecting string sound. As long as the board is not way out of proportion for the strings, it will usually project the sound fairly well.

Planning what string lengths, diameters, and tensions will work best on a given instrument is a rather subtle business. Don't worry. For the instrument plans appearing here, those decisions are made for you. If you wish to pursue this topic further, refer to the sources in the Bibliography. Strings can be made from many different materials. In this book, we will stick with the widely available steel strings.

There are several basic string instrument forms that makers everywhere have most often adhered to, simply because they work well. Three are most common: Lutes (using the term in a generic sense) are string instruments with necks, like guitars and violins. Harps are those with many strings rising from a soundboard, in a plane perpendicular to the board. Zithers are those with many strings running parallel to a soundboard and having no neck. Among the following plans are instruments in each of these forms.

Bowed Psaltery

MODERATELY DIFFICULT

Not many stringed instruments played with a bow have more than four or five strings. That's because it's difficult to individually bow the strings when they are stretched alongside one another. But there is at least one configuration that will give you a zitherlike array of many strings, yet leave each string accessible to the bow. This design makes it possible to equip the instrument with one string for each note over its range. To sound different notes, the player simply moves the bow from string to string, without the need to finger the strings as on a violin. The bowed psaltery described here takes advantage of this configuration.

The key lies in the layout of the strings on the psaltery's narrow, triangular body. In this arrangement, each string extends an inch or so beyond the end of its neighbor. For just that one inch, each string is exposed and accessible to the bow from the side as shown in the photograph below. Special end pins anchor the strings in a way that does not inhibit bow movement from one string to the next.

The name *psaltery* normally refers to certain plucked zithers of the medieval and early Renaissance periods. The instrument described here is not one of those. The idea for the triangular configuration appears to be a 20th-century invention, developed in Germany in the 1930s (this according to the one written reference to the instrument that I have been able to find, an entry in Anthony Baines' *Oxford Companion to Musical Instruments*). About the same time, the Marx Company, an American maker of novelty instruments, produced several variant designs using the same principle. The term *bowed psaltery* was originally applied to the 1930s German instrument and it is now widely used for instruments having this bowing arrangement. Whose idea it was to call a 20th-century instrument by such an ancient-sounding name I do not know.

BECAUSE OF THE TRIANGULAR CONFIGURATION, EACH STRING OF THE BOWED PSALTERY IS ACCESSIBLE TO THE BOW OVER A SMALL PART OF ITS LENGTH NEAR THE END.

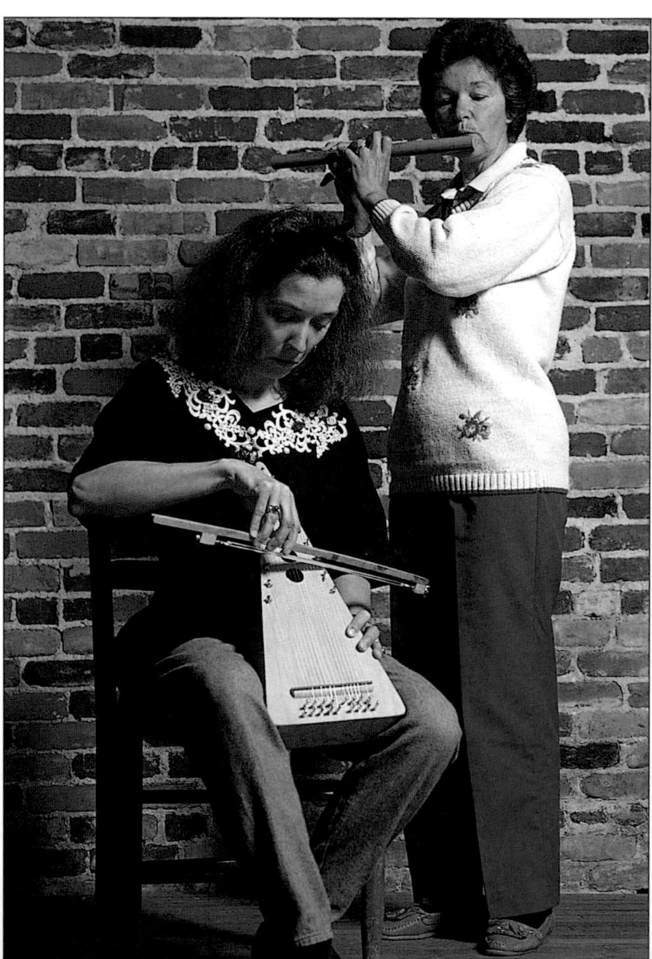

People are used to the sound of bowed strings somewhat damped by contact with a finger, as on a violin. In the bowed psaltery there is no damping contact. The resulting tone is distinctly different, with a finer edge to it. The string continues to ring even after the bow has left it, leaving a luminous wash as the player moves from note to note. It is a charming effect.

This instrument calls for a bow. You can use a violin bow, or you can turn to the plans for the simple string-instrument bow that follow this plan.

Instructions

1. Cut the sides and end block (Figure 1). The only difficult task in constructing this instrument is making the angle cuts on the end block and on one of the sides. After making the cuts, arrange the three parts in their triangle shape and check the fit of the angle cuts. File or sand as necessary to clean up the cuts and correct the angles for a snug fit.
2. Join the three pieces with wood glue. To secure the triangle, glue and tack the joints with four 1-1/2" finishing nails and a 3/4" wood screw (Figure 2). For a more elegant appearance, omit the nails, and clamp or otherwise fix all parts in place with great care for gluing.
3. When the assembly is dry, use a rasp file or electric sander to round the point of the triangle to a gentle curve of about 3/8" radius. Round the other two corners, and sand all the joints smooth. If the surfaces

Materials List

Lumber

- 2 1/8" x 10" x 20" plywood (Notes-1) ***Front and back***
- 2 3/4" x 2-1/2" x 20" any hardwood ***Sides***
- 1 1-1/4" x 2-1/2" x 9" any hardwood ***End block***
- 1 3/4" x 3/8" x 5" any hardwood ***Bridge***

Hardware & Supplies

- 1 3/16" diameter x 5" metal rod such as the shank of a large nail or narrow bolt ***Top of bridge***
- 34 zither pins (Notes-2)
- Music wire (Notes-3)
- 17 small nuts or washers, exact size not important
- Wood glue
- Wood finish of your choice
- 1-1/2" finishing nails; 1" wood screw

Suggested Tools

- Carpenter's saw or circular saw
- Hacksaw
- Drill with 3/16" and 1" bits
- Electric sander or sandpaper
- Rasp file and flat file
- Hammer
- Paintbrush or rag
- Tuning wrench (this can be purchased when you purchase the tuning pins)

Notes

1. One of the widely available birch or other hardwood veneer plies will do well.
2. Buy a few extras; available from piano supply houses or lutherie supply houses listed in the Tools & Materials appendix on page 139. The standard zither pin (.198" diameter x 1-5/8" made to fit a 3/16" hole) will do. When you order the pins, also get a tuning wrench to fit them.
3. You can purchase the wire in coils from a piano tuner's supply house, or purchase enough steel guitar strings to do the job. For guitar strings, use selected strings from extra-light, light, and medium tension guitar string sets. The chart below gives the required string sizes (according to the wire manufacturers' numbering system and in thousandths of an inch) and required lengths for each size. The given lengths represent an approximate minimum for the job; buy more in case of breakage.

Wire Size #	Diameter	Min length required
#1	.010"	24"
#3	.012"	40"
#5	.014"	45"
#6	.016"	52"
#7	.018"	60"
#8	.020"	24"

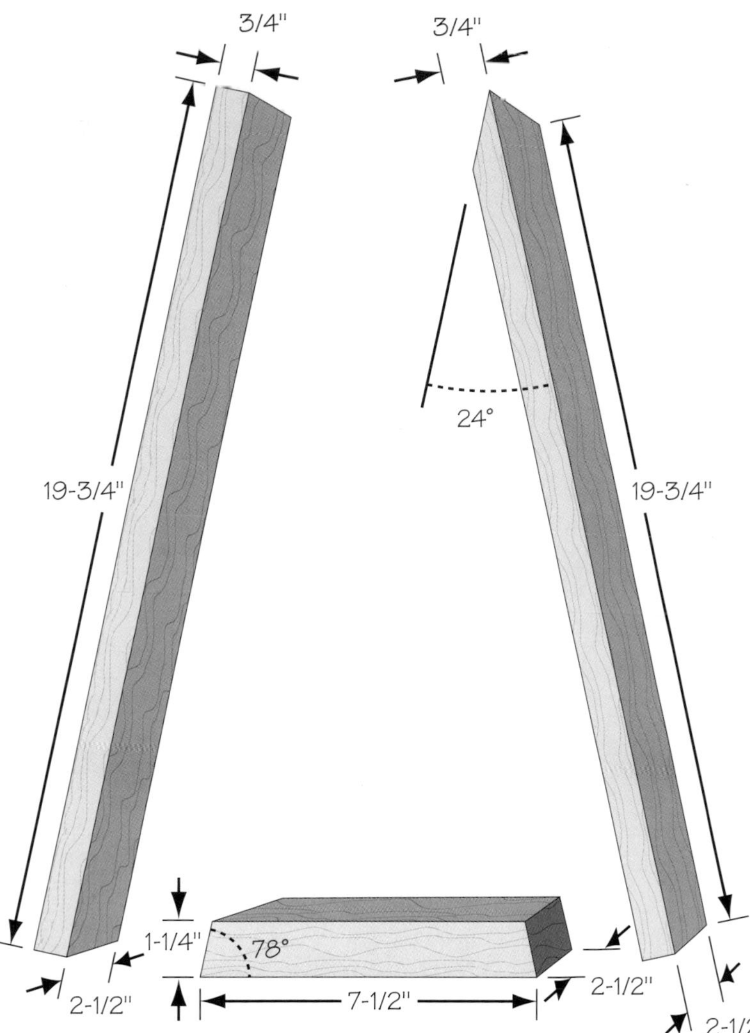

FIGURE 1
DIMENSIONS AND CUTTING ANGLES FOR THE SIDES AND BOTTOM

of the three pieces are not level with one another when the triangle is laid flat, plane or sand them level.

4. To make the top piece, place the triangular assembly on the 1/8" plywood and trace its outline. Turn the assembly over and do the same for the back piece. (Do this on the side of the plywood that won't show). Cut the two pieces, not precisely to the outline, but leaving a 1/8" margin all around.
5. Drill the three small sound holes in the piece that is to be the top using a 1" bit, located as shown at A in Figure 3, page 110. Remove any splinters, and clean and round the edges of the holes with sandpaper or a round file.
6. Glue the front and back in place (with a small overhang all around due to the deliberate oversized cutting). Weight or clamp the assembly well as it dries, being sure that there is positive contact for secure gluing all around.
7. While that dries, prepare the special end pins by modifying some of the regular tuning pins. Follow this procedure to make 17 of them. First, shorten the pin by cutting 3/16" off the top (Figure 4A, page 111). File the cut to make the top smooth and level, and then slightly round off the edges. With a hacksaw, cut a groove in the top. The pin comes from the manufacturer with a hole in it, and the groove should be in the same direction as the hole (Figure 4B). It should be deep at one end and shallow at the other, with a curve to it (Figure 4C).
8. When the glue is dry on the body of the instrument, sand off the overhang on the top and bottom pieces, making a smooth, flush, gently rounded edge. Apply wood finish of your choice now, if you wish to do so.
9. When the body is dry, mark the tuning pin and end pin locations on the top, as shown at B and C

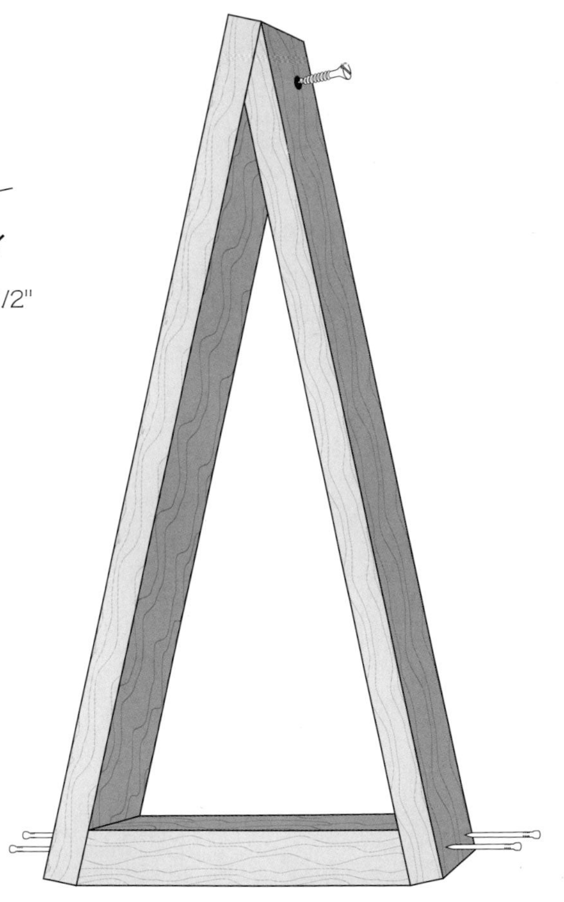

FIGURE 2
ASSEMBLY OF THE SIDES AND BOTTOM

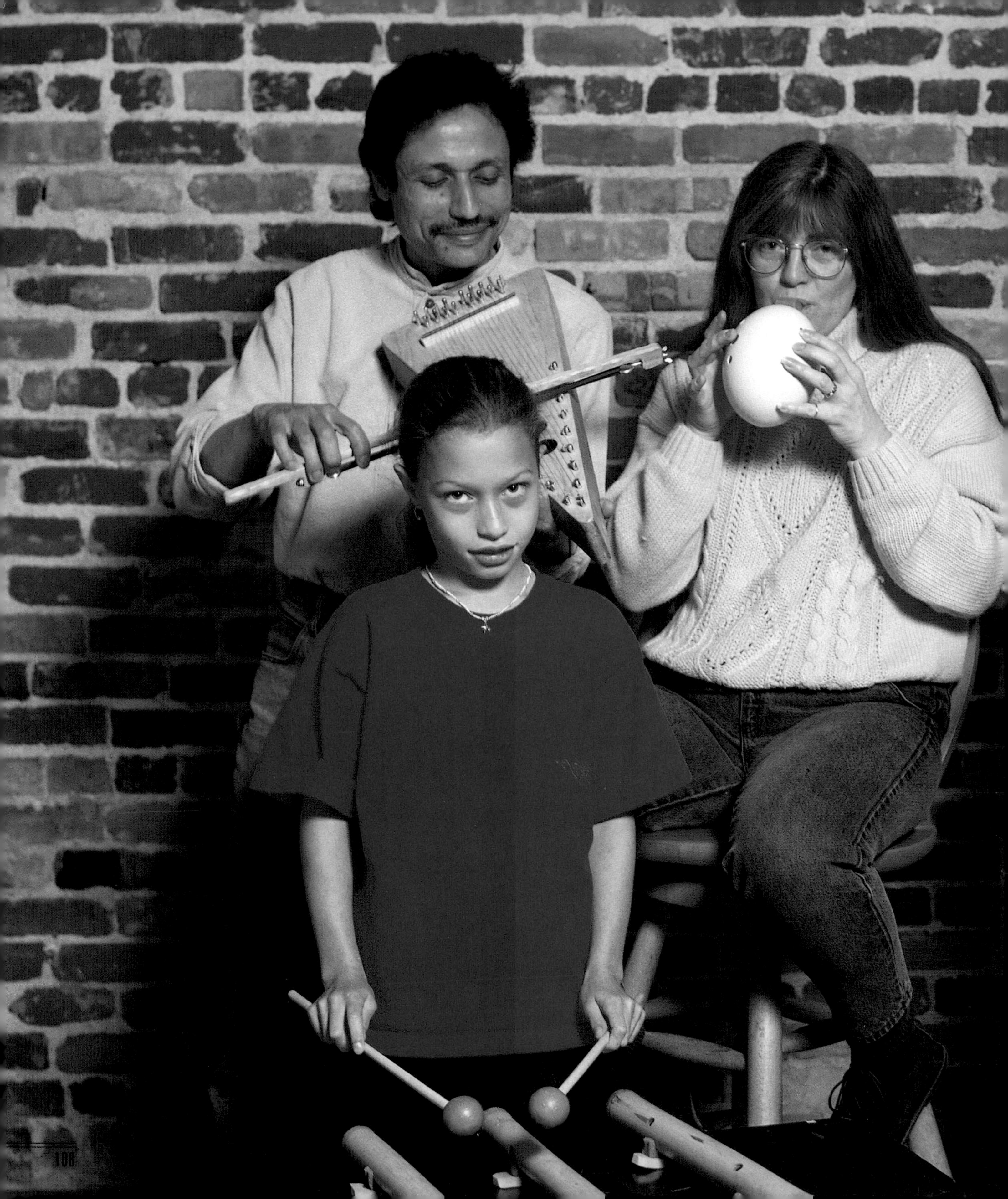

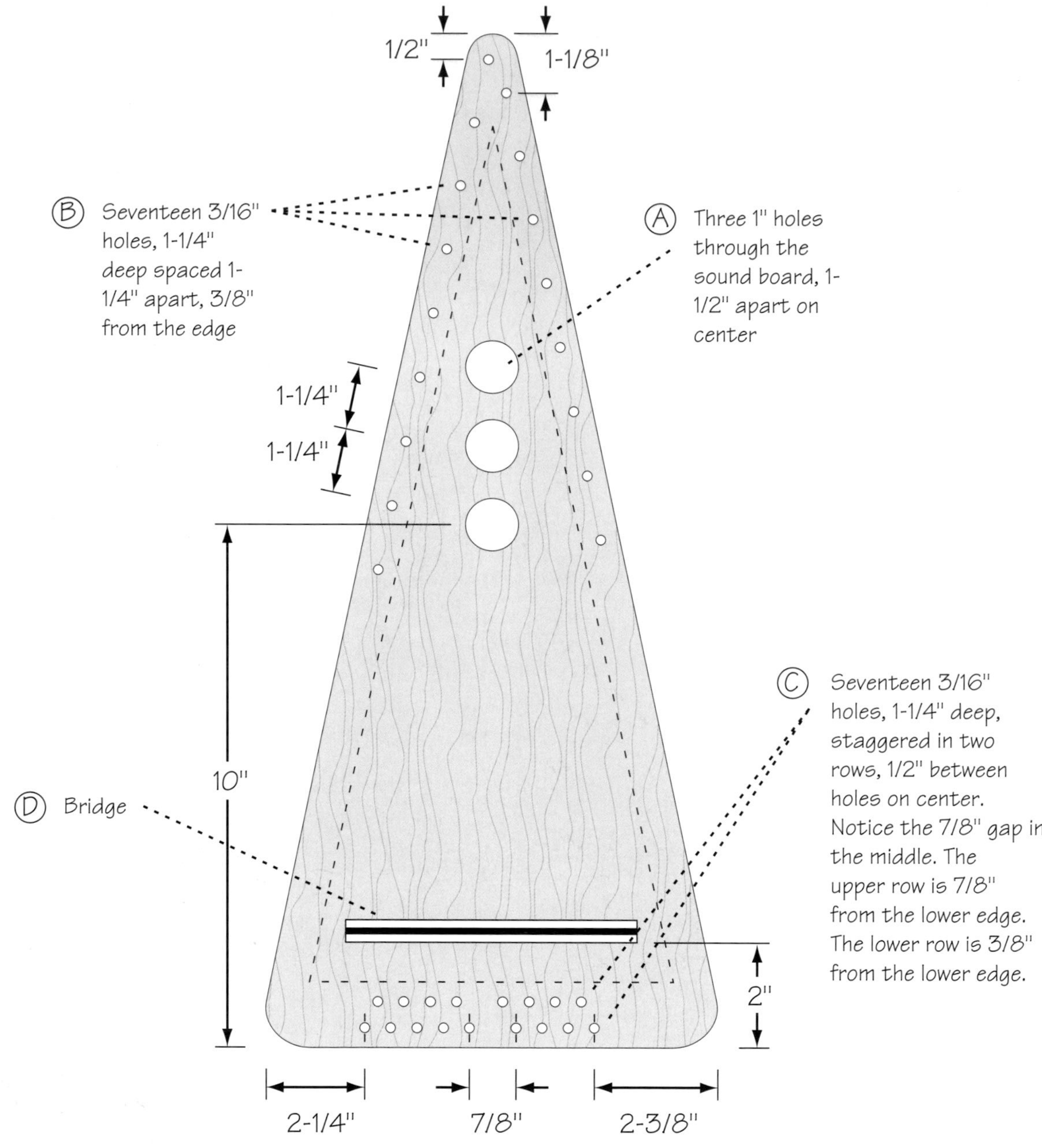
1/2"
1-1/8"
B Seventeen 3/16" holes, 1-1/4" deep spaced 1-1/4" apart, 3/8" from the edge
A Three 1" holes through the sound board, 1-1/2" apart on center
1-1/4"
1-1/4"
10"
D Bridge
C Seventeen 3/16" holes, 1-1/4" deep, staggered in two rows, 1/2" between holes on center. Notice the 7/8" gap in the middle. The upper row is 7/8" from the lower edge. The lower row is 3/8" from the lower edge.
2"
2-1/4"
7/8"
2-3/8"

FIGURE 3

The soundboard. Shows locations for three small sound holes (A), 17 end holes (B), 17 tuning pin holes (C), and bridge (D).

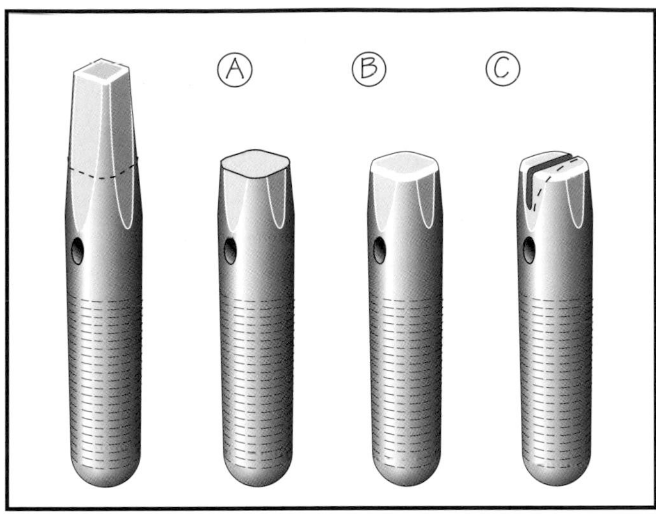

FIGURE 4

Modified end pins. A, top 3/16" is cut off from standard tuning pins; B, the newly cut edges are rounded with a file; C, a groove is cut with a hacksaw deep at one end and shallow at the other.

FIGURE 5

Pitches, sizes and lengths for strings. The string numbered 1L is the farthest to the left; 1R the farthest right; 2L the second from the left, and so forth. The given vibrating lengths may not match those of your instrument precisely but should be within 1/4". If they are not, adjust the bridge position.

String #	Pitch	Wire #	Diameter	Length
L1	F_6	1	.010"	6-1/4"
R1	E_6	1	.010"	6-7/8"
L2	D_6	3	.012"	7-1/2"
R2	C_6	3	.012"	8-1/8"
L3	B_5	3	.012"	8-11/16"
R3	A_5	5	.014"	9-5/16"
L4	G_5	5	.014"	9-15/16"
R4	F_5	5	.014"	10-1/2"
L5	E_5	5	.014"	11-1/8"
R5	D_5	6	.016"	11- 3/4"
L6	C_5	6	.016"	12-5/16"
R6	B_4	6	.016"	12-15/16"
L7	A_4	6	.016"	13-9/16"
R7	G_4	7	.018"	14-1/8"
L8	F_4	7	.018"	14-3/4"
R8	E_4	7	.018"	15-3/8"
L9	D_4	8	.020"	16"

in Figure 3. Drill the 34 tuning pin and end pin holes with a 3/16" bit, to a depth of 1-1/4".

10. Place regular (unmodified) tuning pins in the 17 holes in the end block. Tap them in lightly with a hammer, then screw them farther in with the tuning wrench, leaving about 1/8" of thread showing. Drive the 17 end pins (modified tuning pins) into the holes in the sides, with the grooves in the top pointing toward the tuning pins below. There's no need to screw these in; you can use a hammer to tap them all the way. Be sure to drive them all to the same level, with their tops even; discrepancies in height make playing problems later.
11. Cut the wood for the bridge to 3/8" x 3/4" x 5". Cut the metal rod to 5" to serve as the top piece on the bridge. With a file or a handsaw, make a shallow groove across the top of the bridge to keep the metal rod in position. Put these pieces aside.
12. Now start attaching the strings. The chart in Figure 5 shows the required wire sizes for each string from longest to shortest and their intended pitches. The wires will run from the end pins to the tuning pins, attached at each and as shown in Figure 6A. Notice that an anchor must be attached to prevent the strings from slipping

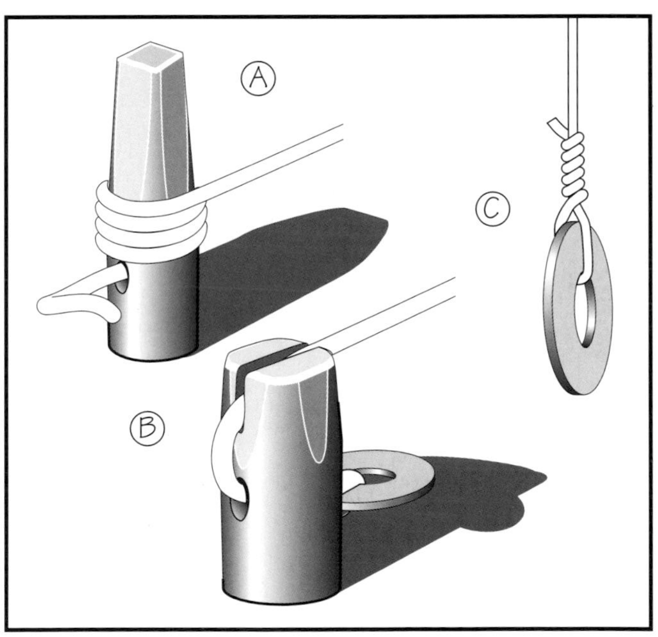

FIGURE 6

Attaching the strings. A, the tuning pin at the bottom of the instrument; B, the special end pin; C, the anchor that prevents the string from pulling through the hole in the pin.

through the end pins (Figure 6B). The easiest way to make the anchor is by running the wire through a small nut or washer and twist-tying it, as shown in Figure 6C.

Put the first string on and tighten it moderately, using the tuning wrench. Slip the bridge with its top piece under the string to its correct location as shown at D in Figure 3. The string will hold the bridge in place. Now tighten the string to its approximate intended pitch, as indicated in Figure 5. Proceed through the remaining 16 strings.

13. With that, the instrument is finished—but for the final tuning. Go ahead and tune all the strings once again, but don't worry about getting it perfect. The tunings will continue to slip as the instrument settles in. Retune periodically over a period of hours. Soon enough you will find it holding its tuning reasonably well, and you will have a lovely, playable instrument.

Playing Technique

Before playing, be sure to rosin the bow well. There are several possible playing positions for the bowed psaltery. One is to use one hand to hold the instrument near the narrow end, with the broad end pressed against your chest near the shoulder. With the other hand, draw the bow across the intended string in the space near the end where it reaches beyond its neighbor. Move the bow from string to string to play melodies.

Variations

You could easily extend the range of the instrument described here by adding strings, up to 25 and more. By altering the stringing, you could create a fully chromatic instrument. Within limits, you can retune this instrument just as it is for different scales.

Bow

MODERATELY EASY

Here are plans for making a small bow using thread or fine monofilament nylon line in place of the traditional horse tail hair. It will work well with the bowed psaltry described in the preceding pages, as well as with many other string instruments and (you might be surprised) lots of nonstring instruments.

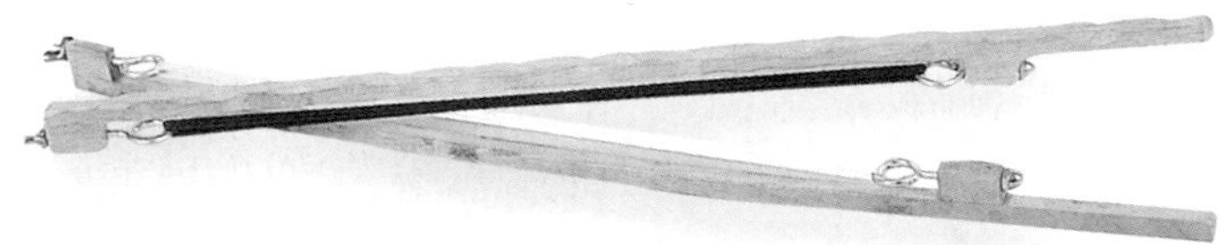

THE WHITE-HAIRED BOW SHOWN HERE WAS MADE IN KEEPING WITH THE PLAN. THE BLACK-HAIRED BOW WAS CUT FROM A SINGLE PIECE OF WOOD, AND HAS ITS SURFACE RE-SHAPED TO CREATE A MORE RUSTIC FORM.

Materials List

Lumber

1 3/8" x 3/8" x 22" hardwood (Notes-1)

1 3/8" x 5/8" x 2" hardwood

Hardware & Supplies

Fine cotton-covered polyester thread, monofilament nylon thread, or similar strong thread (Notes-2)

1 2-1/2" #10 eyebolt

1 2" #10 eyebolt

1 #10 wing nut

1 #10 cap nut

Wood finish of your choice

Bow rosin (Notes-3)

Suggested Tools

Carpenter's saw

Drill and 7/32" bit

Sandpaper

Epoxy glue

2 small C-clamps

Paintbrush or rag

Notes

1. The ideal wood is springy but not prone to splitting. Maple is good.
2. Available where sewing supplies are sold.
3. Available at music stores.

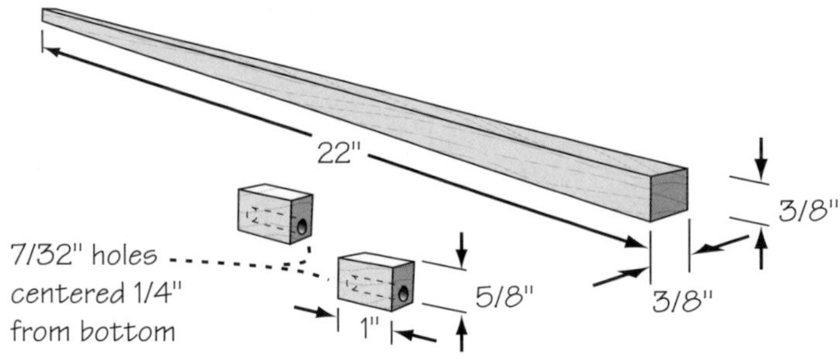

FIGURE 1
THE THREE WOODEN PIECES

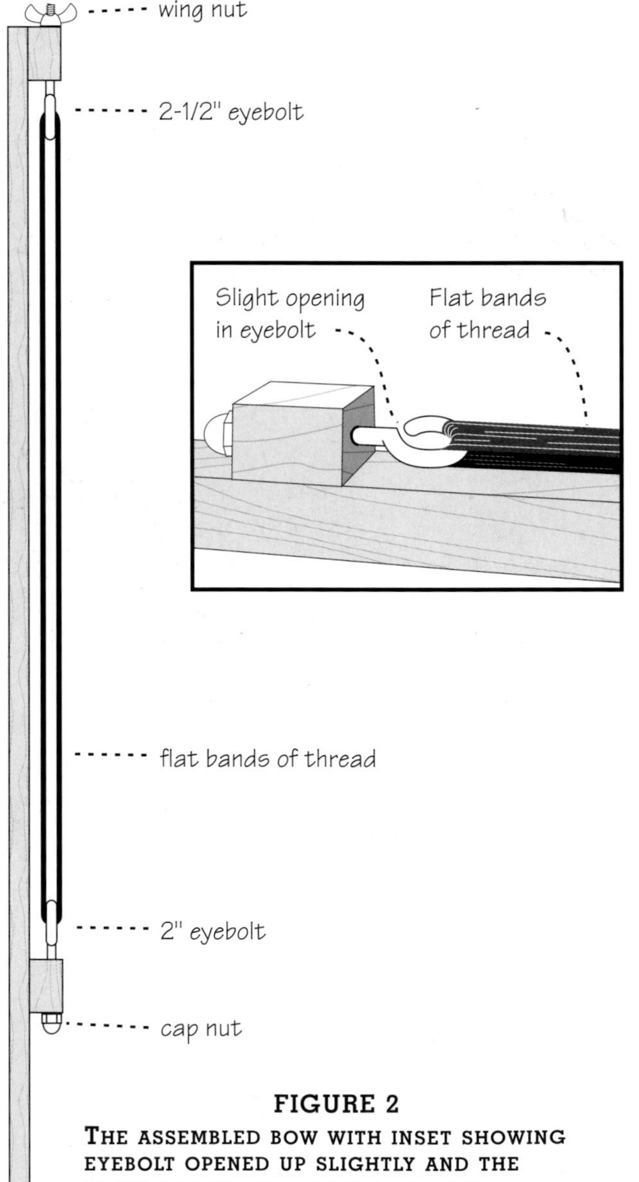

FIGURE 2
THE ASSEMBLED BOW WITH INSET SHOWING EYEBOLT OPENED UP SLIGHTLY AND THE THREAD LOOPED THROUGH THE BOLT

INSTRUCTIONS

1. Cut the 3/8" x 3/8" hardwood stick to 22", and the 3/8" x 5/8" piece into two sections each 1" long. Drill a 7/32" hole through each of the short pieces as shown in Figure 1.
2. Glue the short pieces to the stick (Figure 2). Use high-strength epoxy and clamp well.
3. When the glue is dry, clean up and level the glued joints with sandpaper. Sand the remainder of the bow as needed, slightly rounding over all edges to prevent splintering and give a comfortable feel. Apply a wood finish of your choice.
4. Bend the eyes of the eyebolts very slightly open as shown in Figure 2 inset. Put the 2" eyebolt through the hole at the handle end and tighten on the cap nut (Figure 2). Put the 2-1/2" eyebolt through the far end, and thread the wing nut down about 3/8".
5. Tie the end of the thread to one of the eyes, and begin looping the line back and forth, through the eyes. Continue looping until you have two parallel flat strips about 5/16" or 3/8" wide. Pull each loop just tight enough so that it does not hang slack. (Excessive tension will cause the bow to bend as more loops are added, making previously wound loops go slack.) When you have enough loops, tie the end of the line to one of the bolts.
6. Rotate the eyebolts if necessary, so that one of the strips of thread faces outward, ready for playing. Tighten or loosen the wing nut as needed to adjust the bow hair tension. Rub the thread generously with rosin, and the bow is ready to use.

VARIATIONS

You might choose to make this bow of a single piece of wood cut to shape, rather than several pieces glued together. You can also make a longer or shorter bow of similar design.

The greatest weaknesses of this bow are that it is a bit heavy and the balance less than ideal. You can improve the situation by finding or fabricating screw eyes that are lighter, yet still have a wide enough eye to accommodate a 3/8" band of thread.

Cookery Harp

DIFFICULT

Harps, by their nature, are difficult to design and build. After spending a few days trying to think of an approach to harp making that would be in keeping with the title of this book, I was awakened from my sleep one night by the idea for this little harp. I have had midnight brainstorms before that did not fare so well by daylight, but the cookery harp design, it turns out, works well. Rather than pulling the components apart, the stresses of the strings in this harp work to keep things together, making for a stable and strong instrument requiring no fancy joinery. The sound is as sweet as you could wish.

The cookery harp is built around a sound chamber in the form of an oval roasting pan. The soundboard is not glued or tacked on, but is held firmly in place on the rim of the pan by the pressure of the strings (Figure 1). This little harp has just 12 strings. As with most folk harps, the strings are to be tuned diatonically—that is, to a scale of seven tones per octave, such as the familiar major scale or the natural minor scale—over a range of an octave and a fifth, pitched quite high.

Instructions

1. If your roasting pan has protruding handles at the ends, you will need to remove them, either by taking out the screws that hold the handles, or by cutting them off with a hacksaw and filing smooth where you made the cut.
2. Your pan will probably have a protruding rim or lip. At the point where the neck joins the pan, a portion of the rim will need to be cut away, so that the neck can fit snug against the side of the pan (Figure 1 identifies the neck and the other parts of the harp). To eliminate the

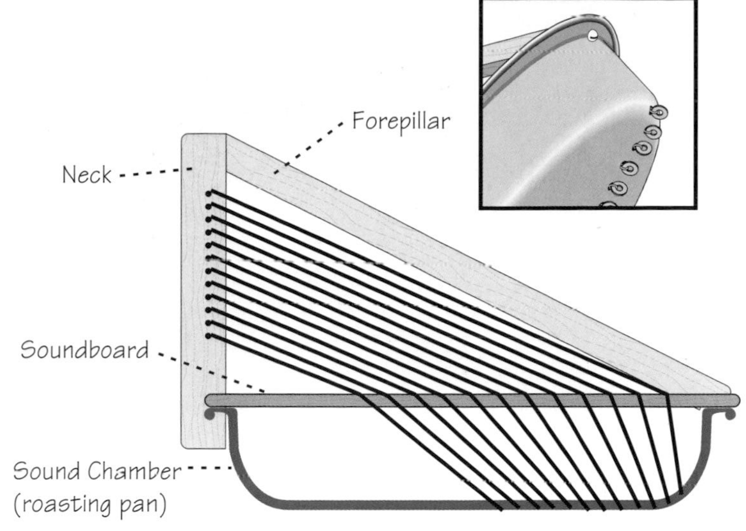

FIGURE 1

Components of the cookery harp design. The stress of the strings forces the soundboard down against the rim of the pot and pushes it snugly in place against the neck. The inward tug of the strings also pulls the neck, forepillar, and roasting pot firmly together. The inset shows how each string has a washer tied at the end which pulls up against the pan's bottom when the string is tightened.

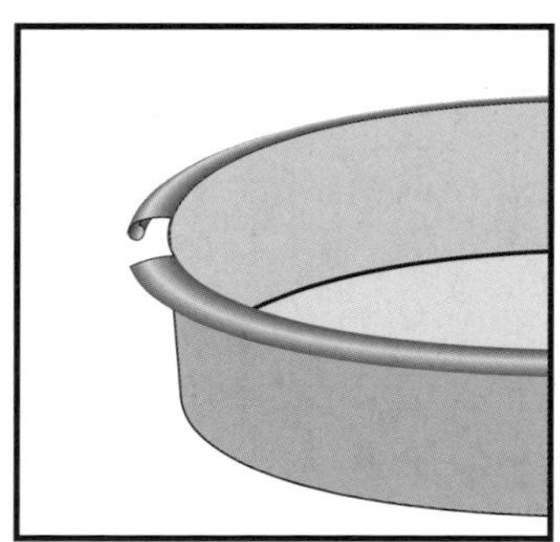

FIGURE 2

The rim of the pot with a section removed to accommodate the neck. The removed section should match the width of the neck at 1" wide.

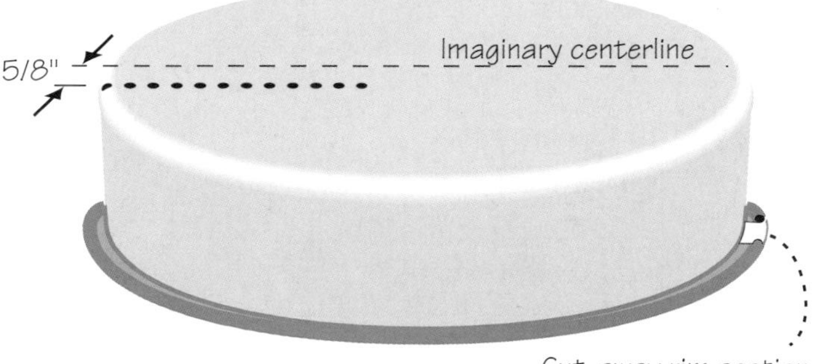

FIGURE 3

The 12 string holes in the bottom of the pan, 5/8" apart, shown relative to an imaginary line drawn down the middle of the pan bottom.

Materials List

LUMBER

1 1/8" x 12" x 18" plywood (Notes-1) ***Soundboard***

1 1" x 1-1/4" x 30" any hardwood ***Neck and forepillar***

1 1/4" x 3/4" x 11-1/2" any hardwood ***String band***

HARDWARE & SUPPLIES

1 10" x 15" roasting pan or lid (Notes-2) ***Sound box***

12 zither pins (Notes-3)

24 3/16" metal grommets

2 #10 x 2" machine screws with nuts and washers

2 #8 x 2" wood screws

1 #8 x 1" wood screw

12 small nuts or washers to anchor the strings; exact size not important

#2 music wire, .011" diameter (Notes-4)

Wood glue

Wood finish of your choice

SUGGESTED TOOLS

Carpenter's saw or circular saw

Band saw, jigsaw, or coping saw

Drill with fractional drill bit set and circle cutter attachment for a 1-1/2" hole

Tin snips and/or hacksaw

Hammer

Rubber or rawhide mallet

Flat file

Sandpaper

Tuning wrench (Notes-5)

Paintbrush or rag

NOTES

1. The given dimensions are approximate. You will need enough wood to cover the top of the pan, including the rim. Any of the widely available hardwood veneer plywoods will work well.
2. This measurement includes the rim of the pan. A longer pan is o.k., but anything less than about 13" long will be too small unless you use fewer strings. These pans are frequently available for little cost at secondhand stores. The pan lid that I used is made of a fairly thin enamel-coated sheet metal. It works well, but I suspect that a slightly heavier gauge metal might have been preferable.
3. You can use the standard size, which is .198" diameter x 1-5/8", made to fit a 3/16" hole. Get a tuning wrench to fit the pins as well. Available from piano tuner supply houses.
4. You only need about 10', but there's no harm in picking up a longer coil. Available from piano tuner supply houses.
5. Purchase this when you purchase the zither pins.

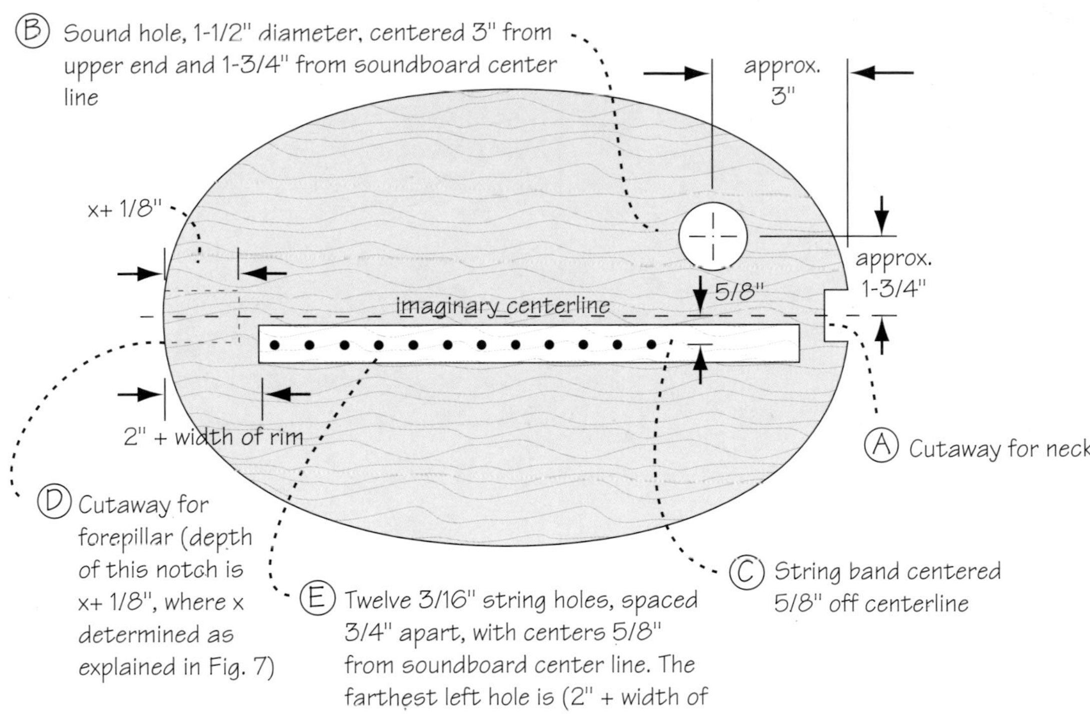

FIGURE 4

THE SOUNDBOARD. A, SIZE AND LOCATION OF CUTAWAY FOR THE NECK; B, SOUND HOLE; C, STRING BAND; D, CUTAWAY, MADE LATER IN STEP 15 TO ACCOMMODATE THE FOREPILLAR; E, STRING HOLE LOCATIONS, DRILLED LATER IN STEP 18. DEPENDING ON THE SHAPE OF YOUR PAN, YOUR SOUNDBOARD MAY NOT HAVE THE OVAL SHAPE SHOWN HERE. YOU CAN STILL LOCATE THE VARIOUS FEATURES OF THE SOUNDBOARD RELATIVE TO THE IMAGINARY CENTER LINE AND THE ENDS OF THE BOARD, IN KEEPING WITH THE DRAWING.

unwanted bit of rim, use tin snips or a hacksaw to cut away a 1" wide section (Figure 2). You may find that you can make cuts just at the sides of the unwanted bit of rim, then break it off by repeated flexing.

3. Drill a row of 12 holes 1/8" in diameter in the bottom of the pan, in the locations shown in Figure 3. The strings will pass through these holes and be anchored there.
4. Trace the shape of the rim of the pan on the 1/8" plywood piece that is to be the soundboard, on the side that will not be exposed (the ugly side). Using a coping saw, jigsaw or band saw, cut the plywood to shape, including the 1" wide inlet where you removed some of the rim, marked A in Figure 4.
5. Make the 1-1/2" sound hole as shown (B in Figure 4) with a circle cutter.
6. Sand all the newly cut edges so they are smooth, and round them to prevent splintering.
7. Cut the hardwood piece for the string band to 11-1/2". Glue it with wood glue onto the front side of the soundboard, in the slightly off-center location shown at C in Figure 4. Clamp or weight it while the glue dries.

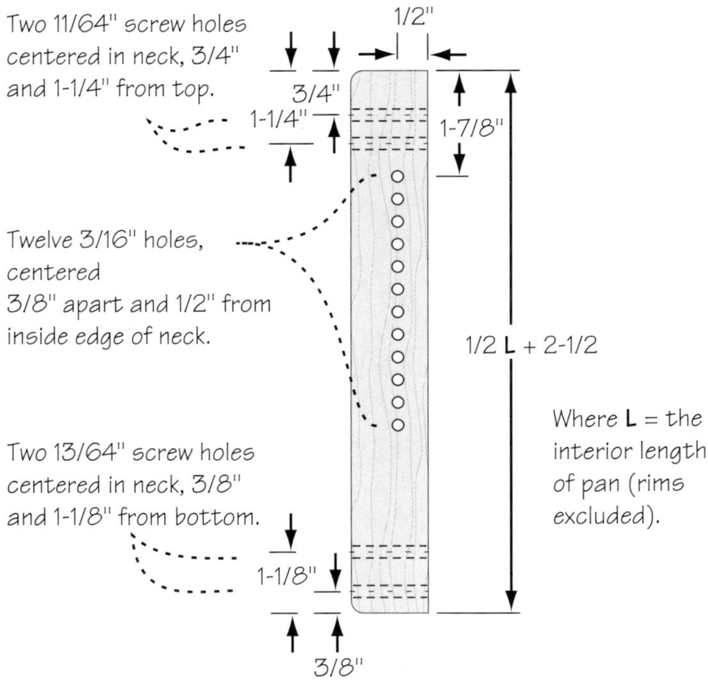

FIGURE 5

THE NECK, SHOWING THE LOCATIONS OF THE FOUR SCREW HOLES AND THE 12 TUNING PIN HOLES. THE OVERALL LENGTH OF THE NECK DEPENDS ON THE SIZE OF YOUR PAN: MEASURE THE INTERNAL LENGTH OF THE PAN (RIMS EXCLUDED), AND CALL THAT LENGTH L. CALCULATE THE NECK LENGTH AT 1/2 L + 2-1/2".

8. The length of the neck depends on the length of the roasting pan you are using. Figure 5 gives a simple formula you can use to come up with the appropriate length for your pan. The figure also allows you to determine locations for the tuning pin holes and several screw holes in the neck. Cut the neck piece to the length you determine from Figure 5.
9. Drill the 12 holes for the tuning pins going all the way through the neck, at 3/16" diameter (for standard zither pins). Drill the two screw holes at the top of the neck with an 11/64" bit and the two at the bottom with a 13/64" bit.
10. To attach the neck to the pan, drill two 13/64" holes in the pan at approximately 3/8" and 1-1/8" below the cutaway rim, as shown in Figure 6A. To ensure that they are located correctly, hold the neck as securely as possible in position against the pan, put nails through the two lower screw holes in the neck, and tap the nails with a hammer to make a mark on the pan. Be sure to hold the neck straight and at the proper height against the pan when you do this. After marking, drill the two holes. Drill a third hole with the 11/64" bit, centered at the

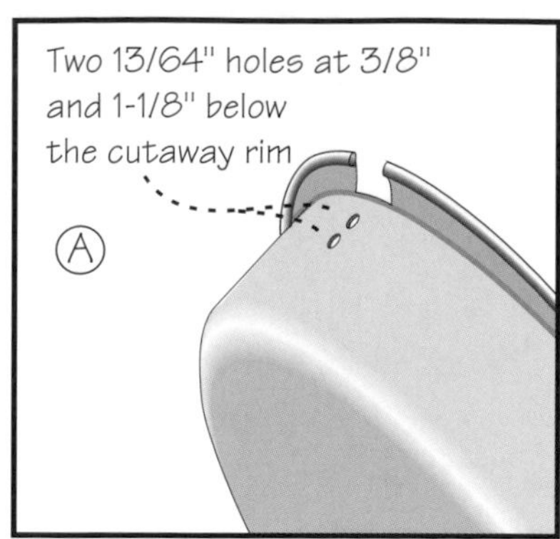

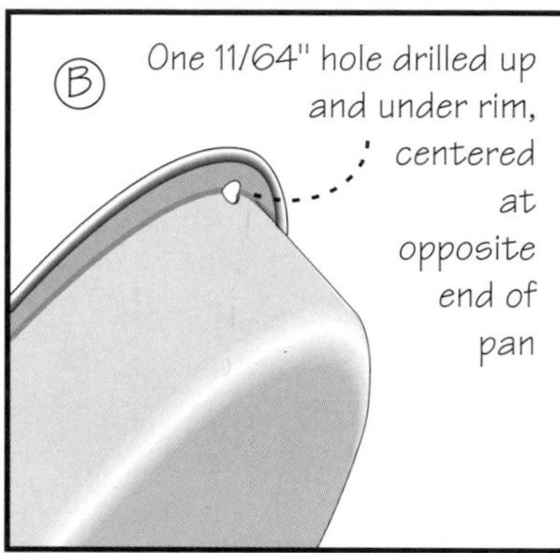

FIGURE 6

Screw holes in the pan. A, shows the ideal screw hole locations for the neck attachment, but you will do well to use the screw holes already made in the neck to mark the exact location, as explained in the text; B, the screw hole for attaching the lower end of the forepillar.

FIGURE 7

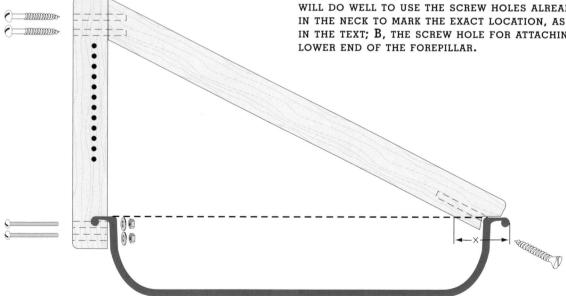

Assembly for the neck, forepillar, and pan. The distance marked X, plus 1/8", will correspond to the depth of the notch cut in the lower end of the soundboard shown at D in Figure 4.

opposite end of the pan where the forepillar will attach, as shown Figure 6B. Drill from the outside, up and under the pan's rim.

11. Figure 7 shows how the neck, forepillar and pan will go together. Attach the neck to the pan as shown, using the two #10 machine screws, with the nuts and washers against the inside of the pan.
12. Figure 8 on page 120 shows the dimensions for the forepillar, once again using a simple calculation based on your pan length to arrive at the overall length. Cut the hardwood for the forepillar to that length. Cut one end to a 62° angle, and in the other make the notch as shown. But rather than taking the dimensions in the figure too literally, I suggest that you first hold the wood for the forepillar roughly in place between the neck and the far end of the pan, and check to see that the suggested dimensions will give you the fit you want. The top end, after the angle cut is made, should rest flush against the side of the neck just at the top, with the notch fitting snugly on the rim at the far side of the pan. If you see a need to slightly modify the suggested dimensions or angles to achieve this fit, do so; then make your cuts.
13. As shown in Figure 7, the forepillar will be held in place by wood screws passing through the screw holes you have drilled in the top of the neck and the far end of the pan. You will need to mark the location for these screws and predrill with an undersized bit. To mark the locations, hold the forepillar in position between the neck and the far end of the pan. Place the 2" wood screws through the two screw holes at the top of the neck. Being sure that the pillar is positioned just right, tap the screws with a hammer so that they indent the correct locations on the end of the pillar. At the opposite end, place the 1" wood screw through the hole in the pan, and tap it to mark the screw location in the opposite end of the forepillar. Remove the pillar, and predrill the screw holes to a depth of about 1-1/2" at the appropriate angles with a 1/8" bit.
14. Replace the pillar and attach it with the two #8 x 2" wood screws at the top of the neck and the #8 x 1" wood screw at the far end. If you are not satisfied with the fit, remove the pillar, make adjustments and reassemble. Then, measure and make a note of the distance marked as X in Figure 7. That's the distance from the lower end of the pan rim to the point where the inner side of the pillar crosses the plane of the pan rim.
15. The soundboard already has a notch at the upper end to accommodate the neck. It will need a deeper notch at the lower end to accommodate the pillar, as shown at D in Figure 4. When the glue that you set earlier on the soundboard is dry, make the notch: it should be 1" wide and 1/8" longer than the measurement described in the previous paragraph, marked X in Figure 7.
16. Leave the neck and pillar attached to one another, but remove them from the pan. Sand them as needed to smooth over the joints, and apply whatever wood finish you wish. You can apply finish to the soundboard now as well.
17. When the finish is dry on the neck and pillar, put the 12 tuning pins in the neck. Which side? If you hold the neck and forepillar so that they look like the number "7," the pins are inserted from the opposite side. Lay the neck and forepillar down on a solid surface, tap each pin in a bit with a hammer, then screw it farther in with the tuning wrench, to where the end of the threads is about 1/8" from the surface of the wood.
18. The locations for the string holes in the soundboard depend upon the length of your pan. Figure 4 will allow you to determine these locations with a simple calculation (see E in Figure 4). Mark the hole locations on the string band, and drill the holes, using a 3/16" bit to accommodate the 3/16" grommets. (The grommets will serve to line the holes and prevent the strings from digging into the wood.) Using a rubber or rawhide mallet, tap two grommets in place in each hole, one top and one bottom.
19. Now you can place the soundboard on the rim of the pan, fit the neck and forepillar over it, and fix the neck and forepillar to the pan once again with the machine screws and wood screw. (At this point the soundboard is still loose, so you can lift it a bit to place the washers and nuts on the inside of the pan.) Check to see that the soundboard notches fit nicely where they meet the neck and forepillar. If they are too narrow or too short, remove the board and make adjustments. If they're a little too large, that's o.k.; the harp won't look as nice but it will play just as well.
20. As shown in Figure 1, each string will run from its tuning pin on the neck, down through the appropriate string hole in the soundboard, and out through its hole in the bottom of the pan. To anchor it there at the bottom, each string will have

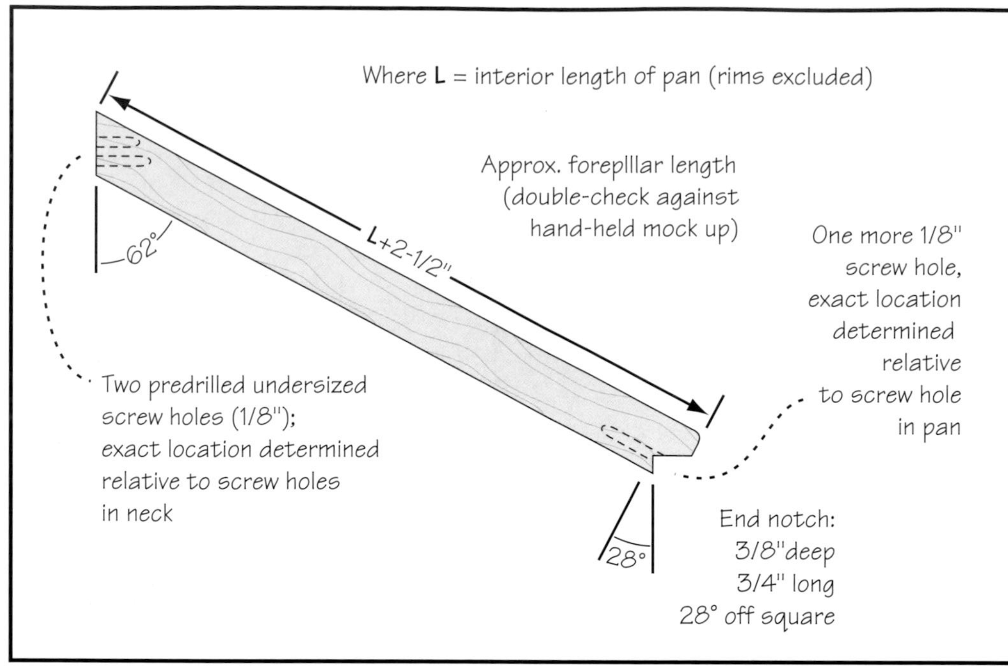

FIGURE 8

THE FOREPILLAR. USE THE INTERIOR LENGTH OF YOUR PAN, CALLED L, TO CALCULATE OVERALL LENGTH AT L + 2-1/2". BEFORE YOU CUT, DOUBLE-CHECK THE RESULTING LENGTH BY HOLDING THE PIECES IN PLACE AS SUGGESTED IN STEP 12.

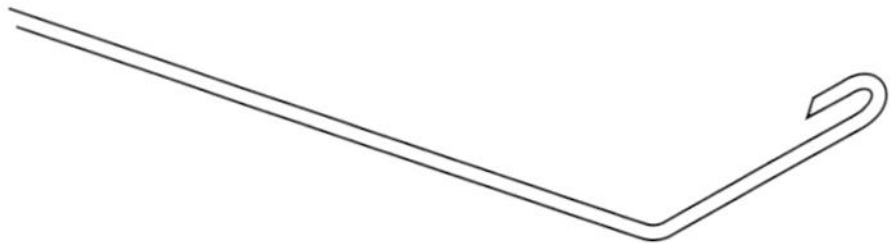

FIGURE 9

HOOK FOR DRAWING THE STRINGS THROUGH HOLES IN THE SOUNDBOARD AND PAN. USE A HEAVIER GAUGE MUSIC WIRE TO MAKE A HOOK THAT IS THIN ENOUGH YET RIGID ENOUGH.

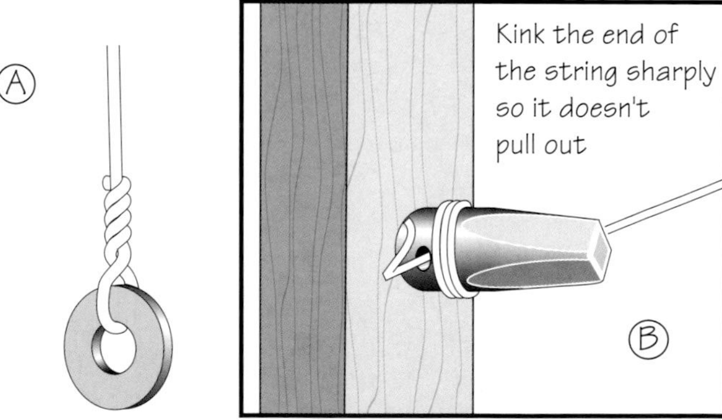

FIGURE 10

ATTACHING THE STRING. A, TO THE ANCHOR AT ONE END; B, TO THE TUNING PIN AT THE OTHER.

a nut or washer tied at the end, which will pull up against the bottom of the pan when the string is tightened. I got a surprise when I ran the requirements for this harp through my string-scaling software: the program suggested using the same size music wire—#2, at .011" diameter—for all the strings. Improbable, it seemed to me, but how very convenient! The software seems to have known what it was doing, because the little harp sounds and feels just right strung that way. (The program is called Stringmaster; see Appendix 1 on page 140 for availability.)

Begin the stringing with the longest string, running from the farthest hole in the bottom of the pan, through the farthest string hole in the soundboard, and up to the farthest pin on the neck. Cut a length of the #2 music wire about six inches longer than the vibrating string length. Sticking that wire through the hole in the bottom of the pan and getting it to poke up through the proper hole in the soundboard can be a most exasperating task, but here are two hints. First, since the soundboard isn't fixed in place, you can lift it a bit to see where the wire is going (as you add more strings it will become more and more fixed in place, but you can still flex one edge up a bit to see in). Second, you can make yourself a little hook out of some thin but moderately rigid wire, as shown in Figure 9 (a heavier gauge music wire works well). Put the hook through the hole in the bottom, guide it up through the proper hole in the soundboard; hook the music wire through it, and pull the wire out through the bottom. Then attach the small nut or washer to serve as an anchor at the end below the pan (Figure 10A). Bring the wire up to the appropriate tuning pin and attach it there (Figure 10B). To tighten the string, turn the pin with the tuning wrench. Do this in such a way that the string ends up leaving the pin about 1/8" or a little less away from the surface of the wood; don't let it

wind its way too far up the pin. Proceed this way through all 12 strings.

21. Tune the strings as follows: Measure the length of your longest string. If it is longer than 13-1/2", tune it to C5, and tune the remaining 11 strings to a diatonic scale above it, which puts the shortest and highest-pitched string at G6. If the longest string is shorter than 13-1/2", tune it to D5, and tune the others to a diatonic scale ascending to A6.

    As you add more strings, the soundboard will pull down more and more firmly against the pan. It will bow inward under the pressure, and that's o.k. By the time you have put on several strings, the tunings for the previous strings will have slipped drastically. Don't worry; finish the job, and then go back and retune. You will need to retune several times over the next several hours or days as the new harp settles in.

Playing Technique

Standard playing position for the harp has the sound box leaning on or toward the sitting player's chest, placing the highest strings closest to the player. The hands are placed on each side of the row of strings, and the player uses all 10 fingers to pluck. As an alternative with the cookery harp, you can turn the instrument around so that the longer strings are toward you. This makes the shortest strings a little easier to get at.

Variations

If you get your hands on a much larger roasting pan, you can make a cookery harp with more strings and a larger and lower range. For a gentler sound, string a cookery harp with bronze or brass (commonly used for wire-strung harps) or even nylon, rather than steel.

The cookery harp, strung and tuned as described here, sustains a little over 200 pounds of pressure from the strings. That's quite modest as harps go; still, if your roasting pan is made of thin metal, it may be enough to cause it to collapse in the region where the strings are anchored. (The cookery harp shown in the photos here collapsed a bit, then stabilized, with no ill effects.) If you suspect that your pan may be too weak to take 200 pounds, consider reinforcing it with a strip of wood about 1/2" x 3/4". Place the strip on the outside of the pan, with string holes drilled through it so that the string anchors hold the strip against the pan. Alternatively, get a stronger pan.

Cooler Guitar

DIFFICULT

It takes know-how and special tools to make a guitar. Most difficult is the making of the guitar's soundboard and box—locating high-quality woods, planing the soundboard to the right thickness, making the struts, bending the sides, joining the pieces, and so on. How can we talk about making a guitar without exceeding the reach of this book?

We can do it by taking advantage of one of the great secrets of instrument making on the cheap: polystyrene foam, such as Styrofoam™. By virtue of being extremely light yet fairly rigid, polystyrene foam turns out to be an amazingly effective sound-radiating material. For the guitar described here we will use a polystyrene foam picnic cooler, in place of the wooden sound box. Basically, we will make a stick with strings on it, and attach a couple of two-dollar picnic coolers to the ends of the stick. The result will be funny looking, but you will be surprised at how well it works. The cooler guitar sounds as loud and as sweet as—well, at least as loud and sweet as an inexpensive commercially made guitar. But you can build it yourself and at minimal cost.

To be sure, the cooler guitar's tone quality differs from that of other guitars: it is brighter and less woody sounding. Having two separate sound radiators (the coolers) creates an unusual and very pretty stereo phase-shifting effect. But, without an enclosed sound box for air resonance, the tone in the bass lacks the fullness of a well-made wooden guitar.

The form of the finished instrument is a bit unwieldy. The plan includes a body support piece to help keep the guitar steady against the player's body. The coolers can be removed for storage or transportation, and replaced quickly and easily when time comes to play.

Commercially made acoustic guitars come in several styles. The most important distinction is between folk guitars made to take steel strings and classical guitars made to take nylon strings. The polystyrene foam sound box sounds best with steel strings, so the cooler guitar plans are designed to match typical dimensions for a steel-string guitar.

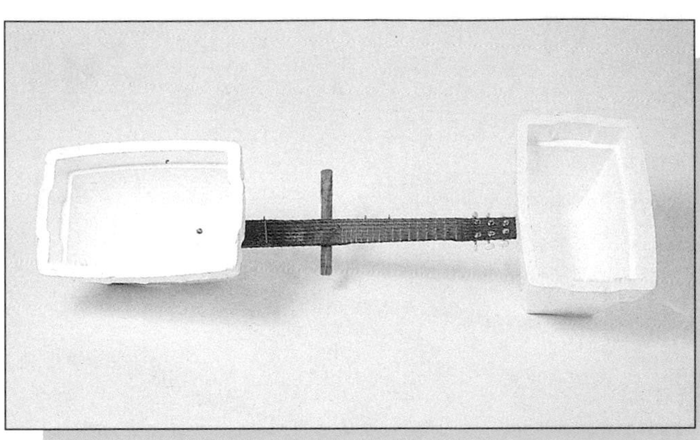

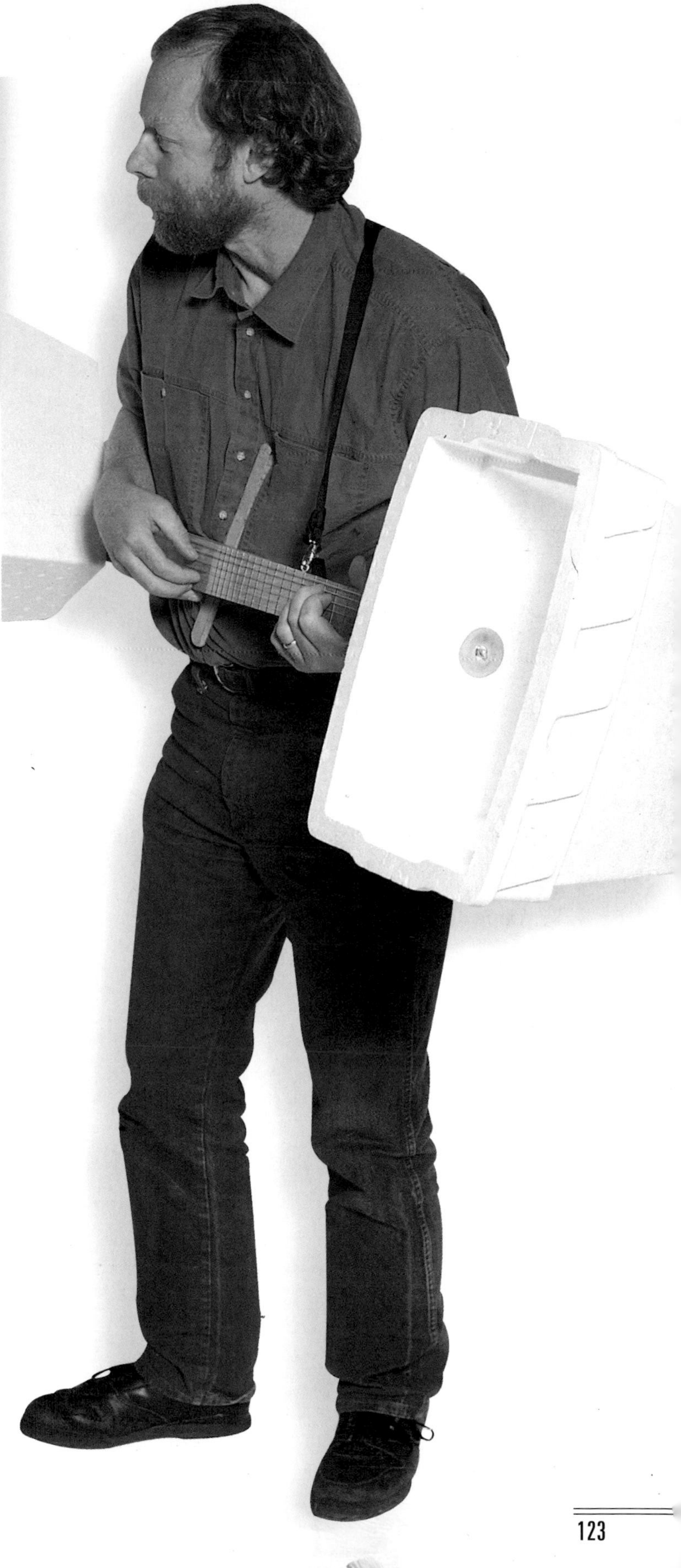

Following the cooler guitar plan in this book is a plan for an alto cooler guitar. The alto is identical to the regular cooler guitar except that it is smaller and plays in a higher range. Construction procedures for the two are the same except for some dimensions appearing in the drawings, and the same instructions will serve for making both instruments. In the cooler guitar instructions you will see parenthetical references to alternative dimensions and drawings for the alto. If you are building the regular cooler guitar, you can ignore these references.

Please be forewarned: For the cooler guitar and its littler sibling to play well, the neck must be very accurately shaped. For that reason, these two instruments are the most difficult appearing in this book.

INSTRUCTIONS

1. Cut and shape the hardwood board for the neck to the shape and dimensions shown in Figure 1 [for the alto guitar: Figure 1-alt]. Notice that the sides of the neck are broadly rounded, like a guitar neck, over a portion of its length. For this shaping, you can use any of several tools. The simplest (though not the fastest) is a coarse rasp file followed by progressively finer files and/or sandpapers. If you have a guitar around, keep it in sight so it can serve as a model for neck shape. Bear in mind that our instrument will have no separate fingerboard laid over the neck; the neck alone will correspond to both the neck and fingerboard of the standard guitar. As for the "region of curvature" indicated in Figure 1: ignore it for the moment; leave the neck flat at its original thickness over all but the cutaway at the very end.

Materials List

Lumber

1 1" x 2-3/4" x 41" hardwood board (Notes-1) ***Neck***

(For the alto guitar: 15/16" x 2-1/2" x 32")

1 1/2" x 1" x 10" any hardwood ***Body support piece***

Hardware & Supplies

2 polystyrene foam (Styrofoam™) picnic coolers (Notes-2) ***Sound box***

1 set of 6 steel string-type tuning machines (Notes-3)

4' standard fret wire for steel-string guitars (Notes-4)

1 set of steel guitar strings (Notes-5)

1 3" long nail or section of straight wire (Notes-6) ***Bridge***

6 1/8" eye diameter x 1/2" screw eyes

3 fender washers; outer diameter 2" or more, inner diameter 1/2" or less

2 #10 eyebolts 1-1/2" long

1 #10 x 1" machine screw and 2 large washers

Neck strap-attaching hardware (Notes-7)

Wood finish of your choice

Suggested Tools

Ripsaw and crosscut saw, or power saw (band saw or circular saw)

Electric drill and bits in these sizes: 3/64", 1/16", 3/16", 11/64", 5/16" (Notes-8)

Fret-slot saw (Notes-9)

Center punch and hammer

Hand plane and/or other tools for truing a surface (jointer, surface planer, electric hand plane, belt sander)

Coarse rasp file and finer flat file

Wire cutters

Rubber or rawhide mallet

Metal straightedge 30" or longer

Small screwdriver

Sandpaper in various grits

Paintbrush or rag

Notes

1. Use a strong, hard, heavy, stable wood; I recommend hard maple. The piece you use should be well seasoned or kiln-dried, good and straight, uniform in grain, and free of knots.
2. These are available at supermarkets and variety stores, especially during the summer months, in a variety of sizes. A good size for the guitar that seems to be widely available is about 17" long by 11" wide by 12" deep. Try to get coolers of the sort now available that have been manufactured without generating environmentally destructive fluorocarbons.

   Alternatively, you might try to intercept old coolers or similarly shaped pieces of polystyrene foam packaging material on their way to the landfill.
3. Buy tuning machines that are individually mounted, not the kind having two sets of three on brackets. You can purchase tuning machines from the lutherie supply outlets listed in Appendix 1 on page 139.
4. The frets that cross the guitar's neck are cut from a specially shaped wire called fret wire. Standard dimensions for guitar fret wire are top, 2mm wide x 1.1mm high; tang, .5mm wide. Available from lutherie supply houses.
5. Unless you are a masochist, use light-tension strings. Available at music stores. [For alto: a very light string set will be required: try the electric guitar string set sold as "regular light." Electric guitar strings are generally of lighter gauge than acoustic, but otherwise are not different from acoustic steel strings.]
6. It will be best to have several diameters to choose from, in the range of 3/32" - 3/16".
7. What you use depends upon the design of the neck strap you use or make.
8. The 3/64" bit may require a special purchase, as it is not included in most fractional drill bit sets.
9. You will need a saw that makes a cut just over 1/64" wide to hold the frets. Guitar makers use special backsaws with very narrow blades. You can use a coping saw with the smallest available blade. Place the blade on an anvil or other metal surface and tap the teeth all along on both sides with a hammer to narrow the kerf. Cut a small sample of fret wire and tap it into a cut made in scrap wood by the blade with narrowed kerf. If it holds, fine; if not, narrow the blade further by sanding or filing. Have a couple of blades on hand (they're not expensive) in case you don't get the width right the first time.

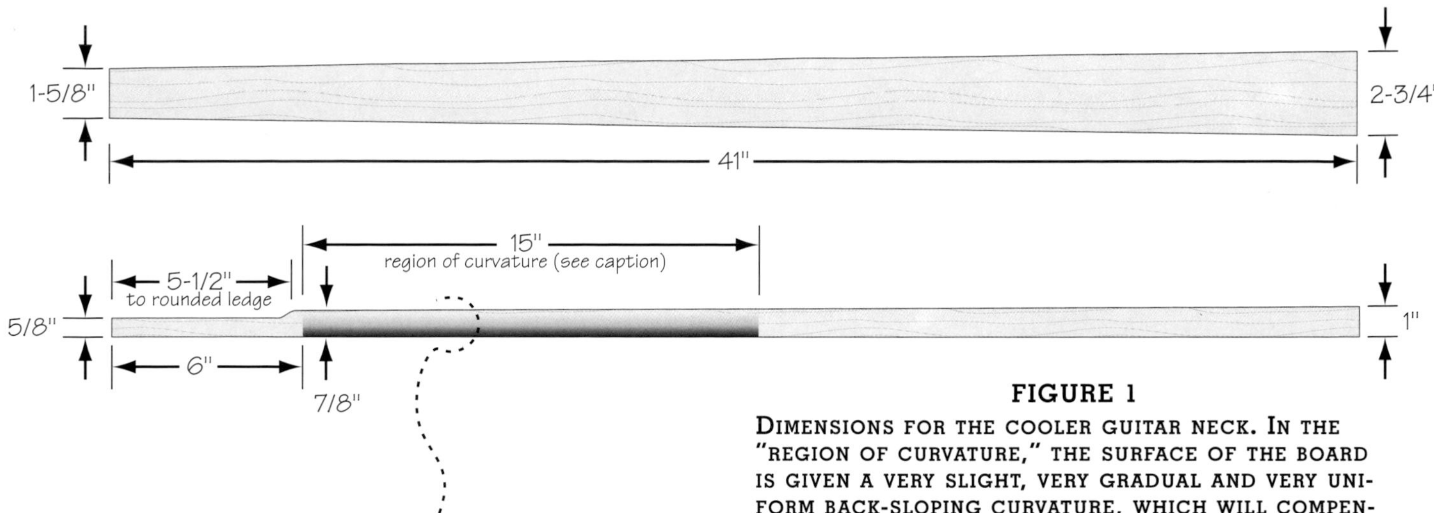

FIGURE 1

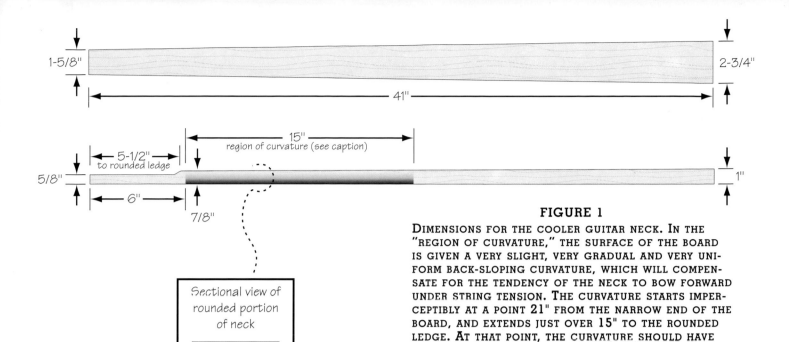

DIMENSIONS FOR THE COOLER GUITAR NECK. IN THE "REGION OF CURVATURE," THE SURFACE OF THE BOARD IS GIVEN A VERY SLIGHT, VERY GRADUAL AND VERY UNIFORM BACK-SLOPING CURVATURE, WHICH WILL COMPENSATE FOR THE TENDENCY OF THE NECK TO BOW FORWARD UNDER STRING TENSION. THE CURVATURE STARTS IMPERCEPTIBLY AT A POINT 21" FROM THE NARROW END OF THE BOARD, AND EXTENDS JUST OVER 15" TO THE ROUNDED LEDGE. AT THAT POINT, THE CURVATURE SHOULD HAVE HAD THE EFFECT OF THINNING THE 1" BOARD TO 7/8". DON'T ADD THIS CURVATURE IN THE INITIAL SHAPING (STEP 1); DO IT AS PART OF THE FINAL FINGERBOARD SHAPING IN STEP 2.

2. After cutting and shaping, let the wood sit for a few days, in case it wants to shift slightly as a result of changes in moisture content brought on by the shaping. Then check the playing surface of the neck for straightness over its full length with a dependably straight metal yardstick or meter stick. Sand or plane as necessary to make it perfectly flat. Then add the slight back-sloping curvature indicated in Figure 1 and described in the caption [For alto: Figure 1-alt]. (Unlike classical guitars, many steel-string guitar fingerboards have a slight lateral curvature as well—a crown, or convexity. If this feature is important to you and you feel up to the exacting task of shaping it, you can do so at this point.)
3. On most guitars, the piece over which the strings pass on their way to the tuning machines, which defines one end of the string's vibrating length, is called the *nut*. As shown in Figure 2, on this guitar a "zeroth" fret will replace the nut. *(Zeroth*

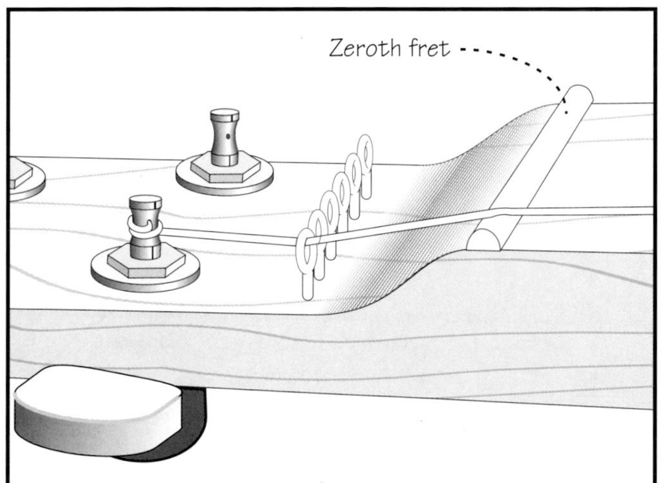

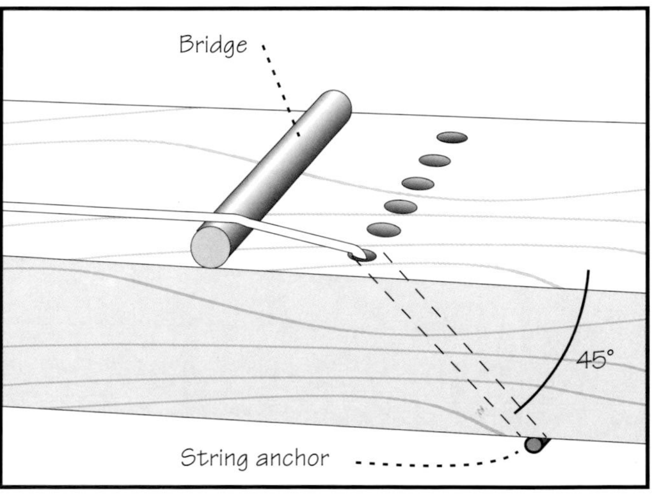

FIGURE 2

THE PATH THAT THE STRINGS WILL FOLLOW, FROM ANCHORING POINT AT RIGHT TO TUNING POSTS AT LEFT

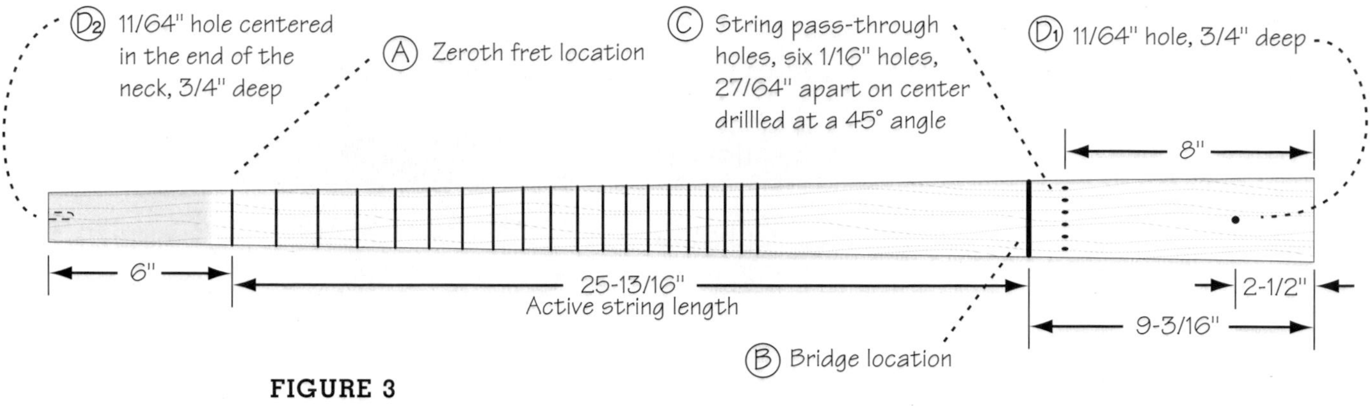

FIGURE 3
THE OVERALL LAYOUT OF THE NECK

refers to the fact that this fret comes before the fret that is normally called the first fret.) To make sure that the strings are pulled down firmly against the zeroth fret, they will pass through screw eyes located just beyond the zeroth fret. At the opposite end, the strings will pass over a bridge in the form of a short segment of metal rod crossing the board. Just beyond that, the strings will pass through holes in the board, anchoring on the opposite side. Figure 3 [for alto: Figure 3-alt] shows the locations for all these features. With a pencil, mark the location on the neck for the zeroth fret (marked by A in the figure) and the bridge (B in the figure).

4. Again referring to Figure 3 [for alto: Figure 3-alt] mark the locations for the six pass-through holes (marked by C in the figure). These holes are to be at a 45° angle, as shown in Figure 2. Accurate lateral spacing of these holes is important. To ensure correct placement, indent the spots with a center punch prior to drilling. Then drill the six holes with a 1/16" bit. The precision of the 45° angle is less important; if the holes don't come out perfectly aligned on the back side, that's o.k.
5. Figure 3 [for alto: Figure 3-alt] also shows the screw hole locations, marked D1 and D2 in the figure, for mounting the polystyrene foam cooler to the board. Drill these two holes with an 11/64" bit to a depth of 3/4".
6. The end of the guitar's neck where the tuning machines are mounted is called the *head*. The head of the cooler guitar is the thinner section at the end of the neck. Figure 4A shows more detail for the head, including the locations for the screw eyes. Here too, accurate lateral spacing is important. Punch and then predrill the holes for the screw eyes with the 3/64" bit, but don't insert the screw eyes yet.
7. To mount the six tuning machines, you will need to drill holes through the head for the tuning machine posts. Figure 4A indicates approximate locations for these holes, but the actual sizes and locations will depend on the particular machines you are using. For hole size: make them just big enough to accommodate the posts and bushings if any, typically 5/16". For hole location: the concern here is that each string should be able to follow its course from its screw eye to its tuning post as shown in Figure 4B, with minimal bending and without having to wend its way around other posts. To achieve this, the two uppermost holes should be located so as to put the tuning machines nearly abutting each other, as close to the center of the head as the casings of the machines will allow. The two lower holes should put the machines as far apart (as close to the edges of the head) as possible. The two middle holes should be somewhere in between. In the longitudinal direction, the posts are 1-1/4" apart on center. Before drilling, double-check your hole positions to be sure that the tuning machine hardware will indeed fit in that position, and that each string's course from screw eye to tuning post is unobstructed or nearly so, and requires no sharp bends. Then drill.
8. Figure 3 [for alto: Figure 3-alt] gives you a visual sense of how the frets will be located. The chart in Figure 5 [for alto: Figure 5-alt] gives precise fret locations. Mark the fret locations with pencil lines across the neck. Bear in mind that due to

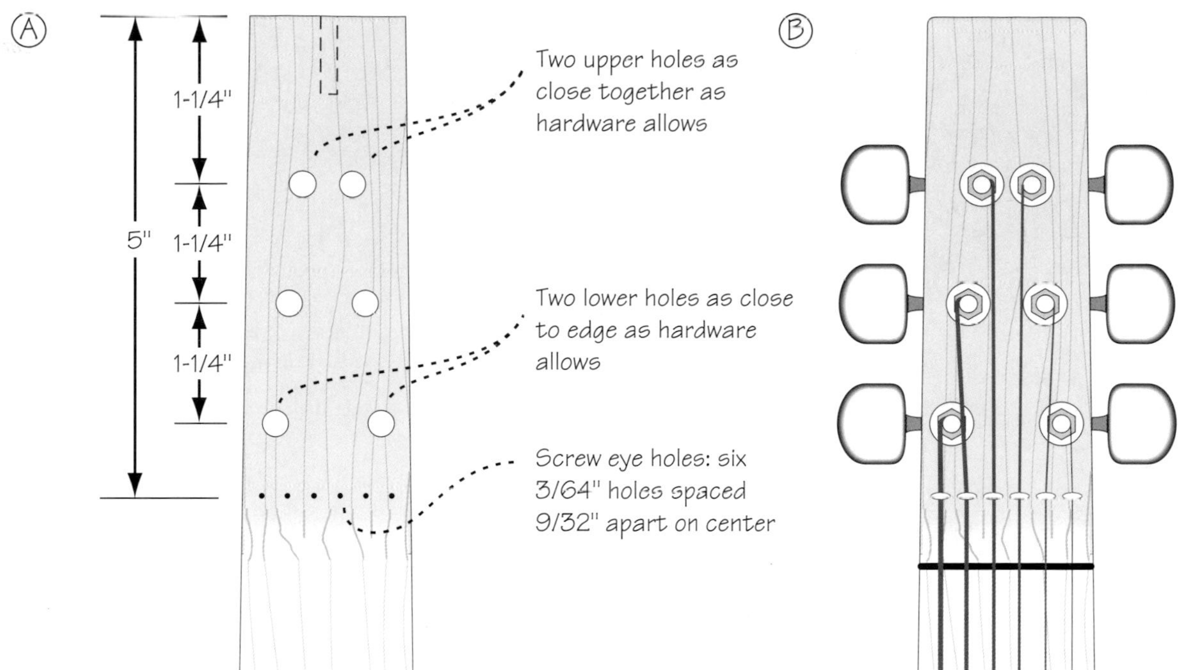

FIGURE 4

The guitar head. A, shows the locations for the tuning post holes and the predrilling holes for the screw eyes. As described in the text, tuning post hole size depends on the specifics of your tuning hardware. So does the lateral placement of the tuning post holes; B, this is what the head will look like with the strings and hardware in place. The tuning posts should be located so that the path of each string from its screw eye to its tuning post requires no sharp bends and is unobstructed or nearly so.

the slight narrowing of the neck over its length, the fret lines are not precisely perpendicular to the sides, but to an imaginary center line down the middle of the neck.

9. A section of fret wire will be cut for each fret, and the lower part of the fret wire, called the *tang*, will be hammered snugly into slots cut into the fingerboard—that is what holds the frets in place. This leaves the upper part of the fret, called the *bead*, as a ridge over the surface of the fingerboard. Cut the narrow slots using a special backsaw or the specially prepared coping saw blade described in note 9 for the tools listing above. Do not try to cut the slots freehand. Figure 6 shows a way to use a framing square or other broad straightedge to make a clean, square cut. Be sure to cut all slots to a depth greater than the height of the tang.

Fret Number	Location (centimeters)	Location (inches)
0	0	0
1	3.65	1-7/16
2	7.1	2-25/64
3	10.35	4-5/64
4	13.5	5-9/32
5	16.3	6-13/32
6	19.05	7-1/2
7	21.6	8-33/64
8	24.05	9-29/64
9	26.35	10-11/64
10	28.5	11-7/32
11	30.55	12-1/32
12	32.5	12-51/64
13	34.35	13-33/64
14	36.05	14-3/16
15	37.65	14-53/64
16	39.2	15-7/16
17	40.65	16
18	42.0	16-35/64
19	43.3	17- 3/64

FIGURE 5

The fret locations. The numbers given here represent the distance of each fret from the zeroth fret. Both metric and inch measurements are given, but you will find the metric measurements much easier to work with.

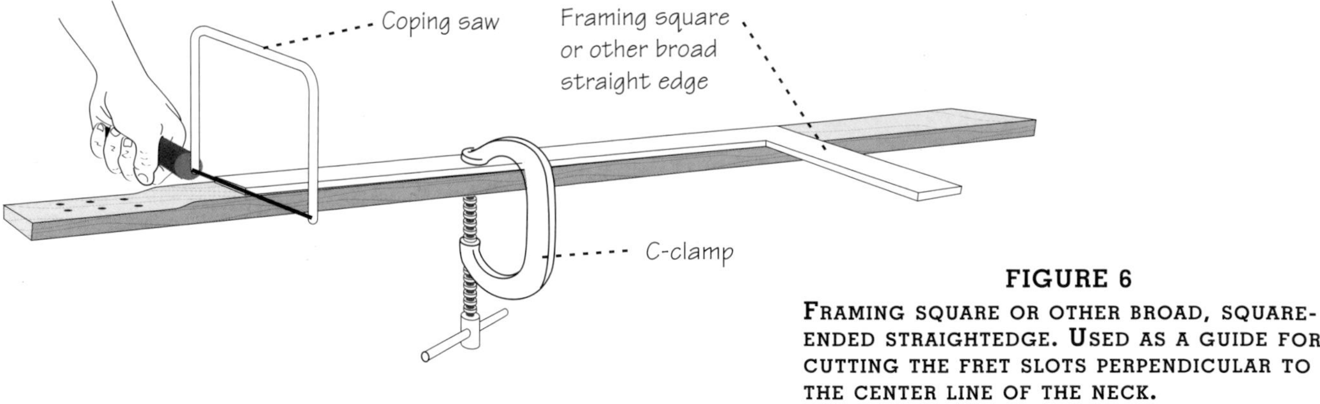

FIGURE 6

Framing square or other broad, square-ended straightedge. Used as a guide for cutting the fret slots perpendicular to the center line of the neck.

10. For each fret, use wire cutters to cut a section of fret wire just a little longer than is required to cross the neck. Tap it firmly and snugly in place with a rubber or rawhide mallet. When all frets are in place, use a metal straightedge to check whether they are level with one another (with allowance for the slight curvature of the neck). If some are high, they may not have been tapped in all the way, or maybe the groove was not cut deep enough. Correct the problem as necessary. If some pop up and won't hold in the slot, the slot is too wide. You can fix this inelegantly by gluing the frets down with epoxy.
11. Use wire cutters to snip off the overhanging fret ends as close as possible to the edge of the neck. Then file the remaining overhang flush, being careful not to lift the fret by filing in the wrong direction. An electric belt sander with medium grit paper will make quick work of this job.
12. Now is the best time to apply a wood finish of your choice on the neck and head. But leave the fretted portion of the neck unfinished, since finish applied there will wear off and gum up the strings.
13. When the finish is dry, mount the tuning machines. Figure 7 shows a typical arrangement. The hardware is usually provided with tiny wood screws for mounting, which may require screw holes predrilled with a 1/16" or 3/64" bit. Predrilling locations will depend on the tuning hardware you're using.
14. Set the six screw eyes in the predrilled holes near the base of the head. Screw them down to where the top of the inside of the hole in each eye is about 1/8" below the level of the zeroth fret.
15. The cooler guitar's shape and balance are somewhat different from a standard guitar. To keep it steady against the player's body, we will add a body support piece to the back of the neck. It is a 10" piece of wood, located where the neck contacts the player's body, with a pivoting mount that allows the player to adjust its position. Cut the body support piece to size and drill the 3/16" hole through it (Figure 8A, page 130). Drill the 5/32" hole in the back of the neck to a depth of 3/4" at the location indicated in Figure 8B [for alto: Figure 8-alt B]. Place a 1-1/4" #10 machine screw through the body support piece with a washer on each side, and screw it into the predrilled hole in the neck, forcing the threads as you go. Screw it down snug, so that the support piece pivots but with good resistance.

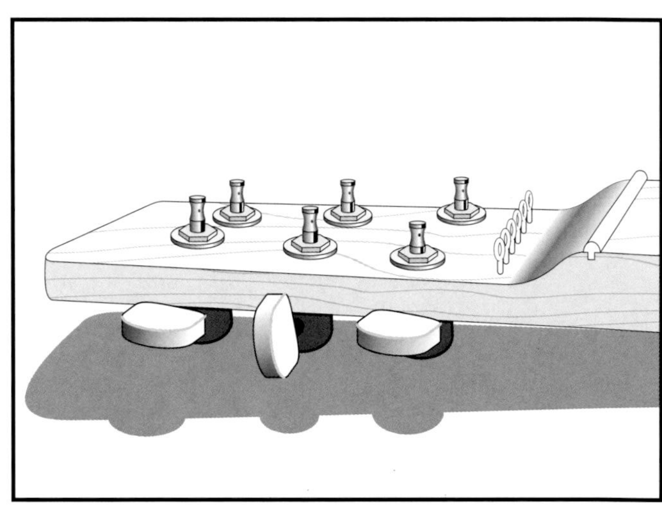

FIGURE 7

Typical tuning machine mounting arrangement

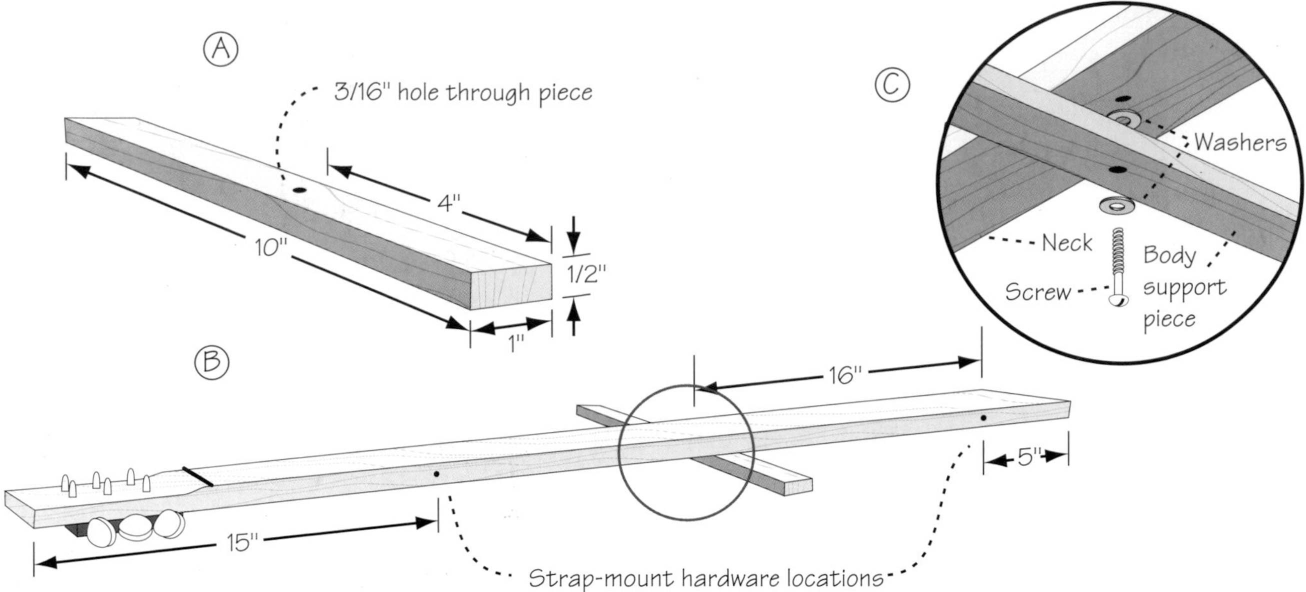

FIGURE 8

THE BODY SUPPORT PIECE. A, DIMENSIONS AND HOLE LOCATION; B, MOUNTING POSITION. ALSO SHOWN: LOCATIONS FOR SUPPORT STRAP ATTACHMENT HARDWARE; C, CUTAWAY VIEW SHOWING DETAILS OF THE BODY SUPPORT PIECE MOUNTING.

16. The differences in shape and balance also make it difficult to play the cooler guitar without a strap. Attach strap-mounting hardware at the locations shown in Figure 8B [for alto: Figure 8-alt B]. Depending on the strap you intend to use, screw eyes in the proper locations may be sufficient, or you may wish to use the special strap-mounting buttons that appear on commercial guitars. For more on straps, see step 21 below.
17. For the cooler guitar bridge we will use (initially, at least) a 2-1/2" section of metal rod about 1/8" in diameter. Cut the 2-1/2" section from a large nail or any other suitable source, and de-burr the ends with a file or grinder.
18. Time now to put on the strings. Figures 2 and 4B show the paths the strings follow from the anchorage at the bridge end to the tuning machines at the head end. Lay the neck face up before you with the head on the left, and mount the sixth string (the thickest) nearest to you. Proceed through to the first (the thinnest) on the far side of the neck. Leave the bridge off initially, and use the tuning machines to tighten the strings to where they are just barely taut. Slip the bridge under the strings, and slide it to the bridge location you marked earlier. Now bring the strings up to standard guitar pitch: 6th string = E_2, 5th = A_2, 4th = D_3, 3rd = G_3, 2nd = B_3, 1st = E_1 [for alto: 6th = B_2, 5th = E_3, 4th = A_3, 3rd = D_4, 2nd = F#4, 1st = B_4].
19. Even though the sound radiator has not yet been attached, you can now play the neck, although it will not be loud. This allows you to make fine adjustments to the guitar's *intonation* (accuracy of pitch, as determined by fret locations) and its *action* (the feel of the strings as you play them, determined largely by the height of the strings over the fingerboard).
    A. First check the action. Experienced guitarists can do this simply by playing. Do the strings feel too stiff and difficult to press down? If so, the action is probably too high. Do the strings buzz against adjacent frets when you play at different points along the neck? If so, either the action is too low, or the heights of the frets are uneven. Check your impressions against a ruler: the ideal height for the strings on a steel string guitar is usually considered to be about 1/8" above the top of the fret at the 12th fret [a little lower for the alto guitar]. To adjust the action, remove the bridge (you will probably have to loosen the strings to do this). If the action needs to be raised, substitute a larger rod or make some sort of narrow shim to insert under the rod. If the action needs to be lowered, substitute a

narrower rod or flatten the underside of the rod a bit with a file. In this process, bear in mind that a small difference in bridge height makes a big difference in playing feel. A slightly higher action on the bass side of the instrument may be preferable. If uneven frets are causing a buzzing, you will have to remove the strings and make whatever adjustments are called for to level them. If the stress of the strings is causing the neck to bow excessively, the problem may be more difficult to resolve short of removing the frets and reshaping the fingerboard (giving it more back-curve to compensate for the bowing). But here's a hint: with a bowed neck you may still be able to get an excellent low action over the first 10 or 12 frets simply by substituting a very low bridge. The upper frets will then be unplayable—but how often do most guitarists actually play them anyway? (Some do frequently; some almost never do.)

B. When you are happy with the action, check the intonation. You will do this by comparing the octave harmonic for the highest and lowest strings to the fretted notes that should produce the same pitch. Lightly touch the first string with a left-hand finger over the 12th fret (don't press it down), and pluck with the right hand at about one-fourth of the string's length from the bridge. Lift the left hand finger immediately after plucking. You will hear the light, ethereal tone known as a harmonic. Now press the same string down behind the 12th fret and pluck again. Ideally, though the tone quality may differ, the two pitches will be the same. If the harmonic tone is higher, shorten the string by moving the bridge slightly toward the zeroth fret. If lower, do the reverse. (It may be necessary to loosen the strings to move the bridge.) Compare the two pitches again, and readjust if necessary until the two pitches match. Repeat the process with the sixth string. Be sure to keep the side of the bridge under the first string in its place; angle the bridge slightly if necessary to accommodate the sixth string adjustment. By the way: remember to count the zeroth fret as zero, not one, when you count up to the 12th fret for the foregoing operation.

20. Now for the sound radiators. The coolers will be held in place by eyebolts (actually serving as thumb screws) threaded directly into the wood of the neck, much as was done with the body support piece. This way they can be easily removed for storage or transport, or for replacement should they get damaged. You already drilled the screw holes in the board back at step 5. Figure 9 shows the attachment of the coolers. You can use the 1-1/2" #10 eyebolts to punch the holes for the eyebolts to pass through. Be careful not to break

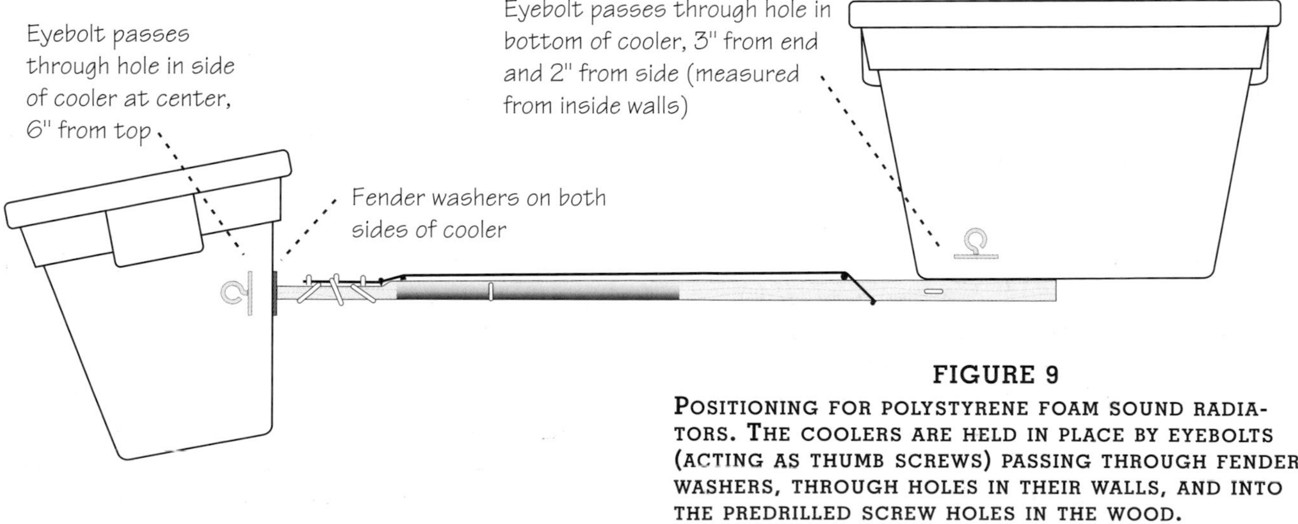
Eyebolt passes through hole in side of cooler at center, 6" from top
Eyebolt passes through hole in bottom of cooler, 3" from end and 2" from side (measured from inside walls)
Fender washers on both sides of cooler

FIGURE 9

Positioning for polystyrene foam sound radiators. The coolers are held in place by eyebolts (acting as thumb screws) passing through fender washers, through holes in their walls, and into the predrilled screw holes in the wood.

away too much polystyrene. Then use the eyebolts and large fender washers to fasten the coolers to the board. Screwing them in the first time will require some effort, as you will be forcing the threads as you go. Screw them down just snug. With that, the cooler guitar is complete, except...

21. If you don't already have a shoulder strap to use with the cooler guitar, you will probably need to acquire or make one. I leave the strap design details up to you. For my own instrument, I use a simple homemade shoulder strap that connects to strap mountings in the form of screw eyes at the locations shown in Figure 8. In addition, I use an elastic strap around my back, hooked to the same screw eyes, to hold the instrument snug against my body. That really makes it steady and secure—very helpful in playing.

Playing Technique

Play the cooler guitar like any other guitar. Here are some tips on getting comfortable with it. Turn the body support piece, which rides against the player's chest or stomach in typical playing position, to an angle that stabilizes the instrument and feels comfortable. You may also wish to adjust the position of the lower-end cooler (pivot it on its mounting screw) either to make more room for your right hand or to provide a right-hand support.

Variations

The dimensions given here are for a typical steel-string guitar. For a classical guitar, the neck is wider and the strings farther apart, as follows: Neck width at zeroth fret; 2-1/8"; neck width at bridge; 2-13/16". To achieve these widths at the zeroth fret and the bridge, make the board width 2" at the narrow end and 2-15/16" at the broad end. Typical spacing between strings at bridge: 1.1cm (7/16"); spacing between strings at zeroth fret; .84cm (21/64").

You can electrify the cooler guitar by placing a piezoelectric transducer (contact microphone) somewhere along the board. These transducers are available at music stores at varying costs and levels of quality. With a little more effort you can attach an electric-guitar-style electromagnetic pickup under the strings. Then you can put the coolers aside and just play the stick through an amplifier.

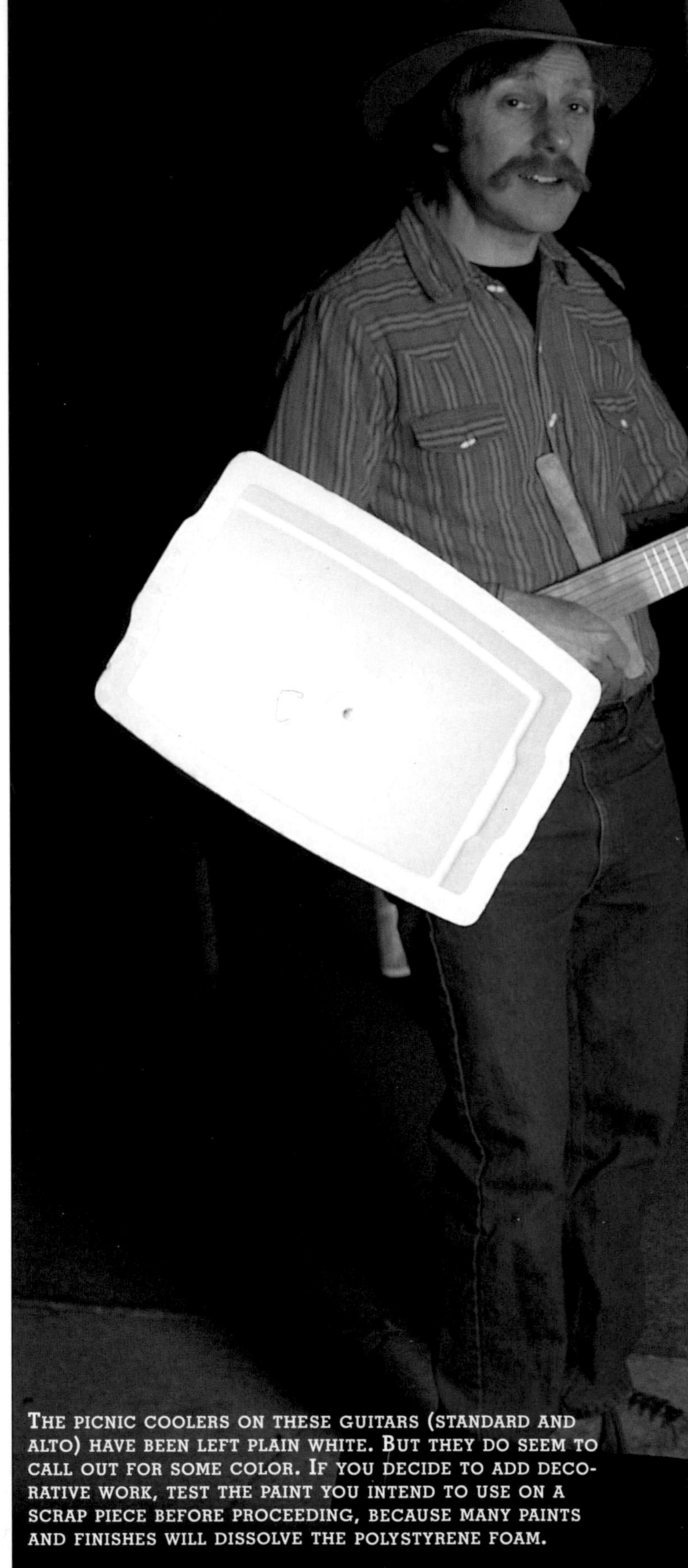

THE PICNIC COOLERS ON THESE GUITARS (STANDARD AND ALTO) HAVE BEEN LEFT PLAIN WHITE. BUT THEY DO SEEM TO CALL OUT FOR SOME COLOR. IF YOU DECIDE TO ADD DECORATIVE WORK, TEST THE PAINT YOU INTEND TO USE ON A SCRAP PIECE BEFORE PROCEEDING, BECAUSE MANY PAINTS AND FINISHES WILL DISSOLVE THE POLYSTYRENE FOAM.

Alto Cooler Guitar

DIFFICULT

Small guitars in diverse forms can be found in many parts of the world. Popular among them are the *cuatro,* played in parts of South America and the Caribbean, and the Hawaiian ukulele. The design here is for an alto guitar with six strings, much like the full-sized cooler guitar of the last plan but at two-thirds the string scale. I decided to make this small six-stringer in part because I've always wanted to have such an instrument myself, and in part because the polystyrene foam resonators sing so lucidly in the upper middle registers that are the heart of this instrument's range. The suggested tuning is standard guitar tuning, but transposed up a fifth: B_2 E_3 A_3 D_4 $F\#_4$ B_4.

Instructions

Follow the construction procedures for the previous plan's full-sized cooler guitar. The only differences will be in certain dimensions. Drawings with correct dimensions for the alto guitar appear below. They are cross-referenced in the instructions for making the full-sized guitar, so you will be able to easily find your way to the correct figures as you proceed through the instructions.

Playing Technique

If you use the transposed guitar tuning suggested above, the cooler alto guitar will play very much like a standard guitar, but higher. Pieces normally played on a standard guitar often sound light and lovely at the higher pitch level, with the crystalline tone quality of the cooler alto.

As with the full-sized cooler guitar, the balance and feel of the instrument is slightly different from a standard guitar. See step 21 and the comments about playing position in the "Playing Techniques" section for the cooler guitar, page 133.

Materials List and Suggested Tools

See the materials and tools listings in the preceding plan for the cooler guitar, page 124.

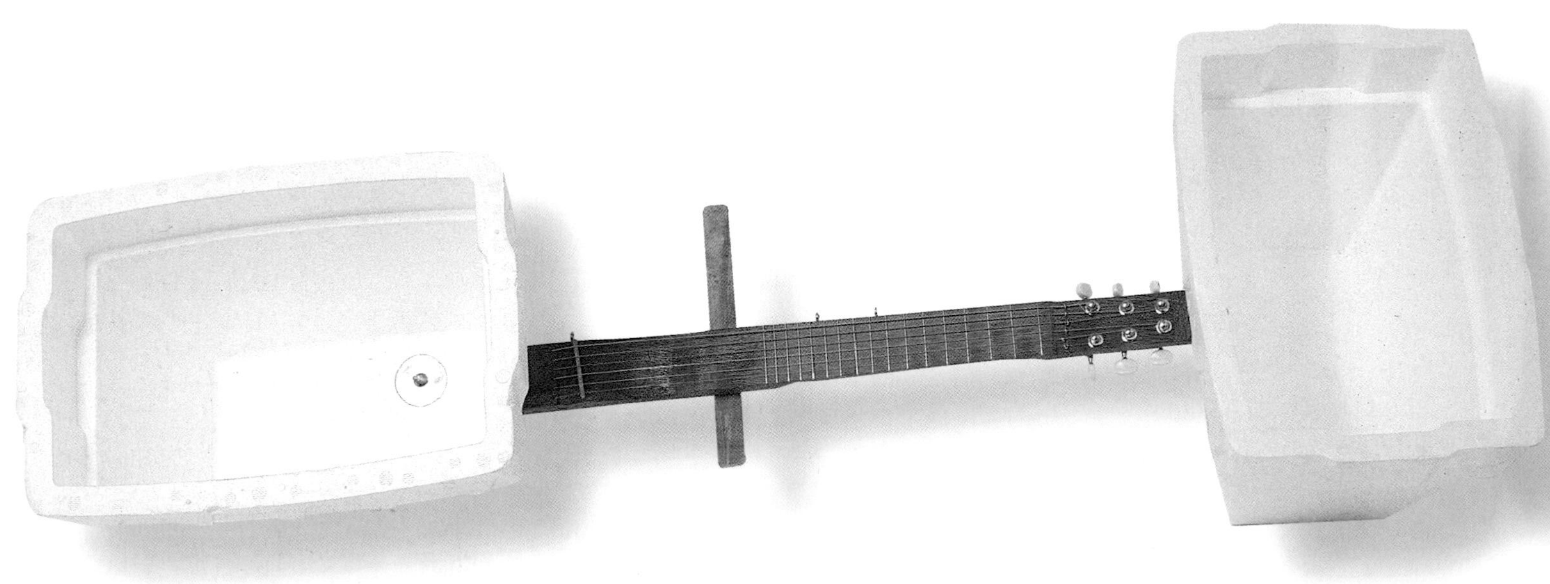

1-5/8"
2-1/2"
32"

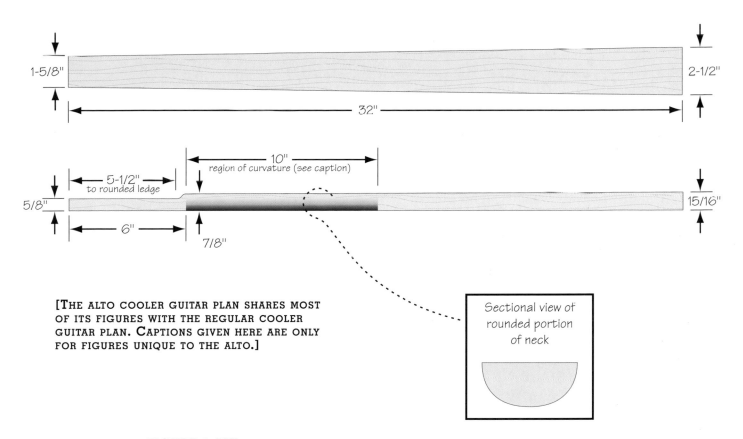

10"
region of curvature (see caption)
5-1/2"
to rounded ledge
5/8"
15/16"
6"
7/8"

Sectional view of rounded portion of neck

[The alto cooler guitar plan shares most of its figures with the regular cooler guitar plan. Captions given here are only for figures unique to the alto.]

FIGURE 1-ALT

Dimensions for the alto cooler guitar neck. In the "region of curvature" the surface of the board is given a very slight, very gradual, and very uniform back-sloping curvature, which will compensate for the tendency of the neck to bow forward under string tension. The curvature starts imperceptibly at a point 16" from the narrow end of the board and extends just over 10" to the rounded ledge. At that point, the curvature should have had the effect of thinning the 15/16" board to 7/8". Don't add this curvature in the initial shaping (step 1); do it as part of the final fingerboard shaping in step 2, after letting the wood sit a few days. In doing the thinning, go slow and easy; be careful not to overdo it.

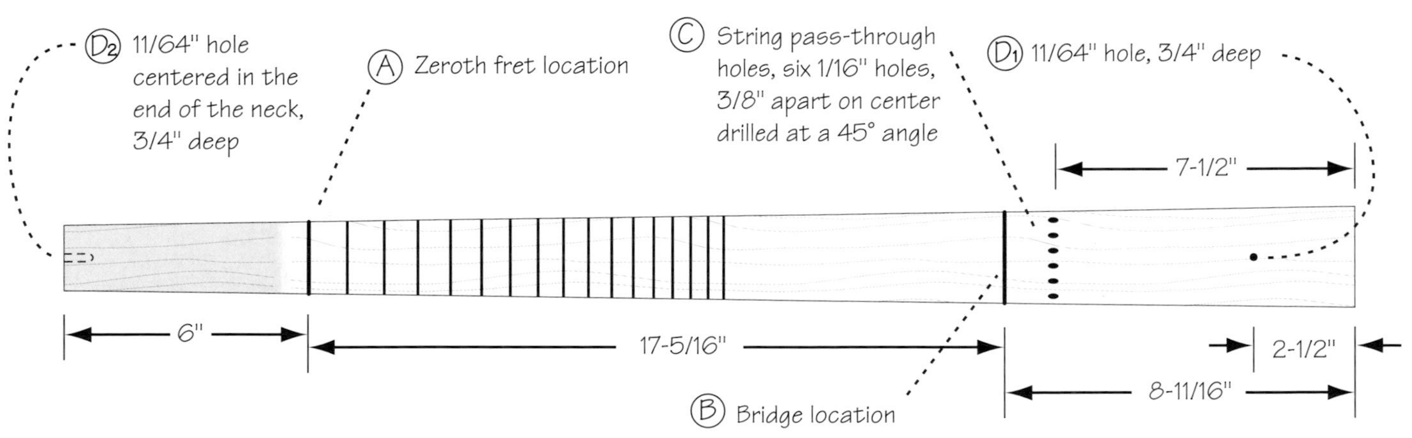

FIGURE 3-ALT

The overall layout of the neck

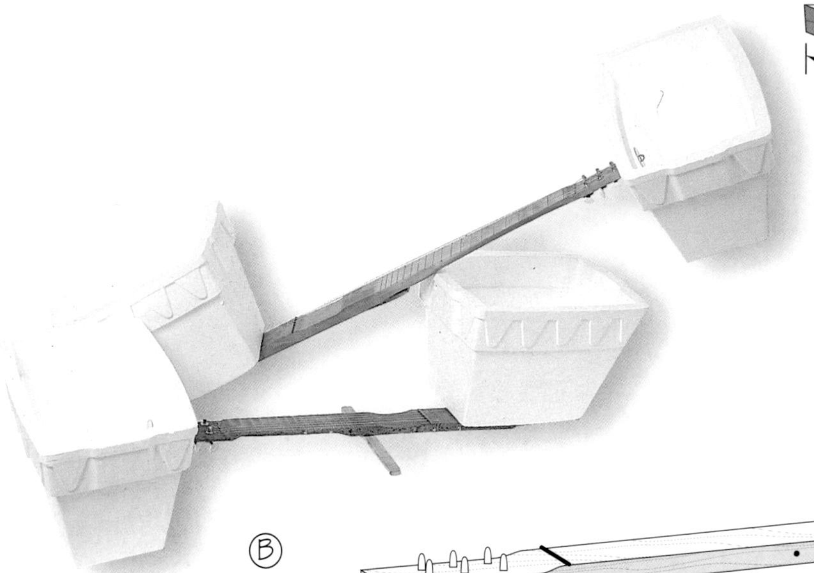

Ⓐ

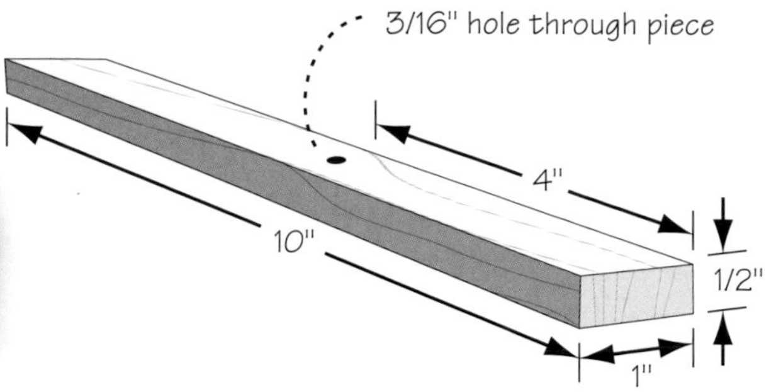

3/16" hole through piece

4"

10"

1/2"

1"

14"

Ⓑ

5"

12"

Strap-mount hardware locations

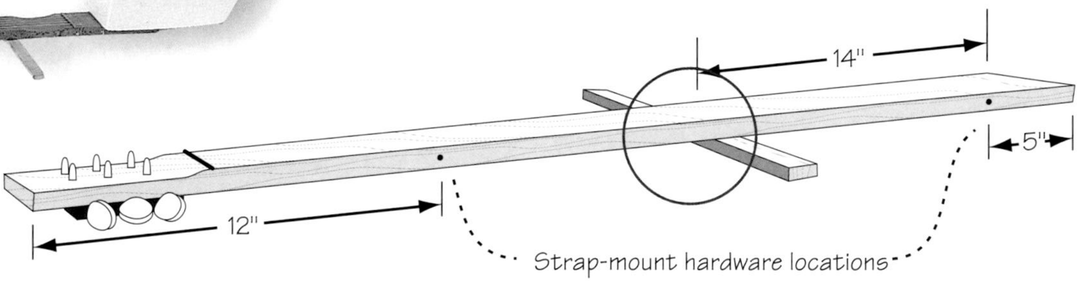

FIGURE 5

Fret locations. The numbers given here represent the distance of each fret from the zeroth fret. Both metric and inch measurements are given; you will find the metric measurements much easier to work with.

Fret Number	Location (centimeters)	Location (inches)
0	0	0
1	2.45	31/32
2	4.75	1-7/8
3	6.9	2-23/32
4	8.95	3-17/32
5	10.9	4-19/64
6	12.7	5
7	14.45	5-11/16
8	16.05	6-5/16
9	17.6	6-59/64
10	19.05	7-1/2
11	20.4	8-1/32
12	21.7	8-35/64
13	22.9	9-1/64
14	24.05	9-15/32
15	25.15	9-29/32
16	26.15	10-19/64

Ⓒ

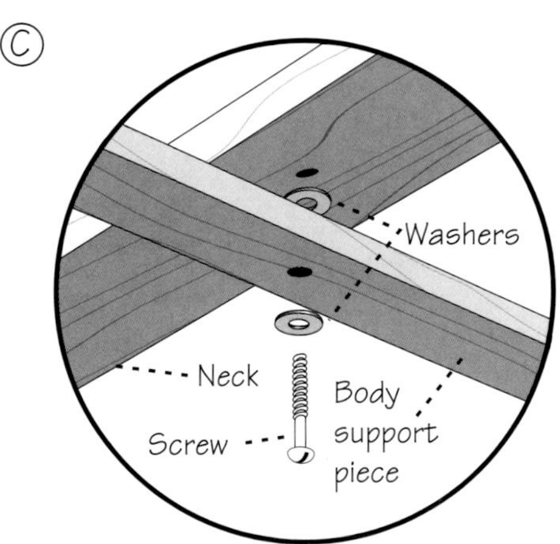

FIGURE 8 B-ALT

Mounting position for the body support piece. Also shown: locations for support strap attachment hardware.

Calculating Fret Placements

The fret location measurements I have given for the plans appearing in this book apply only to instruments with string scalings identical to those of the instruments in the plans. For anyone who wishes to make fretted instruments with different string scalings, here are generally applicable rules for fret placement.

Other things being equal, vibrational frequency for strings is inversely proportional to active string length: the shorter the vibrating string segment, the proportionally higher the frequency and corresponding pitch. Frets should be placed so as to shorten the string's vibrating length by the right proportion to yield the desired new pitch relative to the unfretted string pitch. Based on this proportionality, people with the requisite background in math and tuning theory can figure fret placements for whatever musical intervals they wish. For the rest of us, here are some simple rules.

To locate frets so as to yield a chromatic scale in standard 12-tone equal temperament, the first fret should be placed so as to shorten the string's vibrating length to 0.9438 of its open length. That means, place the fret at a distance of [0.9438 x (open string length)] from the bridge. Each subsequent fret should be placed so as to shorten the length relative to the previous fret by the same proportion. After 12 applications of the rule, you should find yourself locating the 12th fret at half the open string length, yielding twice the original frequency to produce the octave.

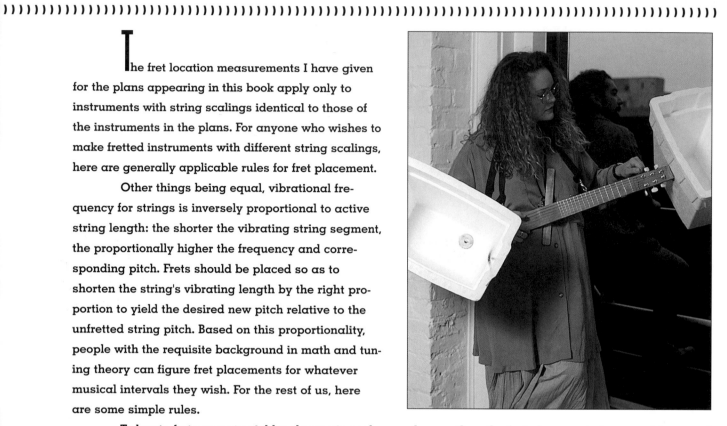

However, there is an important consideration to be added here. The fret locations that this calculation yields do not take into account the fact that in actual playing the pressing down of the string over the fret stretches the string slightly, making the pitch sharper than the fret placement alone would suggest. You can adjust for this by basing your calculations on a fictitious string length of 99.3% of the actual length (less if the action will be very high, closer to 100% if it will be very low). Then, if possible, do what we did in the plans in this book: make the bridge location adjustable. This will allow you to make after-the-fact corrections if the frets turn out to yield inaccurate pitches (step 19 on pages 130–131 in the cooler guitar plan explains how to make the adjustments).

Another approach some makers have used is "the rule of 18." Place the frets so that each successive fret shortens the vibrating string length by 1/18th relative to the previous fret. This gives a result very close to the theoretical ideal for 12-tone equal temperament, but with a small correction built in.

Appendix 1

Tools and Materials

This appendix contains information on tools and materials that will be useful in making the instruments discussed in this book and in exploring a broader world of instrument making as well.

Tools

A list of suggested tools appears with each project in the book. A perusal of those lists will show that you can build most of the instruments with common hand tools. You will get a lot of benefit from at least one power tool—one that is not too expensive, difficult to use, or dangerous: an electric hand drill. The drill, along with a few not-too-expensive attachments, will give you some of the benefits of power tools without requiring the same level of expenditure or the same degree of shop experience. Among the accessories that will be most useful: a complete set of fractional drill bits, a large countersink bit, grinder bits and/or burr bits, circle saw attachment, and sanding disk. For more details, see the suggested tools list with each plan.

If you do have access to more specialized power tools, they will make faster work and in some cases yield better results. The most useful among them would include band saw, bench grinder, belt sander, circular saw or table saw, drill press, electric planer (hand planer, surface planer and/or jointer), hot-glue gun, jigsaw or sabre saw, and router.

Please use your tools wisely. Follow common-sense safety procedures, wear goggles or face mask and a breather (dust mask) when appropriate, follow instructions on tools and products.

Materials

Most of the materials required to make the instruments described in this book are available from hardware stores, lumberyards, and other common retail outlets. In plans where specialized materials are called for, I have included in the materials list a notation indicating where they can be obtained.

Suppliers

Here is a list of suppliers for specialized materials that you may find useful in connection with the plans in this book or other musical instrument making projects. If you request a catalog from any of these retailers, be sure to send a stamped self-addressed 9" x 12" envelope for their response. Some with especially extensive catalogs may charge a dollar or more for the catalog.

Specialty Music Stores

There are several stores specializing in unusual and hard-to-find instruments and accessories, doing much of their business by mail order. Here are some of them:

- Ali Akbar College of Music Store, 215 West End Ave., San Rafael, CA 94901.
- Andy's Front Hall, PO Box 307, Voorheesville, NY 12186.
- Elderly Instruments, 1100 N. Washington, PO Box 14210, Lansing, MI 48901.
- House of Musical Traditions, 7040 Carroll Ave., Tacoma Park, MD 20912.

- Lark in the Morning, PO Box 1176, Mendocino, CA 95460.
- Musicmakers Kits, 423 South Main St., Stillwater, MN 55082 (specializing in buildable kits for unusual instruments).

Piano Tuner Supply Houses and Lutherie Supply Houses

These are some of the companies specializing in materials used in string instrument building and repair, including woods, strings, and hardware.

- Luthier's Mercantile, PO Box 774, 412 Moore Lane, Healdsburg, CA 95448.
- Stewart-MacDonald's Guitar Shop Supply, 21 N. Shafer St., Box 900, Athens, OH 45701.
- S F Pianos, 657 Mission, San Francisco, CA 94105.
- Pacific Piano Supply Company, 11323 Vanowen St, North Hollywood, CA 91609.

Educational Music Supply Houses

These outlets carry a wide range of musical merchandise and accessories at discount prices, aimed at school band music programs.

- Interstate Music Supply, PO Box 315, 13819 West National Ave., New Berlin, WI 53151.
- The Woodwind and the Brasswind (they also have an extensive percussion catalog), 19880 State Line Road, South Bend, IN 46637.

Wind Instrument Manufacturers

For parts and accessories associated with wind instruments, the best place to go is directly to the manufacturers, part of whose business is the sale of parts to band instrument repair technicians. Two leading U.S. manufacturers are:

G. Leblanc Corporation, 7019 30th Ave., Kenosha WI 53141.

United Musical Instruments, 1000 Industrial Parkway, PO Box 727, Elkhart, IN 46515.

Drumheads

For natural drumheads, precut to various sizes, with or without hoops:

United Rawhide Mfg. Co., 1644 N. Ada St., Chicago, IL 60622.

Drum and Percussion Hardware and Accessories

Stewart-MacDonald's Drum Makers Supply, 21 N. Schafer St., Box 900, Athens, OH 45701.

The Woodwind & the Brasswind Percussion Catalog, 19880 State Line Rd., South Bend, IN 46637.

Natural Materials

Here are sources for shell, bone, gourd and bamboo.

Boone Trading Company, 562 Coyote Road, Brinnon, WA 98320 (tusk, bone, shell, ostrich eggs, horn, turtle shell, etc.).

Tandy Leather Company, 116 W. 25th Ave., San Mateo, CA 94403 (longhorn and steer horn).

Benfane Arts, PO Box 298, West Hempstead, NY 11552 (seashells including conch).

Eastern Star Trading Company, 624 Davis St., Evanston, IL 60201 (bamboo, including large diameter poles).

The Gourd Factory, PO Box 55311, Stockton, CA 95205 (dried gourds).

Industrial Surplus

For an incredible potpourri of useless junk, much of which turns out to be just what you didn't know you needed:

American Science & Surplus (formerly Jerryco), 601 Linden Place, Evanston, IL 60202.

Software

The string scaling software referred to in the text is a DOS program called *Stringmaster*, available from Mark Bolles, 1405 Little Leaf, San Antonio, TX 78247.

Appendix 2

Bibliography

This bibliography includes selected English language works on musical instruments of the world, texts on acoustics and intonation theory, and collections of instrument-making plans.

It is not exhaustive in any of these areas. In particular, I haven't included the myriad books devoted to specific instrument types. If you have an interest in learning about a particular instrument, begin by looking it up in the *New Grove Dictionary of Musical Instruments* (available at large libraries), which is organized like an encyclopedia. Most of its articles contain bibliographies that can help guide your research.

For further research into specialized topics, there are also newsletters or journals devoted to most standard instrument types, as well as many obscure ones (jaw harp and musical saw, for example). You can find periodicals devoted to particular instruments by perusing the music section of one of the periodicals directories, such as *Ulrich's International Periodicals Directory*, in the reference section of the local library. The only periodical devoted to new and unusual instruments of all sorts is *Experimental Musical Instruments*, edited by the author of this book, available from PO Box 784, Nicasio, CA 94946.

General Sources on Musical Instruments

Baines, Anthony. *The Oxford Companion to Musical Instruments*. Oxford: Oxford University Press, 1992. Just under 400 pages, organized as an encyclopedia, with entries providing fairly detailed information on a broad range of western and nonwestern instruments. Less complete than the New Grove listed below, but far more affordable.

The Diagram Group. *Musical Instruments of the World: An Illustrated Encyclopedia*. New York: Facts on File, 1976. A browser's delight; beautifully illustrated, but far less detailed and complete than the Baines listed above or the New Grove listed below.

Marcuse, Sibyl. *Musical Instruments: A Comprehensive Dictionary*. New York: W.W. Norton Co., 1975. A dictionary of musical instrument names and terminology. Very complete for historical instruments (with virtually nothing on 20th-century instruments), but the entries are very brief.

Sachs, Curt. *The History of Musical Instruments*. New York: W.W. Norton & Co., Inc., 1940. For many years an important scholarly resource, now somewhat outdated in both content and approach.

Sadie, Stanley, ed. *The New Grove Dictionary of Musical Instruments*. New York and London: Macmillan Press Ltd., 1984. In three volumes; organized as an encyclopedia. This is by far the most complete source for information on instruments of all sorts. The cost is over $300.

Acoustics and Intonation Theory

Barbour, J. Murray. *Tuning and Temperament*. East Lansing, MI: Michigan State College Press, 1951. A long-time standard reference in the field of intonational theory.

Benade, Arthur H. *Fundamentals of Musical Acoustics*. New York: Dover, 1976, revised 1990. An extremely valuable, if fairly demanding and at times idiosyncratic, overview of the topic.

Benade, Arthur H. *Horns, Strings & Harmony*. New York: Doubleday, 1960. Simpler and more accessible than the previous listing by the same author.

Doty, David. *The Just Intonation Primer*. San Francisco: The Just Intonation Network (535 Stevenson St., San Francisco, CA 94013), 1993. This is the place to start for tuning theory if your interest is in just tunings rather than equal temperaments or other approaches.

Fletcher, Neville H., and Thomas D. Rossing. *The Physics of Musical Instruments*. New York: Springer-Verlag, 1991. Highly technical; extremely demanding mathematics.

Hall, Donald. *Musical Acoustics: An Introduction 2nd edition*. Pacific Grove, CA: Brooks-Cole Pub. Co., 1991. Designed as a college level textbook. Accessible, lucid, and practical throughout.

Helmholtz, Hermann. *On the Sensations of Tone*. New York: Dover Publications, 1954. Helmholtz' pioneering study of musical acoustics, first published in 1885, is still read as a foundational text today.

Olsen, Harry F. *Music, Physics and Engineering*. New York: Dover Publications, Inc., 1967. A compendium of technical information.

Partch, Harry. *Genesis of a Music*. New York: Da Capo Press, 1979. Partch's account of the development of his musical ideas and instruments remains an important source for both intonational theory and practical acoustics.

Collections of Instrument Plans and Descriptions

Banek, Reinhold, and Jon Scoville. *Sound Designs: A Handbook of Musical Instrument Building*. Berkeley, CA: Ten Speed Press, Berkeley, CA, 1980. About 50 unconventional designs presented in accessible, readable style.

Francis, Lindo, and Alan Trussell-Cullen. *Hooked on Making Musical Instruments*. Auckland: Longman Paul Ltd., 1989. About 50 simple instruments that can be made by children.

Grayson, John, ed. *Sound Sculpture*, and *Environments of Musical Sound Sculpture You Can Build*. Vancouver: A.R.C. Press [Aesthetic Research Center of Canada], 1976. A variety of essays and plans for sound exploration, culled from several builders. Long out of print and now rare.

Partch, Harry. *Genesis of a Music*. New York: Da Capo Press, 1979. In addition to its theoretical information, Partch's manifesto contains detailed descriptions of his unique instruments.

Hunter, Ilene, and Marilyn Judson. *Simple Folk Instruments to Make and Play*. New York: Simon & Schuster, 1977. A collection of good, workable, simple children's instrument-making projects.

Roberts, Ronald. *Musical Instruments Made to be Played*. Leicester: Dryad Press, 1968. Plans for simple instruments both conventional and unconventional.

Sawyer, David. *Vibrations*. Cambridge: Cambridge University Press, 1977. Contains 28 unconventional designs.

Shepard, Mark. *Simple Flutes: Play Them, Make Them*. Tai Hei Shakuhachi, PO Box 293, Willits, CA 95490, 1992. Accessible, lucid description of the principles behind simple flute design.

Sloane, Irving. *Making Musical Instruments*. New York: E.P. Dutton, 1978. Detailed notes for making banjo, snare drum, Appalachian dulcimer, Hardanger fiddle, and recorder.

Walther, Tom. *Make Mine Music!* Boston: Little, Brown & Co., 1981. Instructions for about 25 instruments that can be made by children, along with activities and philosophical musings.

Waring, Dennis. *Making Folk Instruments in Wood*. New York: Sterling Publishing Co., 1979. Plans for about 50 instruments, some conventional and some unconventional.

Glossary

Note: Italicized words appearing in these definitions are themselves defined elsewhere in the glossary.

A-440 The *pitch* A above middle C, which has been standardized at a *frequency* of 440 cycles per second. This pitch serves as the tuning standard for most western music today.

Absolute pitch *Pitch,* in contexts where relationships or *intervals* between pitches are not important, but specific pitches as uniquely identified by *frequency* are

Acoustics The scientific study of sound

Aerophone Wind instrument

Air resonance *Resonance* associated with a partially enclosed body of air

Amplitude Breadth of vibratory motion. Audible *vibrations* of larger amplitude carry greater energy and are perceived as louder.

Action An instrument's playing mechanism, especially as the mechanism contributes to the feel of the instrument under the player's fingers. "Piano action" thus refers to the mechanism that translates key movement to the movement of the hammer that strikes the string; "guitar action" refers to the positioning of the strings over the fingerboard and the resulting playing feel.

Chordophone String instrument

Chromatic scale A *scale* of 12 tones per *octave,* containing both the natural notes and the sharps or flats of the western scale (e.g., all the tones available on the piano)

Cross fingerings In wind instruments with side holes, cross fingerings are fingerings in which one or more additional holes are covered below the first open hole.

Diatonic scale The major and minor *scales* used in much western music, containing seven tones per *octave*

Edge tone A *vibration* in the atmosphere created when a narrow air stream strikes an edge, as with flutes

Embouchure The manner in which the lips are applied to the mouthpiece in wind instruments

Free bar A vibrating body in the form of a bar, tube or rod, mounted nonrigidly, leaving it free to manifest the free-bar modes of vibration. It can be contrasted with bars held rigidly at one or both ends.

Frequency The number of complete vibratory cycles per second in a given *vibration.* A sound's frequency determines its *pitch* as perceived by the ear: the more cycles per second, the higher the pitch.

Fundamental Most musical sounds contain a blend of vibrations at many *frequencies.* The lowest of these is often called the fundamental, and its *pitch* is usually perceived as the defining pitch for the sound.

Globular flute An *edge-tone* instrument in which the air chamber is short and fat, or more or less round in shape, rather than long and tubular

Harmonic A tone whose *frequency* is an integral multiple of a given *fundamental* frequency. Most musical sounds contain a blend of many frequencies including a fundamental and additional *overtones.* When the overtones have this integral multiple relationship to the fundamental, they are called harmonics.

Harmonic series A series of pitches whose frequencies bear the relationship *f, 2f, 3f, 4f*...

Idiophone Musical instrument in which the initial vibrating body is a solid, unstretched material

Interval The musical relationship between any two *pitches.* Between a very high and a very low pitch, there is a large interval. Between two nearly identical pitches, there is a small interval.

Intonation *Tuning,* or "in-tune-ness"

Inverse proportion Two quantities are said to have a relationship of inverse proportion when one becomes larger as the other becomes smaller in corresponding amounts; e.g., doubling one quantity causes the other to be halved.

Inverse squared Two quantities have an inverse squared relationship when one quantity becomes smaller at a rate corresponding to the square of the rate at which the other becomes larger; e.g., halving one causes the other to increase by a factor of four.

Just intonation Any *tuning* system in which the *intervals* are based on the ratios between the *frequencies* of the *pitches,* with a preference for simple ratios having no large prime numbers in the numerators or denominators. The standard western tuning system, *12-tone equal temperament,* is not a just intonation (the underlying mathematics are not ratio-based, and, aside from the octave, the frequency relationships are irrational), but it is designed to approximate important intervals of just intonation.

Lamellaphone A musical instrument using plucked prongs, such as kalimba or mbira and many small music boxes.

Lay The portion of a single-reed instrument mouthpiece that lies under the reed. Its shaping is important in reed performance. The term may also be used in connection with double reeds.

Lip-buzzing The technique of buzzing the lips into a wind instrument mouthpiece to produce a tone, as with trumpets and trombones

Membranophone Musical instrument in which the primary vibrating body is a stretched membrane—i.e., a drum

Mode of vibration Pattern of vibratory movement in an object or substance. Most vibrating objects are capable of many modes of vibration and can manifest them simultaneously.

Octave The *interval* between two pitches having the same pitch name, e.g., between middle C and the next C above. The ratio of the *frequencies* of two pitches an octave apart is 2:1. Tones an octave apart are perceived as sharing a close identity, to the point that they are often identified as being the same note.

Oscillation Back-and-forth movement, as with *vibration*

Overblow In wind instruments, to play the instrument in such a way that the tone jumps to an upper *register*

Overtone Most musical sounds contain a blend of many *frequencies.* The lowest of these is normally called the *fundamental;* the additional tones above it can be called overtones or *partials.* Overtones may or may not be *harmonic,* depending on their frequency relationship to the fundamental.

Overtone tuning The relationships or *intervals* between the *overtones* within a given instrument's sound. Often, *harmonic* overtone relationships are preferred, and it is sometimes possible, by altering the form of the instrument's sounding elements, to tune the overtone's relationships in order to bring them into harmonic alignment.

Partial *Overtone*

Pentatonic scale A *scale* of five tones per *octave.* There are many possible pentatonics, including some of the world's most widely used scales.

Pitch The listener's sense of how "high" or "low" a musical sound is. It corresponds to the physical property of vibrational *frequency,* with higher frequencies corresponding to higher pitches.

Radiation The transmission of sound energy from a vibrating object or substance to the surrounding atmosphere, and its continuing spread through the atmosphere

Reed One or two strips of material, often cut from a natural cane reed, fixed in an arrangement that allows them to open and close rapidly over the passageway into a wind instrument under air pressure from the player. This allows the air to enter the instrument in a series of rapid pulses, setting up the *vibration.*

Register In wind instruments, the range of tones available when the instrument tube operates in a particular *mode of vibration.* Most tubular wind instruments have a fundamental register in which the tube's *fundamental* mode dominates the tone; a second register in which a higher mode comes to the fore and acts as a surrogate fundamental over a higher range; and, in some cases, a still higher third *register.*

Register hole In wind instruments, a small hole relatively near the mouthpiece, which aids in throwing the instrument into an upper *register*

Relative pitch *Pitch,* spoken of in a context where absolute pitches as uniquely identified by their *frequency* are not important, but the relationships or *intervals* between pitches are

Resonance The especially strong response of any vibrating system to being excited at or near one of the frequencies at which the system is naturally inclined to vibrate

Scale The set of *pitches* used in a particular piece or genre of music. For teaching and analytical purposes, the pitches of the scale are usually arranged in ascending order.

Soundboard Wooden sound *radiating* surface, such as the face of a guitar. By extension the term may also refer to nonwooden radiating surfaces, such as the drumlike face of a banjo.

Sound box A partial enclosure such as the body of a guitar or violin that enriches the sound by adding the *air resonance* of the enclosure

Stick-slip The mechanism by which *vibrations* are generated in bowed instruments, as well as in other friction instruments and in nonmusical squeaks

String scaling The science of selecting the best string lengths, diameters, and materials for a given musical application

Timbre Tone quality

Tuning 1) A set of *absolute pitches* or *relative pitch* relationships that can be used as the raw material for making music—similar in concept to *scale.* 2) The process of adjusting the pitches produced by an instrument to agree with a particular tuning or scale.

Twelve-tone equal temperament The standard *tuning* system in most western music today, employing 12 equally spaced pitches per octave

Vibration Rapid, small-scale back-and-forth movement. Vibrations occurring in the atmosphere are perceived by the ears and brain as sound. In many musical instruments vibrations first occur in solid materials such as strings, drumheads, or xylophone bars, and are *radiated* to the surrounding atmosphere, allowing them to become audible. On a subtler level, most vibrations can be seen as manifestations of recurring wavelike movements.

Index

Thanks

Thanks very much to the friends and friendly musicians whose photographs appear in this book. They include:

Anna-Maria Apostolopoulos
Andy 1/2-Baker
Kamuina Badimu
Ivo and Django Ballentine
Ann Batchelder
Evan Boswell
Sara Brown
Robin Cape
Darlene Clark
Joanna Clarke-Sayer
David Cohen
Thomas Crowe
Terry Lee Edgerton
Frank Edwin
Wayne, Barbara, Rita, and Leann Erbson
Matt Ferguson
Lou Garrison
Robert L. Geyer
Allison Hawn
Penny Jamison
Jonathan Jones
Janet, Thomas, Nathan, and Stefan Kelischek
Carol Kronus
Chris Lenderman
Marion and Cleve Mathews
Trey Marley
Amy Diane McClelland
Robert Moog
Jessica Munday
Matthew O'Connell
Reuben, Cheryl, Nicole, and Lauren Orengo
Zhai Panmao
Don Pedi
Holly Puleo
Kelly Robinson
French and Austin Sconyers
D Smith
Scott Smith
Sam Soemardi
Daniel S. Solts
Sandra Soto
Frank Southecorvo
Bob and Jill Vollmerhausen
Jonavan and Javonda Walker
Nan Watkins
William Wiley